After the Absolute

Richard Rose, 1917-2005

After the Absolute

The Inner Teachings of Richard Rose

David Gold
with
Bart Marshall

REALFACE PRESS

Published by Realface Press
info@realface.com

© David Gold 2002

ISBN: 9781795850988

Also Published by Realface Press

Christ Sutras*: The Complete Sayings of Jesus from All Sources Arranged into Sermons,* compiled and composed by Bart Marshall

Bhagavad Gita*: The Definitive Translation,* translated by Bart Marshall

The Perennial Way*, Extended Edition,* translated by Bart Marshall

The Triune Self*: Confessions of a Ruthless Seer,* by Mike Snider

The Conquest of Illusion*,* by J.J. van der Leeuw, 90th Anniversary Edition, edited by Bart Marshall

Think and Grow Rich*,* by Napoleon Hill, 80th Anniversary Edition, edited by Bart Marshall

Letters of Transmission*: The Enlightenment Method of Zen Master Alfred Pulyan,* edited by Bart Marshall

Magic, White and Black*,* by Franz Hartmann, M.D., edited by Bart Marshall

The Torah*: The Five Books of Moses* King James Bible Readers' Version, by Bart Marshall

Pearl of the Orient*,* screenplay by Bart Marshall

Verses Regarding True Nature*,* poems by Bart Marshall

Contents

Forward	1
Chapter 1. The Meeting	9
Chapter 2. The Invitation	21
Chapter 3. Benwood	29
Chapter 4. The Absolute	38
Chapter 5. The Path	51
Chapter 6. The Farm	65
Chapter 7. After the Absolute	74
Chapter 8. The Intensive	87
Chapter 9. Happiness	101
Chapter 10. Between-ness	116
Chapter 11. The Chautauquas	130
Chapter 12. Transmission	144
Chapter 13. Citizen Rose	156
Chapter 14. Success	171
Chapter 15. Entities	184
Chapter 16. The Krishnites	194
Chapter 17. Murder	206
Chapter 18. The Gun	215
Chapter 19. The Stagehand	230
Chapter 20. Isolation	244
Chapter 21. Seduction	257
Chapter 22. Nostalgia	265
Chapter 23. Fear	270
Chapter 24. Outcast	282
Epilogue	293

Richard Rose (upper right)
with his mother and brothers

Foreword

by
Joseph Chilton Pearce

Acknowledgments of greatness are generally postmortem. We seem to need a bit of "psychological distance" to see the full stature of some fellow human if that stature is out of the ordinary. The Roman church grants sainthood only well after the fact, usually, when the possibility of actual contact with said saint would take a bit of doing.

This allows and encourages what Mircea Eliade spoke of as "mythological overlay," in which we tend to attribute greater-than-life characteristics to a deceased person. Thus Abraham Lincoln grew so strong posthumously that he reportedly had picked up a chicken house seven men couldn't lift and carried it ten miles, the weight and mileage increasing with the passing years.

Eliade also points out, however, that such overlay doesn't take place with ordinary persons; only genuine heavy-weights are apt to bring on this historic process. So beneath the fanciful hyperbole with which we deck our dead heroes generally lies a personage powerful enough to attract such fancies. Over time such theatrics add to that very magnetic attraction *for* overlay, leading to inevitable distortion, but there is generally fire somewhere beneath all that tale-telling smoke.

In regard to someone still with us, however, we generally hear the equivalent of that famous query: "Can any good come out of Galilee" or, in the case of Richard Rose, "...the West Virginia mountains?" A reporter once went to Oxford, Mississippi to gather impressions held by the local citizenry concerning their famous native son, Nobel laureate William Faulkner. "William who?" was the common rejoinder, "You mean Bill *Faulkner*? That old *drunk*?" Indeed, a prophet is not without honor....

In the case of Richard Rose, the subject of the following chapters, we find neither a Nobel Laureate nor an old drunk, but a West Virginia farmer who had, all evidence indicates, achieved the highest spiritual state, that spoken of in classical eastern terms as one with God. Even more heretical to our western ears is Rose's own comment of having "become God."

Just as expressed in the old adage: "If you're so smart, why aren't you rich?" our first reaction to the report of a West Virginia farmer having become "one with the Absolute" would be "Why wasn't he on the cover of Time magazine?" Or, "Why hasn't anyone heard of him?" Where was his following? Who were his PR managers and business accountants? Where were his bank accounts in Switzerland, his hideaways in the Bahamas or Fijis?

David Gold intends that we should, indeed, hear of Richard Rose. From early college days, Lawyer Gold was a student of Rose, and hung in there for decades, surviving Rose's disciplinary demands. Now, with help from his friend and fellow-student, Bart Marshall, Gold has given us an account of this most unordinary of farmers, as seen by one disciple. Gold worked fifteen years on this manuscript, and our debt to him is incalculable. For here is what will surely prove to be a timeless and classic spiritual treatise.

Further, Gold's telling of this tale is one of the most gripping, intensely interesting, dramatic, and indeed romantic-heroic-mythic, yet poignantly human accounts I have ever read. It would make a fantastic, if unbelievable film, and is a profoundly important document. This book throws light on the perennial what-and-why enigma of our species, reveals the makings of a "new cosmology," and surely gives glimpses into as-yet undeveloped potentials we humans hold within us. That all this is found in an utterly absorbing narrative proves the old adage that truth is stranger than fiction.

As the narrator of the following, David Gold is everyman, the archetypical human longing to transcend that destructive dark shadow that haunts our species. Gold speaks to me because he is speaking all for us, and his account is not just a superb narrative but the universal drama, with the evolution of a species the underlying plot.

Richard Rose's own history proves yet another adage—that the creative "spirit" that sparks things "bloweth where it listeth" and no man knows its comings and goings. Rose, while coming out of a Catholic background, went beyond any and all inherited frameworks, and calls to question nearly every notion we have of religions in general and the making of a saint or man of God in particular.

Surely the ironclad and rather mechanistic, inviolable lock-step stages of enlightenment espoused by popular spiritual philosophers is called to question by the likes of Rose. While an intensely self-disciplined man, with a steely self-control, Rose followed no set discipline in his search for self, and his actual moment of awakening to his true nature came out of the most unlikely of all possible trigger-events, and in the most unexpected way. (Which actually bears out the truth of what a will-o-the-wisp "spirit" is.)

Rose thunders at us the conventional theme that our first and greatest challenge as humans is to become aware of who we are. Equally he states both an eastern and "Gospel" truism that we are ourselves the very God we so avidly seek elsewhere. In his ceaseless attempt to get his students to "see" who he was and become likewise, Rose employed "non-ordinary" phenomena of the first order, the heady stuff of miracles, that food for the ego's power-hunger that feeds so much of our new-age literature (though possibly few souls, as found in the Gospels, nothing new here.)

Becoming one with the Absolute, or going beyond one's fragmentations into a state of wholeness, leads to miraculous powers, it seems, but miraculous powers can be had without becoming one with the Absolute, and Rose's focus was on that unity-state, not miraculous gimmicks. I saw fakirs in India who could do things that defied every concept we have concerning reality—who could completely reverse the ordinary causal processes of our world, within their own straits. But these were "psychic phenomena" and the gulf between psychic and spiritual is wide. The spiritual can encompass and even engender the psychic, but not the other way around, just as the infinite contains the finite, but not vice-versa.

Rose referred to a state called *between-ness*, which involves suspension of our ordinary split between thought, feeling, and action. That is, we average citizens think one thing, feel something else, and act differently to either most of our time, making us truly a house divided against itself . We all exemplify Freud's famous trio of id, ego and super-ego, eternally at war with each other. We "do that which we would not do and do not do that which we ought to do, and there is no health (or wholeness) in us"' as Paul and the Book of Common Prayer lament.

In a state of actual wholeness of being, an undivided house, we have dominion over our world, a condition not as yet explored by us humans. Dominating nature a la science-technology is vastly different than this state of dominion, and Rose's "between-ness" is the gateway to that dominion. There one can function "in the world" but free of its crippling and harsh judgments and restrictions.

The Institute of Heartmath speaks of "entrainment between heart and brain," an alignment of frequencies clearly detectable on EEG and ECG machinery. In this state of entrainment between head and heart all the body oscillators go into sync and one's entire being is a single, integrated frequency. This opens up whole neural areas of brain previously unused, and makes available heretofore unexplored domains of experience and action.

Alignment between heart-frequency and brain frequency is a new expression of an old problem, how one's individual will and a universal or "global" will can be brought into alignment. What one does with such alignment isn't quite open to individual whim and fancy, either, but subject to a further state, a "higher frequency" which the fusion of head and heart brings about.

There is also a condition of mind called "unconflicted behavior," through which non-ordinary events can be brought about (and, in fact, disastrous influences set into motion). Unconflicted behavior is simply functioning without internal conflict—easier said than done, but not necessarily either unifying or benevolent.

Id, ego, and superego can go into sync so that thought, feeling and action are an undivided whole and one can then invest every vestige of self in a venture without reserve, throw caution, logic, emotion and rationality to the wind and, holding only to one's intent, bring about a "suspension of the ontological rules." At that point almost anything is possible and a person can employ this effect in ordinary affairs, take on tremendous power in situations and determine outcomes to an indeterminable extent.

There is, however, no divine universal ethic monitoring the results. The function works positively or negatively, since such niceties as good-bad, positive-negative are the very criteria set up by our ordinary logic and reasoning—and which are set aside in order to function as unconflicted behavior. (Nothing can so debilitate us as moral conflict.)

In Heartmath entrainment and Rose's "between-ness" the same single-minded intent and suspension of self-concern is necessary, but without the kind of investment or concern over outcome that ordinarily drives us. One's intent isn't for a singular goal or event, but for an alignment of wills, which alignment then determines outcome along lines unavailable to, and not restricted by, reason and logic. The negative possibilities of unconflicted behavior can't manifest in such entrainment, since a unified system can't work against itself.

Unconditional commitment to some act—yet with a total indifference to either the content, course of action, or outcome of that action—is similar to the central theme of Carlos Castaneda's semi-mythic hero, don Juan. It is the state of "faith" central to the teachings of Jesus, clearly stated by Krishna in the *Bhagavad Gita*, and implied in James P. Carse's *Infinite Play*.

One must be in some form of this state to willfully bring about non-ordinary phenomena, but far more importantly, this is the very state necessary to "merge with the Infinite" or become "one with the Absolute"—whatever metaphor fits one's spiritual aesthetic. So between-ness offers unlimited potential in our ordinary world, or the chance to go completely "beyond this world."

Rose considered his state of oneness-with-the-Absolute Zen-like, but, as with Zen or any spiritual "way," problems arise when the teacher prescribes for the student a path and goal by which they, too, might become one with the Absolute. For we then have a closed, finite, goal-oriented struggle, with boundaries and established end results in mind.

This is the heart of the perennial paradox in the Perennial Philosophy. Following goal-oriented, bounded procedures sets up a win-loose game of seriousness, and deadly serious too, because "soul" is concerned. This seriousness inevitably produces a guilt-producing criteria. Infinite openness and play close at that point, boxed into a finite game, which game or pursuit the student is anxious to conclude so that he or she might be "realized" and get on with real life.

And so life is spent trying to "get there" so one can really live—thus missing out on the present moment in which everything takes place. "Today is the day" involves a paradox found in most spiritual disciplines, since most disciplines are ways to "get there," someday, maybe.

The issue is that a finite pursuit can't lead beyond its own boundaries. The finite can't lead to the infinite. They are separate logical sets, so to speak. The logic of one cannot suggest or lead to the other. Yet, stuck in this finite structure as we are, we have no other materials with which to work than our all-too-finite mind and understanding. There is a real, true paradox here, but one which, as George Jaidar would say, is a threshold to a truth beyond paradox.

Classical logic claims, rightly, that we can't have "both Category A and Not-A simultaneously." We can't entertain two different and mutually exclusive logical sets at the same time. An unyielding either-or "law of the excluded middle" separates them.

But this excluded middle, as that between finite and infinite, is the "crack in the cosmic egg," the true *between-ness* through which we can slip to the freedom of the infinite game. We are, however, either "there" or not. There is no bridge between, and we can't think our way there since thought is a product of our very finite orientation.

Rose was caught on the horns of this ageless paradoxical dilemma, as every spiritual teacher has been: how to lead one to the unbounded infinite through finite process. In trying to help others catch his same light, as spiritual teachers seem impelled to do, Rose inevitably set up finite boundaries, disciplines and practices he hoped would break through the students perceptual-conceptual blocks. But such end-goaling, working *for* enlightenment, finitizes the infinite openness involved, and grounds the hapless student in a double-bind, for, as Jim Carse explains it, he who *must* play, *can't* play.

I know of no spiritual teacher who has solved this dilemma, even that giant of history, Jesus. Perhaps, though, the dilemma is more apparent than real. Perhaps the value of someone who has "broken through" and moved to a higher dimension of life is not their guidance so much as their presence, their beingness. "If I be lifted up I draw all humankind toward me" may be the point. The "model imperative" operates here. The great value of our great beings may not be "secrets of the masters" or prescriptions for sure-fire spiritual success, but simply their having actually lived among us, emblazoning their image on our collective consciousness and memory, stirring us from our sleep with glimpses of a new way of being.

I have never met a full "graduate" from any of the many spiritual systems I have come across or participated in since the participants in all those systems seemed eternally struggling to "achieve the goal." Should they do so, perhaps they would simply disappear, drop into anonymity, with only the charlatans hitting the media, waving their enlightenment degrees in the air and competing for the paying students.

An eastern saying is that the true Sufi is always anonymous, never known, except by another true Sufi. Small wonder Richard Rose never made the big-fish time, not even in his own tiny West Virginia pond. But I think extraordinary people such as Richard Rose pop up continually in history, in varying degrees of intensity, to act as target cells for the rest of us. The target cell phenomenon in found in brain growth, and is a mysterious and awesome event that may well be carried throughout the whole of our life process.

For the first four months or so of growth in our mother's womb, our brain grows as a simple homogenized "soup" of randomly mixed neurons, a chaos of unformed material. This growth hits a "critical mass" somewhere between the fourth and fifth month, at which point certain large and unique "target cells" appear. No one can explain the sudden manifestation of these strange and powerful cells, which immediately send out a signal which reads, in effect: "link up with *me*."

This instantly galvanizes those billions of random cells into a frenzy of activity, throwing out axons and dendrites, pushing and shoving to make dendritic connection with that great cell that has appeared among them. The full signal seems to read more like: "link up with me or a cell that has linked up with me," for through some simple directive that chaotic soup of cells is lifted, with astonishing rapidity, into the most magnificent order known in the universe, a human brain, with its many uniquely different forms and structures functioning in perfect synchrony to build, through their trillions of linkages, the infinitely diverse universe of our experience.

Note that on linking up with the target cell the neuron doesn't become a target cell itself. It becomes a fully functional neuron, linked with its neighbors in powerful, productive and creative ways. An isolated neuron is powerless and rather worthless, but through this transformative and unifying act it then lends itself to creating that fully functional miracle between our ears. Were all neurons to become target cells, an irremediable chaos would apparently result. (At least there would be no brain as we know it.) So the target cell appears to lift chaos into order, not to create other target cells.

In the same way, great beings just suddenly and inexplicably appear among us when some critical mass need demands them. And they don't necessarily have to rush off to do their stint of education in the Himalayas or wherever. When they appear they appear in full-bloom ready to go to work, and not to clone themselves but to bring about a linkage of separated, isolated, alienated and scared-lonely cells into fully human and functional souls, in turn moving to lift a social chaos into a new order.

I felt a great empathy with and respect for lawyer Gold, when he lamented that after all these years he felt he had still failed to realize the potential Rose saw in him. That is, he was still Dave Gold and not Richard Rose II. Most people on spiritual paths nurse a similar feeling of failure.

But, though I have found no fully finished "graduates" of the various spiritual systems encountered, I have observed legions of people who have undergone tremendous personal growth, change, improvement in character and quality of life through their spiritual discipline or contact with a great being—people who live far richer and more rewarding lives, and contribute richly to their society and larger body of earth as a result. And the David Gold I met was a prime example, an exceptional human, mature, kind, intelligent, responsible, the kind of citizen our society and earth need so badly. May his number increase. And in him, I think, Richard Rose succeeded.

So the reader of this book is fortunate indeed, for even reading about Rose can plant a seed in our minds. And target-cell seeds can take root and those roots can split boulders, mountains, worlds, even closed minds and their cosmic eggs. Those seeds become priceless pearls that can lead us to new and fuller life.

The following work is a pearl, a pearl without price, dropped into this endless field of human folly to bring to order that individual finding it. May Rose's hints and cues into that pearl's whereabouts aid the reader in his search. For seek and we shall find, it is said—the only game in town.

Joseph Chilton Pearce

Chapter One

The Meeting

In the winter of 1973 I encountered a strange and enigmatic man from West Virginia named Richard Rose and nothing has been the same for me since. I was in my first year of law school at the time, living at home with my mother to save on expenses and keep her company, my father having died suddenly two years before.

One night my friend Leigh, who had recently been spending a lot of time with a group called the Pyramid Zen Society, talked me into going with him to hear Rose, whom he called a Zen master. I had refused several previous attempts on Leigh's part to get me to a meeting, but he persisted, and each time he brought it up his descriptions and stories of Rose became more superlative, until Rose had begun to take on a magical, almost mythic, quality.

"Leigh," I said, "I have no interest in these things." Which was true. I had no interest in philosophy or religion, or anything even remotely introspective for that matter. I believed I knew who I was and where I was going. After law school I would get married, have kids, make money, maybe have a couple of discrete affairs with secretaries or friends' wives, then retire comfortably and play with the grandchildren. Life. What's to think about? You do the best you can.

"Dave," he said, "you could die any minute. We're all just killing time until we die. Do you understand what I'm saying?"

"Yeah, I guess so," I said. The truthful answer would have been, "No." Even now, after years of inner work, the hard fact of my personal death remains elusive. Yet, for some reason I agreed to go with Leigh that night, and a half-hour after we hung up he pulled into my driveway.

We drove through a light snow to the University of Pittsburgh, where the meeting was held, and I spent most of the ride wishing I was back home watching hockey. When we arrived the room was already packed. We made our way through the noisy crowd to what appeared to be the last two empty seats in the room, one on each side of an older man in a red flannel shirt. As we were sitting down my attention was drawn to two attractive women nearby. It occurred to me that I would at least have something pleasant to look at during the meeting. They were engaged in an animated conversation that seemed to focus on the men in their lives.

"Well, what Alex doesn't know won't hurt him," I heard one say. "If I were you, I'd just go with the flow." They both laughed. The old man next to me was listening, too.

"You can go with the flow if you want to," he said to them loudly, "but every flow I ever saw flowed straight down the sewer." He and a few others who heard him laughed, but the women didn't.

The room was filled with the kind of colorful, eclectic crowd that gathered in the early Seventies when you put the word "Zen" on some posters and tacked them up around a college campus. I felt out of place and impatient for the meeting to get underway. The quicker it started, the better chance I had of at least catching the last period of the hockey game.

I turned to ask Leigh when Rose was due to show up, but he was talking to someone on the other side of him. Everyone in the room seemed to be talking at once. For something to do, I listened in on some of the conversations. Nearby two long-haired youths were extolling the power of drugs to expand the mind. They seemed to have taken their own advice before coming that evening.

"Expand the mind?" The old man next to me chimed in again. "You mean your heads just get bigger and bigger until God himself has to move over and make room for 'em?" He kept a straight face until Leigh and a few others laughed, then he laughed too, with great abandonment and glee.

The rest of the room quieted down somewhat at the sound of the laughter, until only a few conversations remained, the most noticeable of which was between three middle-aged men who sounded and acted like professors. They were discussing the reason for man's existence while occasionally glancing around the room, perhaps to measure the effect of their words on anyone who might be listening.

The old man next to me focused his attention on them for a few moments before interrupting. "I'll tell you why you exist," he said in a voice loud enough to be heard over the other conversations. The room got suddenly quiet. "You're here to fertilize the female, work yourself to death, then drop dead and fertilize the earth." Several people laughed but this time the old man did not join in.

The tallest and most imposing of the three professors looked condescendingly at the "rube" in the flannel shirt who had interrupted him.

"Are you saying, then, that we're just sophisticated animals?" he asked.

"No," the old man smiled, "we're not a bit sophisticated." There was loud laughter, most of it in our vicinity.

The professor shook his head with dramatic sadness. "We'll never build a better world with that kind of attitude. "

"Spare me," the old man replied, his voice filled with disgust. "What are there, four billion ants on this ant hill? And you think they're gonna get their heads together about anything except breeding?"

The same people laughed, Leigh the loudest, and I finally realized that the old man next to me was Richard Rose. So far I didn't think much of him, but he did have a novel way of beginning a meeting, or whatever this was. I turned sideways in my chair to get a better look at him.

On the ride over Leigh had tried to explain to me that Rose had had some kind of "enlightenment" experience when he was thirty, and that he seemed to have some unusual powers. I had to admit that he had a commanding presence, but he looked more like a longshoreman than a mystic—short, broad shouldered, and powerfully built. He was in his late fifties or so, and mostly bald. What remained of his hair was white and cut close to his head. His clothes were clean, but well-worn, giving the impression of a man without much money.

Leigh told me he'd written several books, but his thick, vein-lined hands looked like they'd be more at home with an ax than a typewriter. As I surveyed him, he glanced briefly over at me and I was struck by his piercing pale blue eyes. He had heavy, hooded eyelids, giving him an almost oriental look, and his sparse white goatee added to this impression.

The professor seemed irritated. "I am merely speaking of a simple desire to improve the world. A basic—"

"No one who has seen the Truth would want to change anything but his own erroneous view of things," Rose said forcefully. "Forget about changing the world. There's something much greater and more important to be done. Each person must be concerned with saving his own soul."

"That's right," said a woman near the back of the room. She was in her forties, perhaps, with a few streaks of gray in her long black hair. She wore a lot of jewelry and a loose fitting dress that disguised her ample figure. "God placed us here on earth for a reason," she said in a slow, deliberate manner. "Every human is given the opportunity to learn the lessons necessary to become complete and rejoin God."

Rose looked at her. "That's not what I said. If you believe that, you're kidding yourself. The idea that life is an education for the glorification of God is absurd. Why would an omnipotent being create a bunch of ignorant people then torture them to make them better?"

Rose spoke with the ease and manner of an educated man, but his accent and grammar had a slightly backwoods flavor, and he pronounced certain words with an unusual inflection, such as "glory-fee-cation."

The woman's face reddened. "You have some rather unorthodox presumptions about God."

"What makes you think I have any presumptions about God at all? You're the one that used the word, not me." He looked away from her and spoke to everyone.

"The way people use the word 'God' is shameless name dropping, that's all. We take too big a step when we conjure up some cosmic intelligence who's supposed to transcend all time and space, then pretend to know him on a first-name basis. Everyone tosses the word 'God' around like they know what it means, but they don't know the first thing. Overuse has drained it of any power it once had. Everybody feels so comfortable with the *word* 'God,' they don't feel the need—the necessity—to actually go out and *find* God. To *become* God."

The professor spoke up again. "We'll, since you seem to be such an authority on the subject, perhaps you can settle an old philosophic question for us. Does God exist?"

"Yes," Rose said quietly, "but *you* don't."

There was a long silence that made me, and probably most everyone else, uneasy. Rose just sat there. Finally, a woman in her mid-twenties wearing what appeared to be a waitress's uniform broke the silence. Her face reflected an unusual mix of strength and vulnerability that I found very attractive.

"Don't you believe in helping God make this a better world?" she asked.

"What makes you think God needs any help?" Rose smiled warmly and continued to look at her as if he expected a response. The woman did not speak, but she seemed unable to look away from him. The room fell silent. Rose held his gaze on her for awhile longer and the silence seemed to deepen.

"Don't take life seriously," he said finally. "It doesn't take you seriously. The Cosmos is laughing at you." Then he looked away from her. When he did, she shook her head almost imperceptibly, as if her thoughts had just returned. Rose pulled an open can of soda from under his chair and took a drink. A studious young man with wire-rimmed glasses raised his hand politely. Rose nodded in his direction.

"Mister Rose, you obviously feel you have something to offer the world, but you talk so disparagingly about people."

"There is no world," Rose said. "There are no people."

"Don't you care about humanity?" someone called out.

"Yes, some of them. The ones that can be helped." He paused a moment as if choosing his words. "I'm not out to save the masses. It's impossible to do and I'm smart enough to know it. I talk to *individuals*. If in my entire lifetime I can get a handful of people to reach a few plateaus above their current state of confusion, I'll be lucky."

"But aren't we all God's children?" someone called out. "What about the brotherhood of man?"

"Membership in the clan does not mean we're equal. Is a baby equal to a dying man? Is a genius equal to an idiot? No. And people are on different rungs of the spiritual ladder, too. Most of mankind is on the lower rungs and there's not much that can be done for them. They're too mired in animal behavior to look for something more out of life. All they know—or want to know—is sex, booze, fighting, power, that sort of thing.

"What I presume, though," Rose went on, "is that there are a few people out there who are looking for something more. Looking for something *real*, something that will stick with them. Something they won't end up regretting twenty years down the road. People who aren't satisfied just living out their lives as ignorant animals. These are the people I might be able to help. They want to know *who's* living out this experience, and what might continue to live and experience after death. And if I'm lucky enough to run into those people and they ask for help, then I'll try to work with them any way I can. But before anyone can be helped they have to become somebody who is *capable* of being helped. It's foolish to bail out a leaky boat without also plugging up the hole."

"You mean a person has to change his way of life," Leigh said.

"Right, right." Rose said enthusiastically. "You get attached to the flesh, but after awhile you realize you're no better than a dog in the street. Of course, our egos offer all sorts of noble pretenses for indulging in pleasure—poetic rationalizations about love, and 'experiencing life to the fullest.' But eventually we run out of excuses, and by the time the ego lets loose of us, it's usually too late to do anything about what's up ahead. That's why so many people die screaming."

I expected him to at least smile at his last remark, but he didn't.

"People are just doing the best they can," a woman near the back of the room called out. "Following their bliss as they see it. "

Rose stared at his hands for a moment then looked up again. "Look, if you ever want to discover anything of importance," he said with great seriousness, "you've got to get this Pollyanna crap out of your heads. People think they can indulge in whatever whim overpowers them at the moment, and that somehow this 'spontaneity' is going to transform them into a wonderful spiritual creature that God just can't resist loving. This is nonsense. Life isn't pleasure, it's constant struggle driven by relentless tension. Look out the window. It's a bloody carnage out there. Everything's trying to eat something else, just so it can stay alive long enough to reproduce and provide more food and fertilizer for this slaughterhouse."

"You're condemning us for trying to be happy," someone said.

"I'm not condemning anybody. What people do with their lives is their business. Besides, you can't *talk* someone into virtue. You might as well try to talk a goat out of eating. People have to find out for themselves what has value in their lives and what doesn't. What's worth living for. What's worth doing."

"But you're advising us against *looking* for happiness..."

"No, no. Don't presume to know what I'm doing. Sometimes *I* don't even know what I'm doing," Rose laughed. "It's better that way. But I do know better than to give direct advice. Nobody takes it, anyway. Otherwise, everyone would start off at least as smart as his parents."

For the last half hour or so I had been looking for a chance to insert myself into the proceedings. My initial discomfort with the unfamiliar situation had subsided and I had been trying to think of a question to ask, not so much because I was interested in the answer, but because I wanted to show Leigh and the rest of the room my "stuff."

Most of what Rose said made no sense to me and it seemed that the rest of the people in the room were incapable of offering a strong enough intellectual challenge to Rose to pin him down. I was, after all, a sharp Jewish lawyer-in-training and, as unusual as Rose was, he still stumbled over words, had a homespun manner, and came from West Virginia. In other words, I felt I could *take* him. There was a brief silence after his last remarks so I jumped in.

"I'm new to all this, Mister Rose," I began, "so perhaps you can enlighten me." I slid to the furthest edge of my seat before turning towards him, like an attorney facing a hostile witness.

"Why should a person give up his natural instincts and ego in a world where only the strong survive?" I said. "Who's to say which behaviors we should have and which we should toss away? What's wrong with having a multi-faceted personality, if for no other reason than to protect ourselves from those who might want to take it away and replace it with their own agenda?"

It wasn't totally on the subject he was addressing, perhaps, but it sounded good. I was proud of myself. I wanted to look at Leigh to see his reaction but I felt I should stare at Rose during the showdown.

Rose looked me over for a few seconds before answering. "There's not a damn thing wrong with it," he said firmly, "provided you don't mind being a hopeless robot all your life."

Then he turned away and addressed the entire room. "Now, for instance, this guy here," he said, gesturing to me. "There's no doubt that in his own mind he thinks he's very clever and that he's someone of great importance. He likes to think he's blessed with a superior intellect and is destined to do great things. He thinks he's better than everyone else so he never takes part in what's going on around him. He just daydreams about women and thinks up ways to exercise his ego. But the truth is, he's confused and miserable. He doesn't know anything, and he's never accomplished anything of value. All he does is get by through manipulation, playing petty games with himself and everyone around him.

"He'll probably choose a career that favors deceit and manipulation. Maybe he'll even end up being one of the hucksters who makes the rules for this madhouse. But it won't take away his misery. He lives in a self-imposed world of competitiveness and suspicion, always on guard against the rest of humanity, trying to protect his inflated self-importance. He's smug and ignorant, which is a bad combination. But even so, a part of him senses that something is terribly wrong with him, and he wonders why he's always on edge, why he's unable to enjoy even the most basic pleasures in life, like true human friendship."

When he finished the room stayed silent. I was unable to speak or even move. I sat motionless, my face burning with humiliation and anger. The deft sparring match I had envisioned was a one-punch fight. His words, delivered in smooth unbroken prose, left me stunned. I fought the urge to run. I wanted nothing more than to be someplace else, *anyplace* else. Was what I said so bad that I deserved what he just did to me? Who in the hell did he think he was?

But more importantly, how did he know these things? He was right and I knew it. Only the truth could hurt as badly as his words had. How could he *know*? How could he know and understand a stranger in that much complexity and detail?

Someone broke the silence and asked a question unrelated to my exchange with Rose and the meeting resumed. I heard very little for awhile, staying lost in my own thoughts, relieved to not be the focus of the attention I had so openly sought a few minutes before. I could remember every word he said. Every nuance of his tone and inflection was burned into me. I hated him for humiliating me, and yet there were other strange feelings beginning to form. I don't know how long I stayed within myself, but gradually I tuned back into the room and the sound of Rose's voice.

"If any of you people ever got serious about the work," he was saying, "one of the first things you'd discover is that you don't exist—at least not as you think you do. You look in the mirror now and you're tickled to death with what you see: 'Wow, look what God put on this earth to grace it and make other people jealous.' But after awhile you'll maybe realize that you're nothing but a blob of protoplasm waiting to die and get put in a hole so you won't stink up the place. That's all you are, as far as what you can prove. Everything else is just unfounded belief and wishful thinking."

"Sounds awfully negative to me," a young voice called out. A number of heads nodded in agreement.

Rose smiled. "A negative reaction to a negative situation might turn out to be quite positive."

Suddenly the questions started coming faster.

"Will your system make me happy?"

"I don't know about that, but if you're like me, you'll wind up with a high degree of immunity."

"But are you *happy*?" someone challenged.

"I'm free of happiness."

"Would you say, then, that you have perfect, eternal contentment?"

"Yes, you could put it that way."

"How do you know you're not deceiving yourself?"

"I have no self left to deceive."

"Are you a success?"

"Yes, I believe so. I know exactly what it is I want to do with my life, and I spend a hundred percent of my time doing it. But if you mean money, no, I never cared about money. If you have more than you need, it's a curse.

"Fact is, though, you can use the principles of spiritual work to get whatever you want out of life—money, power, fame—any kind of success or pleasure. The mechanism for achievement is the same no matter where you point it. But sooner or later, life—or death—will bring you face to face with the only thing that has any real value. I spent the first thirty years of my life looking for it, and the last twenty-five trying to find people who might also be looking for it. Not because I want to change them, but because I might be able to drop them a hint. To say, 'Hey, you're banging your head against a wall that won't move,' or 'You're wasting your life on some pleasure trip or petty ego.'"

"What about love?" someone called out.

"What about it?" Rose shot back.

"Love between two people. There's nothing petty about that."

"We may believe that someone loves us," Rose said, "but if we live long enough we'll discover that they really only love that which we can give them. Everyone wants desperately to believe in love, though, because we're so lonely."

No one said anything so he went on.

"This overuse of the word 'love' is a curse. I lived for twenty years with my wife, and never once did I tell her I loved her. I consider it a lie. Everybody's got a different definition of love and they're all wrong. There's no way to communicate love with words. If you respect your woman, you prove it. Your life proves it. You give your life to that woman and those children, that's all."

"And people will see it, right?" someone said.

"It doesn't matter if they see it or not. It only matters if you know it in yourself and she knows it in herself. That's what counts. But to go around popping off about how much you love people..." He shook his head. "These words mean nothing."

"How about a mother's love for her children?" someone called out.

"The selflessness of motherhood is beautiful," Rose said quietly. "There's an unseen umbilical connection between mother and child throughout their entire lifetime, and perhaps beyond. But it's also true that giving birth to a child is the same as killing someone. In both cases you're doing something you don't really understand."

There was a stunned silence in the room as Rose continued.

"The worst thing about this love and happiness obsession is that it keeps us from taking an honest look at life. If we did, we'd recognize our existence for what is—a moment of consciousness between two oblivions. Every day we live on the edge of the precipice and with the next step, the lights might go out. So the only answer is to make the trip. And until you make the trip, you have no validity."

"The trip?" someone asked.

"Across and back," Rose said. "Die while living."

"You mean like *satori*."

"No, I mean an Absolute condition. The final Experience. Enlightenment."

There were a lot of puzzled expressions.

"Some of the popular Zen books talk about achieving *satori*, which is really nothing more than the 'Wow' experience," Rose went on. "A fellow says, 'I went to this ashram and stayed there so many months or years, then one day it hits me. 'Wow, I got it!' So I had some tea with the head master and we went away laughing together because we both got it.'" Rose frowned. "This is not Enlightenment. Because if this man had experienced Enlightenment they would have carried him out on a stretcher—it's that drastic. You don't die and then laugh and say 'Wow!' Death is more final than that."

Another long silence. Then someone asked the question that hung in the air.

"Have *you* made the trip?"

"Yes, I've made the trip. But what I know isn't going to do *you* any good. The reason more people don't discover the Truth is that they want to receive it bodily and personally, preferably as a gift from another person so they don't have to work for it." Rose chuckled. "But it's impossible to pick up through relative thinking that which another man has discovered through a *direct-mind experience*. All words—even my words—are useless. If you want to know, you've got to go there yourself. And to go there you have to pass through death."

The room stayed uncomfortably silent while Rose looked around at everyone.

"I'm a discoverer, not an orator," he said finally. "A discoverer tells you what he's found, regardless of the consequences to your peace of mind."

"What *did* you find," asked a young girl with a colorful headband. She spoke haltingly, as if afraid of the answer.

"Everything. And Nothing."

"You mean you became one with...."

"No, no. I became *One*. There's nothing to become one *with*."

He glanced around at the puzzled faces. "Don't think you're going to be able grasp this stuff logically, because you won't. I'm talking about a state beyond words, a state beyond the mind, even."

Rose paused for a moment as if considering whether to continue.

"This whole planet is fiction," he said. "A picture show. Sometimes it can be a rather engrossing picture show, but that doesn't make it real. Our heads are programmed to get puffed up with all kinds of infatuations and obsessions. Some of them use up years and decades of our lives. Then when the spell breaks on one of 'em you shake your head and wonder, 'What was that, a bubble?' But you turn right around and get obsessed by something else. Entire lives pass this way, from one petty obsession to another. Eventually, if you're lucky and if one of these obsessions doesn't kill you, you come to realize that life is at best a dream, and at worst, a nightmare."

"But you've already escaped the nightmare," a boy in the front row said. "Why would you want to stick around and inhabit *our* dreams?"

"Oh, I still exist in the nightmare," Rose said. "Everyone on earth exists in the nightmare. The difference is that when you people die you'll just go into *another* nightmare. Then there's a tremendous agony that accompanies the realization you're still not free. My job is to find five people and wake them up now in the hope that they'll each find five more people, and so on. In that way, mankind might be benefited."

The room stayed silent for a long time. Strangely, in the midst of the conflicting emotions that swirled inside me that night, the thought briefly crossed my mind that I actually wanted to be one of those five people. The desire startled me, and it lasted only a few seconds before I dismissed it. But for those few seconds it flashed with an intensity I had never before experienced in my thinking.

I have since come to believe that thought and desire are capable of guiding, perhaps even creating, events. And so I sometimes think, probably overly dramatically, that the whole rocky course of my association with Richard Rose—living under constant confrontation in his house, practicing law in a backwoods West Virginia town, carrying a gun because the local Hare Krishnas put out a contract to have Rose and me killed, and all the rest of it—issued from that single transient desire to know what it was to be Awake.

Chapter Two

The Invitation

Rose's concise public reading of me left me with a confusing mix of thoughts and emotions. On the one hand, I couldn't shake the sense of embarrassment and humiliation I'd felt that night as it happened. In some strange and mysterious leap Rose had exposed my inner character with unerring precision. He not only spoke things I knew about myself and tried to hide from others, but also things I had successfully hidden from myself. I had felt naked and helpless under his gaze and a strong part of me never wanted to see him again.

But another part of me, a strange and unfamiliar part, felt a surge of energy and excitement, as well as a heavy—and yet not unpleasant—sense of foreboding. To have someone know me as thoroughly as Rose did in those few moments left me with an undeniable and almost irresistible feeling of closeness with him. He had seen more deeply into me than anyone had before and, as painful as his words had been, they were not judgmental, only an offhand appraisal of a flawed fellow man.

Yet, as compelling as these feelings were, they were not what drew me back to Rose. In the end I returned because I was curious almost to the point of obsession about how he had performed his little miracle of reading my mind, my psyche, as he had. I was convinced it was a talent I could learn for myself and that it would serve me well as I went about the business of making my mark on the world. And so I resolved to attend more meetings with Rose—enough, at least, to learn the secret of his abilities. Then, as soon as I had the formula, I'd slip out the door and get on with my life.

The following week I drove to the meeting alone and as I stepped off the crowded elevator in the Pitt Student Union I nervously jingled the car keys in my pocket, reassuring myself that this week I could leave whenever I wanted to. It didn't help. As soon as the elevator doors closed behind me my stomach began to twist into a knot of tension that tightened with each step I took towards the meeting room. I paused at the doorway, took a deep breath and pushed myself inside, never dreaming how many times I would repeat this process in the years ahead—hesitating fearfully before doors that led to Rose.

The room seemed even more crowded than I remembered and I tried to slip in before people recognized me from the week before. Once

I was seated, though, I realized my self-consciousness and sense of importance were unfounded. Nobody even noticed me except Leigh, who seemed mildly surprised, and Rose, who gave a polite nod of recognition.

Although the place looked and sounded as it had the week before, something was different. As I glanced around the room I noticed that many, perhaps even most, of these people had not been at last Thursday's meeting. It made me wonder how many actual hard-core followers this man really had. Rose himself appeared different, too. He seemed shorter and perhaps a little more paunchy than the intimidating image I'd carried around in my head all week. He had on a different shirt and pants but they gave the same impression: clean, well-worn, slightly dated.

He seemed to act differently too. Less obtrusive, almost subdued, he allowed conversations to take their course, speaking only when spoken to.

"It's eight o'clock," someone said loudly in a deep voice. "We better get started." The speaker was a short, balding fellow in his early twenties who was seated, along with two other men, behind a wooden table at the front of the room.

"My name is Ray," he continued. "This is the Pittsburgh Pyramid Zen Society. We meet here every Thursday night. Our goal is to find the Truth by retreating from untruth. The method we use is called the Albigen System."

For the next ten minutes or so Ray attempted to explain the principles of the group. His voice was dull and monotonous, and his explanations full of unfamiliar terms and phrases—*reverse vector, conservation of energy, between-ness*. When he finished he asked if there were any questions. There were plenty. The first few he tried to handle as best he could, looking occasionally to Rose as if waiting to be rescued from what seemed an uncomfortable situation for him. Rose did not intercede, however, and Ray was left to fend for himself as best he could for fifteen minutes or so. Then, as the meeting reached a point of maximum awkwardness and tension, Rose gently took over by elaborating on one of Ray's answers. From then on all questions were directed to Rose and the room came alive.

The meeting continued with Rose holding forth until about ten o'clock, when Ray announced that the formal part of the meeting was at an end. Leigh put a coffee can into circulation and asked for contributions to help pay for Rose's gas from West Virginia. People stood up and talked to each other or left. Some drifted towards Rose. Soon there was a small crowd around him and the dialogue continued.

I was sitting nearby so I stayed in my seat and listened in. The questions to Rose were tentative, as if everyone were testing the rules of this more intimate setting. Rose answered each question in turn, never hurrying an answer, treating each person as if the two of them were the only people in the room.

When one boy asked how he could get an appointment, Rose laughed and said, "This isn't like going to the dentist, you know." The boy blushed.

"You can find me in the Student Union an hour or two before these meetings," Rose assured him. "I'm driving a fifty-dollar car with baloney-skin tires and four spares in the back seat. I need to leave West Virginia a couple hours early to allow for blowouts."

His collection complete, Leigh sat down next to me. "That's true," he said, nodding his head towards Rose. "His car's a real junker. I don't know how he makes it here."

"How was the take?" I said, smiling at the coffee can.

"Lousy, as usual," he said, poking around the inside the can. "Looks like about six bucks. Enough for Rose's expenses, I guess." He put the crinkled bills and loose change into an envelope. I took out my wallet and gave him a dollar to add to it.

"Big time," he said, grinning. He put my buck in the envelope then licked the flap and sealed it.

Rose looked up from the center of the crowd and addressed Leigh. "Are we going out for a bite to eat?"

Leigh stood up and announced that everyone was invited to meet at Winky's, a local hamburger joint, for more conversation with Rose. I was tired and felt like I'd had enough for the night. But another part of me was strangely afraid I'd miss something valuable, so I followed the crowd out the door.

The restaurant fell silent as we walked in—maybe twenty of us in all—led by Rose, who, in his long wool coat and faded black fedora, looked like a gangster from the Thirties. As we passed a well-dressed couple they stared uneasily at the strange mix of people in our group. Rose paused at their table and gestured to them reassuringly.

"Don't worry," he said, "I'll have them back in the sanitarium before their medication runs out." He then proceeded to the counter and announced loudly, "I don't know about the rest of you, but I'm hungry enough to eat here."

Rose pulled out an ancient brown leather wallet with frayed white stitches, and ordered two hamburgers and a large cup of coffee. It surprised me that he ate meat, or even that he drank coffee.

"Sometimes the only antidote for poison is another poison," he said to no one in particular.

When his food came he took it to one of the tables Leigh had commandeered for us and sat down. The chairs and tables around him immediately filled up. Still straggling, I was left to sit at a table on the periphery.

Seated across from Rose was a tall, happy-go-lucky youth in his early to mid-twenties. He had a round, peasant's face and a sturdy build, but his speech and mannerisms were those of an intellectual. I had seen him at the meeting, sitting at the table with Ray and a few of the other "insiders," but had not paid much attention to him. Rose called him Augie, and it appeared from the way they interacted that Augie served as some sort of right-hand man for Rose. Augie immediately engaged Rose in lively conversation and laughed with abandon at much of what Rose said. At one point Augie laughed so hysterically he drew stares from around the restaurant. Rose jerked his thumb in Augie's direction and shook his head.

"This is why Augie hangs around this group," he said. "All he wants to do is laugh. He thinks that if he sticks around long enough, when he dies there'll be an army of heavenly cherubs waiting to tickle his rear-end with feather dusters throughout eternity."

Everyone but Augie broke out laughing, including Rose, who seemed to be more amused with Augie's self-conscious discomfort than the joke itself. Suddenly, though, Rose's laugh turned into a violent cough. When he finally caught his breath he took a sip of coffee and wiped his mouth with a napkin.

"Are you okay?" Augie asked.

"Oh yeah. It's just bronchitis. Comes back every year since I froze up in that blizzard."

"When was that?"

"Oh, a long time ago. My kids were still young."

"How'd you get caught in a blizzard?" someone asked.

Rose leaned back slightly his chair and scratched the back of his head for a few seconds. It was one of several gestures of his that I would later come to recognize as indications that a story from his life was forthcoming. As I was to discover during the coming years, Rose was, among so many other things, a consummate raconteur.

"Well," he said, "it was at a time when I was working myself to death trying to secure the family. I had a painting business in town and was also raising cattle out on the farm. I was going crazy, running back and forth between the farm and town at all hours."

As little as I knew about him, I still had a hard time picturing Rose as a married man with children and ordinary cares.

"One day my brother-in-law, Art, asks me to go with him to Los Angeles. I can't remember if one of his people was sick or he had some business out there. But I was ready for a little vacation anyway so I figured, what the hell, let's take a ride."

It was a different Rose who sat in front of us now, relaxed and talking as if we were all old friends.

"We had a nice trip out, not in any hurry. Stopped at the Grand Canyon. Took in the Painted Desert. I never saw anything like the sunset there. The entire sky opened up like it was on fire. Just beautiful. Anyway, we got out to L.A. and two days later my wife called. It was early spring and she told me a freak blizzard just blew down from Canada. The whole state was covered with a foot of snow."

A chubby girl in the Winky's orange-plaid uniform appeared and offered refills on the coffee. Rose thought for a moment before accepting.

"This stuff's poison, you know," he said as she filled his cup. "Wrecks your kidneys." When she left he poured in several packs of sugar and continued.

"Anyway, we jumped in the car and headed straight back to West Virginia because I'd left my cattle grazing out there on the farm—not expecting snow that time of the year—and now they had no way to get in out of the weather. If they stayed outside there was no hope. They'd either freeze or starve.

"So we high-balled it out of there and drove non-stop. Made it in less than forty-eight hours," Rose said with a tinge of pride. "And this is on old Routes 40 and 66, before the interstates went through. I had an old Buick I'd picked up for forty bucks. She wasn't too reliable, but once you got her cranked up she could really fly. I was doing a hundred miles an hour through Indiana when we blew past this state trooper standing by his cruiser on the other side of the road. You should've seen him scramble. Art starts cursing under his breath.

"'Quit worrying,' I told him. 'It's less than ten miles to Ohio. We'll be across the border before he gets his car turned around.'" Rose chuckled and blew steam off the top of his coffee. "Never saw that cop again."

I glanced around the silent restaurant. We were the only customers left.

"Well, I dropped Art off in Benwood then drove out to the farm." He turned towards Augie. "Now this is the 'back' farm I'm talking about, the one the Krishnites have now, not the one you fellows stayed at during the Intensive last summer."

Leigh had mentioned that Rose had a farm, but never anything about a second, "back," farm. And I wondered what the Hare Krishnas had to do with anything. Rose continued.

"The last two miles to that farm were down a dirt lane, and even in dry weather you could only get a vehicle within a half-mile of the place. When I got to the lane the snow was higher than the car so I had to walk the rest of the way."

He shook his head. "Those were a couple of rough miles. Some of the drifts were over my head and I'd have to just run through them, hoping I made high ground before I suffocated. All I had on were a pair of street shoes and a spring jacket. I was half frozen by the time I got there. My shoes were soaked, I couldn't feel my toes. And like I figured, some of the young cows were already down and the rest were scattered all over the farm.

"It took me an hour to clear the snow away from the barn door just so I could get to that damn horse." Rose's eyes lit up when he mentioned the animal.

"He was one despicable creature, I mean to tell you. Couldn't turn your back on him. He'd ram you from behind—cracked a couple of my ribs once. Sometimes it took me two hours to put him in harness for plowing. Then he'd settle down and let me lead him to the field. Soon as I hitched up the plow, though, he'd lay down. Didn't matter how hard I cracked him, he wouldn't get up until I unhitched the plow," Rose chuckled and shook his head in grudging admiration.

"You couldn't keep him outside in a pasture, either. He'd jump over or bust through whatever fence was out there. That's why I had him locked up in the barn—you just couldn't catch him once he was loose. The thing was, though, that horse may have been a demon, but he was one tough animal. Once I got him saddled up that day and put the spurs to him, he took off through that snow like it was a cloud of smoke.

"There were a hundred and seventy acres on that farm and we rode over every one of them looking for cattle. I was just getting 'em rounded up when the snow got worse. Pretty soon I couldn't see a thing and neither could the horse. He started getting spooked and hard to control. Everything was a sea of swirling white.

"'About that time he steps in a groundhog hole and stumbles, which makes him really go crazy. He starts rearing and bucking and the next thing I know I'm hanging off the side of him, one foot hooked in the stirrup, while he takes off running, bouncing my head on the ground. He dragged me that way for a half-hour through the snow and the thickets, up and down the hills. Even through a creek or two."

"But you held on?"

"Had too," Rose said matter-of-factly. "Besides, I knew that sooner or later he'd wear himself out. Sure enough, he finally slowed down, and I was able to get myself back up into the saddle. Eventually we finished rounding up the cattle and got 'em out of the weather."

Rose paused to take a look around the restaurant. A young man with bad acne stared impatiently from behind the counter. Another leaned on a mop.

"Geeze, what time is it?" Rose asked, gathering up his loose trash.

"What about the bronchitis, Mister Rose?"

"Oh. Well, after the livestock was safe in the barn, I went into the farmhouse and collapsed on the floor. My guts were frozen inside of me. I mean, literally *frozen*. I was chilled bad. And I didn't have any dry wood in the house so I couldn't build a fire. For three days I couldn't move. I just laid there on the floor, coughing, waiting for my insides to thaw out. My lungs have never been the same since."

There was a short silence, then Rose and everyone seemed to get up simultaneously.

"Why didn't you just pull your foot out of the stirrup and drop off the horse, instead of letting the him drag you all over the farm?" Augie asked.

Rose picked up his tray. "Oh I could have gotten loose easily enough, that's true. But I'd given my word not to. I knew when I took that horse out of the barn he stood a good chance of getting killed out there. So before I saddled him up I made a promise that either both of us were coming back, or neither of us were."

Rose dumped his trash in a bin and started towards the door.

"Was the horse worth it?" I said, half-jokingly.

He turned suddenly and stared directly at me without a trace of a smile. His voice was firm, and louder than a normal conversational tone.

"It doesn't matter whether the horse was worth it or not," he said, narrowing his eyes at me. "What matters is *I gave my word*. Once you do that, you either keep it, or die trying."

Then he raised his arm and poked a short, stout finger into my chest.

"And that's the way *you* have to practice law!" he said. Then he stared fixedly at me for a few seconds before finally turning away and heading out the door.

I was stunned by his force and directness. It was the first and only thing I'd said to him that night, and once again he had pounced on it, catching me completely unaware and confounding me to the core. For what seemed like a long time I stared after him, not really seeing, waiting for the blood to stop pounding in my ears.

I was the last one out the door, and as I walked I was barely conscious of my surroundings. Out on the sidewalk Augie was getting some parting instructions from Rose. I moved into the circle of conversation in time to hear that Augie was planning a trip to Rose's farm that weekend, and that he was apparently bringing some new people down.

"Just make sure there's no witches this time," Rose said to him. Augie smiled self-consciously while several of the others laughed. With a wave of his hand Rose turned and started towards his car, then stopped a few feet away and turned to face us again.

"Oh yeah," he said, pointing his finger at me once more, "if he wants to come along, that's all right, too."

Chapter Three

Benwood

The next night Augie called to say when he would pick me up. "Eight o'clock, sharp," was how he put it, his tone implying strongly that he was a man of punctuality and that he'd leave me behind rather than delay his trip by even a minute.

So Saturday morning, still filled with equal parts curiosity and doubt, I was ready by 7:30. At 7:45, afraid he might miss the house and be too impatient to spend much time looking, I moved out into the bitter December cold to wait on the front stoop. At 9:15 I was still there, bouncing from foot to foot, blowing into my gloves. No Augie. I peered through the window and looked at the mantle clock for the hundredth time.

Waiting on the stoop that morning I replayed the last ten days in my mind and tried to understand why I was standing in the biting cold waiting for a ride to see some backwoods guru. Almost in spite of myself I had to admit that I liked the man. I liked his outspoken opinions and biting sense of humor. I liked the way he handled himself with a strange combination of confidence and humility. I liked the way it felt when he looked me in the eye and told me how to practice law.

But I was also afraid of him. He was a mystic, a man with power. As yet, I didn't know how much power, but I wasn't sure I was ready to find out. I was afraid, I think, that if I ventured too deeply into his world I'd never get out again and back into mine. The longer I stood on my mother's porch the more I felt like a little boy waiting for the camp bus to arrive and take him away from all that is warm and familiar. And by the time Augie's white Ford van finally roared into the driveway, tires squealing, horn honking, I found myself wishing he'd never found the place.

As I opened the car door I anticipated an effuse apology for his being two hours late. I was prepared to be magnanimous, but cool enough to let him know I wasn't pleased.

"Hop in, we're late," he said flatly, jamming the gearshift into reverse.

I looked around. There was no passenger seat and the space where it should have been was overflowing with clutter.

"Where?" I said, forcing a smile.

He didn't smile back. "Be creative. Let's go."

I crouched in a tiny open area and slammed the door. "Are we picking up the others?" I asked.

"No, they're coming from Cleveland," Augie said curtly. He backed down the driveway and took off quickly, seemingly in no mood for conversation.

I looked around for some way to make my ride more comfortable. Between us were two enormous rolls of carpet that stretched from the back door to the windshield. The rest of the van was filled with tack strip, rolls of padding, five gallon buckets of glue, and a variety of tools. Toward the front was a box full of Pyramid Zen Society posters and a half dozen copies of Rose's book, *The Albigen Papers*. A sleeping bag and dirty pillow were jammed behind the front seat, and dog-eared copies of *The Teachings of Huang Po*, and *The Bhagavad-Gita* were stuck up on the dash. I fashioned a seat out of a glue bucket and hoped for the best. When we finally turned onto Interstate 79 and began to make good time Augie seemed to relax a little so I decided to draw him out.

"You knock off a carpet store or something?"

"I lay carpet for a living," he said, turning to me with a grin. "If you call this *living*."

My guarded laughter was all the encouragement he needed to keep talking. From then on the challenge was not how to make conversation, but how to squeeze in a word.

Working with Rose kept him on the road, he said, setting up lectures, starting groups. In the year or so they had worked together, they had settled into a workable pattern. Augie would go to a new campus and set up a lecture date for Rose. Then, after Rose's lecture, Augie would find the most interested student there and persuade him to start a Zen study group on campus.

"But Rose is unpredictable," he said. "Nothing ever goes smoothly. You never know what he's going to do or say next. One time there was this decrepit old lecher at one of the lectures—looked like a drunk off the street—who kept demanding that Mister Rose help him. Rose tried to ignore the guy but he wouldn't shut up. 'Help me, help me,' the guy kept saying. Finally Rose says to him, "I'd like to help you, pal, but I left my gun in West Virginia." Augie laughed and shook his head. "We didn't get many converts that night. People prefer gurus who say they love everybody.

"At another lecture Rose kept getting harassed by this big Hare Krishna guy with a bunch of his followers. Rose tolerated him for awhile, then when he'd had enough he told the guy to get out. The big guy folds his arms and says that this is a public meeting in a campus building and he's not leaving. Rose says, 'Oh, you're leaving all right. That much has been established. The only thing left to decide is whether it's by the door or window!' Augie laughed so hard at the memory he could hardly speak. "We're on the sixth floor. 'Door or window,' Rose says."

"Did the guy leave?"

"Hell, yes. They all left. Good thing, too. Rose was serious."

When he stopped laughing Augie went on to explain that once he'd organized a campus group Rose would come to some of the meetings and Augie would be the group monitor until he could groom a replacement. When Rose was satisfied with the new monitor, he'd send Augie on to the next campus to repeat the process. Rose's purpose, Augie said, was to use these campus groups to find some truly sincere seekers who were serious enough to work with Rose directly.

"What kind of work?" I asked him.

"Inner work. Work on themselves—to become less foolish. Work to reach Enlightenment, like Rose did."

Augie stayed silent for a moment, as if his own words had pulled him into deep thought. He was dynamic, articulate, and apparently quite competent. In this respect he seemed a cut above most of the people I'd seen at the meetings.

"How long has this been going on?"

"About two years."

"You mean there was no group around Rose until two years ago?"

"Not really. When I met Rose he was still painting houses and living with his wife."

"But it seems like he's been doing this all his life."

"That's because he's been *waiting* to do this all his life. Ever since his Experience. It's as if Rose has always had this complete idea for a spiritual group in his head, even though it looked like he'd never get a chance to start one."

A convoy of trucks filled both lanes of the highway. Augie checked his watch impatiently and inched closer to the truck ahead of us in the left lane.

"Rose tried everything. Put ads in magazines, gave hypnosis demonstrations, wrote to anybody who showed any interest at all. Even after he was married he traveled all over the Ohio Valley trying to get people to meet regularly. But he never met anybody who was serious—at least not the way *he* was serious."

The tractor-trailer in front of us finally pulled into the right lane and Augie hit the gas. The van responded with a violent jerk, upsetting my glue bucket and throwing me to the floor. Augie laughed uproariously as I slapped off the dust and slowly replaced my seat with as much dignity as I could.

"That's the thing about Rose, though," Augie went on. "He never gave up. He says that's the formula for success in anything. Persistence. 'If you throw enough mud at the ceiling, eventually some of it will stick,' he says.

"Which is what happened. In the late sixties everything changed. 'A window opened,' is how he puts it. He thinks LSD had something to do with it, although he doesn't know whether acid was the catalyst or just another symptom of the *zeitgeist*. Either way, Rose says, hallucinogens apparently gave people enough of an artificial intuition that they began to pick up what he was saying. Before, when he talked about visiting another dimension and seeing the earth as an illusion in his Experience, people just thought he was crazy. Now, kids had seen enough of a glimpse of that on acid to sense that Rose might be talking about what lay beyond the drug experience.

"Next thing he knows, some of the local kids start showing up at his farm. The word must have got around that Rose was a cool guy to talk to when you were high. I guess this was the sign he was looking for because he threw himself into it a hundred percent. Shut down his contracting business and quit working, even though he couldn't afford to. I'd be at his house all day and the only thing I'd see him eat were day-old rolls from the thrift bakery."

"What about his wife," I said.

"She left about a year ago. The first time I drove down to Rose's house was with Ray—you know, the guy who runs the Pittsburgh group now. We didn't know what to expect, of course. Even so, we about fell over when his wife answered the door. Just never considered that a guy like Rose would be married. She didn't hide the fact that she wasn't crazy about us dropping in, and she kept out of sight the whole time we were there. Within a year she moved out. Too many *brahmachari* coming in and out at all hours, I guess.

"She never really knew about that part of Rose's life. Rose had his Experience before he even met her. The only time he mentioned it to her was on the day they were married. He told her he would always take care of her and always be faithful, but that if he ever saw the opportunity to teach, he'd take it."

Augie glanced over at me. "Of course, she had no idea what he was talking about, I'm sure. Probably thought he meant teach school or something. But by the time I met Rose, their marriage had just about run its course anyway. The kids were grown. His wife had gone back to school and gotten herself a job as a nurse. It just seemed to work out that the group got started about the same time she was supposed to leave."

"What's it like working with him?"

Augie grinned through tight lips and shook his head slowly. "Sometimes it's pretty painful," he said. "Other times there's no place in the universe you'd rather be." He stayed uncharacteristically quiet for a few moments as if considering whether to elaborate or not. When he spoke again it was with a slightly different tone.

"For instance, last summer," he began. "Rose held an Intensive at his farm and a bunch of us came down to stay a couple months. A real mixed bag of personalities and backgrounds, but all of us excited about doing some serious work with a Zen master. So Rose took us out to the farm and showed us where we could pitch our tents and park our vans, or whatever, then he went back to stay at his place in town — Benwood, where we're going now.

"We figured he'd be out again in the morning to get us started on the 'Zen,' but he didn't show up. Or the next day, or the next. We waited a week and he never showed. Finally we got up the nerve to drive into Benwood to see him. When he came to the door he just looked at us and said, 'Yeah, what do you want?'

"We shuffled our feet and stammered something about not knowing what he wanted us to do. 'We're bored,' we told him.

"'Good!' he says. 'That's what I've been waiting for. Now you're all thinking along the same lines at least. When you first came here you were all lost in your own dream worlds, ready to run off in a dozen different directions. Come on in, we'll talk,' he says.

"So he put us to work that summer, tearing down a house he owns in town — board by board. Then we took the lumber out to the farm and used it to build a bunkhouse. Well, I'm not very good with my hands — talking is what I do best. Matter of fact, the reason I lay carpet is to try to get better at practical skills. So Rose noticed this, of course, and wouldn't even let me use most of the tools or get up on the roof of the building — afraid I'll hurt myself or somebody else. He gave me the most menial tasks, like straightening nails to reuse — Rose can really squeeze a nickel.

"Anyway, while I'm doing these menial jobs I amuse myself by capping on everyone else, you know, putting them down. This doesn't wear too well on people and they complain to Rose. He tells them to stop being babies and to learn how to beat me at my own game. When I hear this, I figure I've got *carte blanche* to really lay into these guys, and I do.

"Next thing I know, though, Rose starts in on *me*, really ripping me. At first he was witty and humorous, like he usually is when confronting people, but after a couple of days he dropped the humor and just hammered me, not even trying to be funny. For the first few days I thought, 'Okay, he's teaching me a lesson. I deserve it.' But he just kept going for maybe a couple weeks. I couldn't sleep or eat. All I could do was think about what he was doing to me, and why. All day every day he'd just lay into me about absolutely everything I said or did. Even the guys I'd been capping on began to feel sorry for me.

"Then one night I was really in the depths of despair, sitting outside in the dark with my dog feeling sorry for myself—I had brought my German Shepherd, Dharma, to the farm with me. Well, Dharma went over to this certain area of the farm where everyone went to take a crap. Rose doesn't believe in deep pit outhouses because he doesn't want it to get in the water table. So anyway, that night Dharma went over to this area and rolled in all the fresh shit he could find. Then he came running back and climbed all over me, literally covering me with human excrement."

Augie shook his head at the memory. "I knew that if Rose heard about the incident he'd make the most of it, so I tried to get cleaned up without anyone seeing me. No luck. A couple of the others spotted me—and smelled me—so I had to tell them what happened. And sure enough, a couple nights later we were in town in Rose's kitchen for a meeting and one of the guys tells Rose about my incident with Dharma.

"Rose had a field day with it. He says, 'I always knew that dog was a Zen master. He's just as sick of taking shit from Augie as the rest of us, but he can't speak up and tell him. So he conveys it with a wordless *transmission*—he gathers it all up and gives it back to him!'

"On and on he went. At first everybody was laughing. I even tried to laugh and take the joke for awhile. But Rose wouldn't let up. It went on for hours. Literally hours. I felt absolutely crushed under the weight of it. Eventually the other people in the room couldn't even take it any more—no matter how much they disliked me. Everyone was looking at their shoes and avoiding eye contact with Rose. Except one guy, Al, who ended up getting really angry at Rose and just glaring at him. I've always remembered that Al did that. It meant a lot to me. Finally, around midnight, Rose abruptly stopped talking and we left."

"Was that the end of it?"

"In a way, yeah. A few days later I was at the bunkhouse construction site — watching the others work on the roof. Rose walked up behind me and put a hand on my shoulder. 'That wasn't so bad,' he said. 'You'll live.' Then he walked away and it was over. The rest of the summer it was like it never happened."

"How did you feel about Rose personally while all this was going on?"

Augie paused for a moment, as if unsure how, or whether, to answer me. "That's a funny thing," he said. "My feelings for Rose then and now run the complete gamut. He can infuriate and confound me beyond anything I've ever felt, then two minutes later inspire and move me literally to the point of tears. I've always felt this intense emotion around Rose, but it frightened and embarrassed me. I didn't like the feeling that I might break down and cry at any second, so I fought it. I've since heard Rose call it 'voltage.' He says some people just *feel* him — feel who he is.

"I felt it off and on all that summer, even while he was pounding away at me. Part of me wanted to ask him about it, but I was afraid he'd make fun of me, or think I was weak or unmanly, I guess.

"But then near the end of the summer we were all gathered in the kitchen in Benwood one night. Rose was in rare form, cracking jokes, telling stories, and generally keeping everyone in stitches. The whole house was filled with a feeling of total warmth and friendship — not a trace of tension. I think that's why I decided to say something to him that night — because I felt safe among friends, and because of the mood of the room.

"I was sitting close behind him and off to one side, just out of his peripheral vision. Then at one point in the conversation, while everyone else was laughing at something Rose had said, I leaned over and said something to him about this feeling. But I still didn't have the courage to really spell it out, so I couched it in vague terms. I said, 'You know, Mister Rose, I sometimes think that if I just let go, something might happen to me.'

"He immediately turned to me without a moments hesitation — with a totally transformed, ineffable expression on his face — and says to me, 'Yes, but you'd have to cry. And Augie doesn't cry, does he?'

"He might as well have hit me with a brick. It felt like my head literally snapped back. My mind began to race uncontrollably until I thought I wouldn't be able to hold it together. Like my mind was some kind of engine revving way past the redline, faster and faster until it seemed there was nothing to stop it from coming apart.

"Then, at a certain peak moment I became aware that I was not the person having this frightening experience, that I was observing myself have it from another vantage point. And I knew with great certainty that at that moment I was being offered the chance to see myself, to see who was watching. That if I turned my mental head, I would see who I really was."

"Wow. Did you?"

"Hell no, I was terrified. That was the last thing in the world I wanted to do at that moment. I knew that whoever I saw would not be me, would not be Augie. I was absolutely terrified of who I would see. Terrified of seeing who I really am."

"What was Mister Rose doing while all this was going on?"

"Rose had turned away from me right after he spoke, and went back to talking with the other people at the table. I felt like I had receded from the room, but I was still aware somewhat of Rose, though not of anyone else. Later people told me my eyes were as big as saucers and tears were rolling down my face, but since Rose was ignoring me, they did too.

I was transfixed by his story. "Then what?"

"At a certain point—perhaps when I refused the opportunity to see myself—my mind began to gradually slow down until I started to have thoughts again. I felt myself reenter the room. Then, just as I was becoming aware of the people and surroundings, Rose casually turns back to me and says quietly, 'Mine eyes have seen the glory of the coming of the Lord.'"

Augie stopped talking and I didn't ask any more questions. We passed under a large blue and gold sign welcoming us to "Wild, Wonderful West Virginia," then, a few miles later, turned off the interstate and started up a steep hill past modest brick houses with pickup trucks in the driveways. I was uncomfortable with the silence.

Some miles later we descended into the valley and turned onto a four-lane road that paralleled the Ohio River. I stared out at the comfortless blue-collar panorama, the steel mills and junk yards, the stone quarries and deserted factories that lined the river banks.

"Rose scares me," I said.

"He scares me, too," Augie said quietly. "He scares anybody with enough intuition to sense who he is."

We drove past Wheeling, got off at the exit marked "Benwood," and headed down a narrow street that must have been the main road before the four-lane highway went through. Augie drove slowly, almost tentatively, probably going through his own version of the mental preparations that occupied my thoughts. I tried to dispel my nervousness by concentrating on the details of Benwood as we drove.

With the Ohio River on one side and steep mountain slopes on the other, there wasn't much room for a town. The houses were narrow and built close together. Everything looked old and rusty and in need of paint. Weeds grew in the tiny yards. There weren't many people walking around, but those I saw looked tired and lifeless. The women had fat arms, the men, hard-boned faces with deeply etched lines. Finally, we turned into a large asphalt parking lot next to a smoke-blackened brick building. The faded sign read, "Union Junior High School." Augie pulled up next to the only other vehicle in the lot—an old white bread truck—then shut off the engine.

"Well," he said with a tight smile, "it's show time."

Chapter Four

The Absolute

I got out of the van and followed Augie across the street. We passed several dreary frame houses darkened by years of factory smoke before pausing in front of the steep concrete steps leading to 1686 Marshall Street. Augie stopped for a moment and looked up at the tall, narrow house, built into the hillside. It was painted a steel gray that blended almost perfectly with the winter sky that day, and it seemed to peer down at me with a Gothic solemnness from atop the steep steps.

"It ain't much, but we call it home," Augie said with a grin, obviously enjoying my apparent discomfort at the scene.

Suddenly, there was a thunderous crash and squealing of metal that seemed to shake the pavement beneath us. I jumped back involuntarily and jerked my head around looking for the source. Augie erupted into delighted laughter and pointed to the long rows of freight cars being coupled at the railroad junction a few blocks away.

"You ought to try sleeping here some night," he said, then started up the stairs. I stared at the gaunt, joyless house for a few seconds before following him and decided that sleeping there was the *last* thing I wanted to try.

We passed the front door and went around back to a small porch that held an old refrigerator and several tires. Augie paused to take a breath then knocked loudly.

"Here goes nothing," he said.

After a moment the door swung slowly open and a stern face came into view.

"Christ," Rose bellowed, seeing who it was and flinging open the door. "The way you were banging I thought it was the cops or the IRS." Giving us an exaggerated once-over he added, "Maybe I'd be better off if it was."

Then he broke into an infectious grin. "Come on in. Come on in."

As soon as we'd closed the door behind us he offered me his thick, muscular hand. "Good to see you," he said. His firm, friendly grip and warm tone immediately melted my nervousness and left me with a brief sensation of well-being.

Then he turned to Augie. "You're late," he said, gesturing to the room. "Your charges from Cleveland have been here for over an hour."

I was so absorbed in Rose's greeting that only then did I take in the surroundings. We were in a kitchen crammed full of people sitting around a large formica table in an assortment of mismatched chairs. There were three old refrigerators, all of which appeared to have received a recent coat of an odd peach-colored paint, and against one wall was an antique porcelain sink. The gas stove had two burners lit, but nothing cooking on them, and in a corner was an enormous brown gas heater, creaking and popping. The only wall not covered with plumbing or appliances contained a large, hand-made shelf jammed full of books, papers, and writing supplies.

"Hang on," Rose said, disappearing into the hallway. "Let me see if I can find a couple more chairs."

While he was gone Augie introduced me to the ten or so people there from the Cleveland group. Soon Rose returned with an oak footstool in one hand and a tall red step-chair in the other.

"Best I can do," he said, pushing them towards the table. Augie grabbed the footstool and I was left with the step-chair, which was uncomfortably high and had no arms. I pulled it closer to the table and tried to rest my elbows there, but the angle was wrong. The table itself was covered with pens and spiral notebooks, and an old iron typewriter. Mixed with the papers were a variety of cups and spoons, no two of common origin.

"Want some tea?" Rose asked us, picking up a dented kettle.

"Thank you, yes, " I said. Augie declined and instead pulled a large bottle of Diet Pepsi from his ski jacket.

Rose filled the kettle with water and placed it on one of the already-flaming burners. "Well, Augie," Rose said, gesturing to the gathering, "at least you sent me a better crowd than last time. There don't seem to be any witches in the bunch, at least."

"You're never going to let me forget that, are you," Augie grinned. "You know, the only reason I brought them was —"

"A few weeks ago Augie shows up at my doorstep with two scraggly women, looking just as proud as can be," Rose said, interrupting him and addressing the rest of the group. "Pelts. I send him out looking for serious seekers and all he's worried about is numbers. He thinks his mission in life is to see how many pelts he can drag home to the master's house," Rose laughed.

A few people frowned at being compared to animal hides, but Rose either didn't notice or didn't care.

"Awful looking women. One had long black hair that hung down across her face, which was a blessing. Every now and then, though, she'd lean her head back and the hair would fall away from her face. God almighty. It was like stage curtains opening on a Greek tragedy." Everyone laughed, Augie the loudest.

"I'll tell you though, as soon as those women walked into the kitchen I noticed a strong smell of sulfur," Rose went on, "and I knew immediately they were possessed."

There were a few raised eyebrows at the table. Rose looked them over and redirected the story to one of the skeptics.

"Of course," he said, "the psychiatrists would say they hadn't taken a bath, or they'd been eating matches or something. But this one woman in particular... What the hell was her name?"

"Leslie," Augie said.

"Right, right. I'm terrible with names. She had this floating eye—each of her eyeballs worked independently. Anyhow, I kept seeing this shadowy figure standing behind her. So finally I said to her, 'Do you mind if I ask you a personal question?' And she said, 'No, go right ahead.' So I said, 'Do you have an entity that travels with you?' And she says, 'Oh yes, I have five of them.'"

As he said this, Rose mimicked her squeaky voice so humorously that I surprised myself by bursting out laughing. Rose looked over and directed the rest of the story to me.

"So I asked her, 'Do you mind showing me where one is?' And she says, 'Not at all,' and points right to this shadow I see hanging over her left shoulder. You should have seen Augie," Rose said, forming his fingers into big circles around his eyes. "His eyeballs was like this."

Augie shook his head and laughed. "It was a circus upstairs that night," he said. "Those two women had the room at the end of the hall, and three of us guys were sleeping in the middle room. None of us wanted to be near the door. Every time I woke up the other guys had moved behind me, so that I was the closest to the door. Then I'd stand up with my sleeping bag and move behind them again. Before the night was over we were huddled in the far corner sleeping on top of each other."

Rose and Augie started laughing again, each chipping in a fresh detail now and then, getting more giddy with each memory. Rose was actually holding his sides as if they hurt. For what seemed a long time they stayed lost in their laughter, leaving the rest of us to get what humor we could from the situation. I found it contagious, but most of the people at the table seemed uneasy. When they finally stopped laughing the room was silent for a moment while Rose and Augie coughed and wiped their eyes.

"You know, Mister Rose," Augie said, his voice becoming more serious, "I found out later that Leslie had been a part of an underground movement that planted a bomb and killed someone at the University of Wisconsin."

"Well, that explains how she picked up the entities, then," Rose said matter-of-factly. "Or else she had them beforehand and they're what got her involved in the blood letting."

The idea that entities and possession might be real phenomena, not just the stuff of horror movies, was totally foreign to me. I wanted Rose to elaborate, but felt uncomfortable asking him any questions.

"Why would you put up with it?" asked a short red-haired boy named Jeremy. "I mean, why waste your time with people like that."

Rose smiled at him. "Who am I to say?" he said. "Sure I'd like to work with more serious people, people who are already on the edge, people I could push into something enormous. But I have to figure that everyone who crosses my path is sent for a reason, even if I don't know what that reason might be."

"Do you talk about your philosophy with everyone you know or meet, then? At the store? Neighbors?" Jeremy persisted.

"Hell no," Rose replied. The kettle started whistling and he removed it from the burner. "People here in Benwood think I'm a gangster. I encourage that. If they knew I was a philosopher they wouldn't give me such a wide berth."

He took a dented tin cup off the shelf for my tea and scrutinized the inside of it. Apparently dissatisfied with its sanitation, he went to the sink and rinsed it out.

"You can't act the same with everyone," he said. "When you get around hillbillies, you just smile and talk about cows." He dropped a tea bag into the cup and carefully poured in the water.

"Thank you, Mister Rose," I said, as he handed it to me, surprised to hear a slight catch in my voice. Something about his series of simple gestures had unexpectedly moved me.

"Anybody else ready?" He held up the kettle. Several people took him up on the offer and Rose refilled their cups before returning the kettle to the stove and sitting down in an old wooden swivel chair, the kind you see in attics and basements and very old offices. He leaned back, rocked slowly, and sipped his tea. Then he continued with his thought.

"People here have known me and my family all our lives. My grandfather built this house. My father shot a man a few blocks from here. Your hometown is generally the last place anyone will take you seriously. What's it say in the Bible about Christ going back to his village? Something about not doing any great works there because of their unbelief. That's true. That's the way it is."

"Are you comparing yourself to Christ?" Jeremy asked. His tone was challenging and slightly incredulous.

"Well, there's not much we know about the man," Rose said, smiling, "but from what I can read in the Bible I'd say, yes, he probably had an Experience of the Absolute. Which is what happened to me."

"But, but...Christ was the *son of God*," Jeremy persisted.

"So are we all—if we care to be. If we become who we really are. Like Christ says, 'The works that I do you will do also, and more.'"

"What I mean is, I've studied the Bible and—"

"I gave the Bible a good hard look myself, believe me. I was in a seminary for five years, studying to be a priest. Went in when I was twelve and left when I was seventeen. You can't join a seminary that young anymore, but they took 'em early in those days. It was beautiful there for awhile."

"Why did you leave?" someone else asked. Jeremy looked irritated at the change in subject.

"I left because I couldn't get any answers. I'd ask about something that was bothering me, like the origin of time or the limits of the universe, and they'd tell me to forget those kinds of questions and just have faith. Then they'd quote Thomas Aquinas: 'The finite mind can never perceive the infinite,' they'd say. Which as it turns out is true as far as it goes. But what Aquinas never caught on to was that the finite mind can become *less finite*.

"Anyway, these priests got tired of my questions and told me I had to just perform God's will as the Church decreed it, or else. Told me I could go to Hell for doubting. I mean, even then I began to sense the manifest absurdity of it all. Here we're given this microscopic intelligence to work with, yet God's going to damn us eternally if we can't guess what He wants from us—and He's not talking!

"And so," Rose said over the laughter, "I rejected it all."

"Mister Rose," Augie said, "don't you think it's unusual, though, for a person to be as curious about religion and philosophy as you were at that age?"

"Maybe, I don't know. Part of it had to do with my mother, who was a devout Catholic. She had me convinced that priests talked directly to God. This intrigued me. But even as a small child I had a certain curiosity. One of my earliest memories is writing over and over on a piece of paper: 'Many are called. Few are chosen.'"

"Do you think your early interest in these things is what eventually caused your Enlightenment experience?" Augie asked.

"Oh, I don't know, maybe." Rose grinned mischievously. "That, and catching the woman I was going to marry in bed with a lesbian."

There was scattered, uncertain laughter, except for Augie, who howled. Rose took a sip of tea.

"I don't understand," said Jeremy, looking truly puzzled.

Rose grinned at him and paused for a moment before speaking, as if deciding where to start the story, or how much of it to tell.

"When I was in my twenties I pursued a very ascetic lifestyle," he said finally. "I had decided to make my body a laboratory rather than a cesspool. I did yoga and quit eating meat. I meditated for hours at a time. Every six months I changed jobs so my brain wouldn't harden. I had no attachments, nothing tearing at my hide. If my intuition told me something might possibly be of benefit, I gave it a try.

"And most important, I believe, to my eventual discovery, was celibacy. Between the ages of twenty-one and twenty-eight I was totally celibate. I was celibate because my intuition told me it was worth a try, and because all the people I'd read about who'd achieved anything of a spiritual nature had an energy retention plan—they were celibate. Today there's beginning to be scientific evidence that explains why this works. The discovery of prostaglandins and serotonin, for instance— these are the seeds of genius. But back then it was just intuition and a willingness to try anything that might contribute to my becoming a spiritual being. Celibacy just seemed logical, and I liked not having any hooks digging into me."

I looked around the table and sensed the discomfort everyone felt with this topic. None of us liked hearing that celibacy was an important part of the path. Anything but that.

Rose took a sip of tea before continuing. "But when I got to be twenty-eight years of age I took stock of myself and had to admit that even though I'd had some beautiful experiences, I still didn't know anything. I still didn't know who I was or what was going to happen to me when I died. I decided then that I'd been wasting my life with this spiritual stuff. I figured the best thing to do was to forget the search and get on with the business of being a good animal, at least. So I followed this woman I knew out to Seattle. Her family was rich and we got along okay—she liked my poetry, at least—so I figured this would be a pretty good setup. I'd marry her and live off her money." Rose laughed contagiously.

"But once I got out there I went back to my old ways. I kept drifting down to the library to read esoteric books, or ending up in a yoga pose, meditating. I was trying to forget the search for Truth because I was convinced it was a waste of time, but I was too far along to put it down and walk away from it. I couldn't stop. I had *become* the search.

"Anyway, I worked as a waiter at the Seattle Tennis Club. She had a job riveting airplanes. We were on different shifts so we didn't get to see much of each other. But one day I got off early and decided to stop by and surprise her.

"She lived on the third floor of a boarding house, and her room was right across from the steps. When I got to the top of the stairs I heard strange noises coming from her apartment, so I put my ear to the door. I heard her voice, squeaky bed springs, and a deeper voice.

"I raised my fist to pound on the door, but then thought better of it. There was only one bathroom on the floor, so I decided to sit down on the stairs and wait 'em out. They'd have to come out eventually and I'd see who the guy was.

"Sure enough, after an hour or so I heard the sound of heavy work boots. I stood up and the door opens. Out she walks with her lover. Except it wasn't a man. Her lover was a thick-legged woman with short hair."

Rose seemed amused at the memory.

"So I stumbled back to my hotel room in shock — I had a cheap room over top of a Japanese restaurant. Next thing you know I'm propping myself up with my feet tucked under me in a yoga pose to meditate. But I'd barely got started when something happened.

"It began with a tremendous pain right in the top of my head. Now I've had pain before, but nothing like this. Tears were streaming down my face. I couldn't stand it. My head felt like it was going to explode, and I thought, 'Oh boy, three thousand miles from home and here I go.' I was convinced I was dying. Nobody could have that much pain and live. I remember thinking it must be a stroke, and I worried about how my people were going to get my body back home. They didn't have money to be shipping bodies across the country.

"Then, at the peak of the pain, I went out the window. I could see the Cascade mountains from my hotel room, and that's where I went — out the window and towards those snow-capped mountains. I was aware of seeing people on the street, except that I was above them. I passed over the people, and then over the mountains, and I watched this just like I was in an airplane. And I kept going out until I arrived at a 'place.' I don't say where. It wasn't the Cascades or anywhere else I knew. It wasn't on Earth because there was no sun, there was no sky. I simply arrived at a high place, and it was beautiful.

"I became aware at some point that I was in a causal realm — that I was the reason for its existence, that whatever I thought became a reality. In other words, I was *causing* things to happen, to be created, merely by desiring or thinking about them. The thought passed through me then that I was alone and that I wanted to see humanity—all of it. And so they appeared, all of humanity—everyone who had ever lived, everyone who ever *would* live—covering a huge mountain below me, crawling over each other like maggots, trying to get to the top. I was aware that they were engaged in a struggle that had an ultimate spiritual goal, but their immediate lives and pleasures were pathetic. I was still in some sort of astral form at this point—still maintaining an attachment to the body and to these people—and so I felt a tremendous amount of grief and sadness for their seemingly senseless struggle.

"I knew that if I desired I could pick out individuals, that I could see any man or woman who ever lived or ever would live. Because there was no such thing as time. These people were all living now—no matter what the earth time was for their lives—and all I had to do was pick them out, if I wished.

"So I thought to myself, if everyone is down there, then I must be there, too. And I looked down into the maggot pile, and there I was—Richard Rose. I could see myself struggling down there, the little man, happy in his illusion. I could see his whole life pattern.

"And then I thought, 'If that's Richard Rose down there, who's watching all this?' Suddenly I realized I was not just my individual self. I was the whole mass of humanity *and* the Observer watching it all—I was *Everything*. This propelled me into an indescribable experience of what I can only call 'Everything-*ness*.'"

Rose paused for a moment and looked around the table. When he resumed speaking his voice had a distant quality. "There's just no words…no way I can talk about what that was… no way to begin to describe the…" his voice trailed off, "…the *Totality*."

The room stayed silent as Rose took a sip of tea.

"Then, as I was experiencing this Everything-ness, this Totality, I got to wondering, 'If this is Everything, then what's Nothing?' Because even though I was in an Absolute dimension I still carried traces of my relative mind, which is always looking for dualities, for opposites.

"As soon as the thought of 'Nothing' occurred I started falling. I fell through an incredible void and blackness. And I thought, 'Oh boy, this is it. I'm gone forever.' But I wasn't. At the end of Nothingness I was back on Earth, in my room in Seattle.

"And strangely enough, something was *aware* of the Nothingness as I fell, and of the Everything-ness as I took command of creation. That's why I say, in the final analysis, what you are is the *Observer*. That which you see is never you. That which *sees*, that's you.

The room was dead quiet. Everyone was staring at him, many as if they were seeing him for the first time. Finally someone spoke.

"How do you function *here*, having been to where you've been and then finding yourself back where you are now, wherever that is?" The questioner, a prematurely balding youth with sad black eyes, fumbled for words. Rose nodded encouragingly to show he understood.

"I do nothing and yet everything gets done. Upon returning, you are aware of your projections, of feeling beauty and the like, but you always know that it's not real, that it's nothing."

"So what do you do now?" asked the boy seated to my left, a thin, bookish youth with thick glasses.

"I'm not sure I understand your question," Rose said. "I'm not interested in being a functional person, if that's what you mean. I do a lot of things, but I don't make plans."

"I mean, what do you do for a living?"

Rose gestured to his surroundings with both arms. "You call this *living*?" Everyone burst out laughing. I looked over at Augie, who gave me an uncharacteristically sheepish grin.

"Actually, *this* is what I do," Rose went on. "Maybe it's my own peculiar form of vanity, but teaching is my only excuse for living. If it wasn't for the group I'd probably be off in a cave somewhere, muttering to myself."

"Does life get any easier after Enlightenment?" someone asked.

"No," Rose said quickly, "but it gets funnier."

Everyone laughed loudly again, but I could not seem to join in. Thoughts and emotions I didn't recognize were stirring inside me and I felt the need of being alone for a few minutes. Throughout the morning I had seen several other people leave the kitchen through a closed interior door, presumably to use the bathroom, so I stood up and headed that way.

"Upstairs and down the hall," Rose called out after me.

The door led to a dim hallway, and I was hit by a wave of cold air as I stepped into it. It was like walking outside. Apparently the kitchen was the only heated room in the house. The only light in the hall came from a narrow translucent transom window over the front door at the far end. I hurried past several other closed doors, two of them secured with steel padlocks, and ran up the bare wooden stairs, my footfalls echoing in the dark cold.

The three upstairs bedroom doors were open. The room at the top of the stairs appeared to be the women's bedroom, with its dressers and mirrors and neatly made beds. The middle room—furnished with bare mattresses on the floor, cardboard boxes full of clothes, and orange crates for tables—was obviously inhabited by males. The third room was plastered with psychedelic posters and probably belonged to Rose's teenage son, James, whom Augie had told me still lived there with Rose.

The bathroom was warmer than the hallway thanks to a small space heater that glowed in the partial darkness. A huge claw-foot bathtub stood off to one side, and above the commode was a list of do's-and-don'ts designed to make one-bathroom communal living somewhat workable. I read them as I stood there. At the bottom of the list was the signature "R." As I washed my hands I glanced at myself in the distorted old mirror above the sink. Taped to the top of the mirror was a piece of paper with a question in block letters: "WHAT IS YOUR REAL FACE?"

I stared at the image of myself beneath these words for a moment, then shook my head, almost in a shudder, and hurried out the door, closing it behind me.

At the top of the steps I heard the muffled sound of Rose's voice followed by the sound of laughter, including his. Like a paranoid child, I found myself worrying that they might be laughing at *me*. I stopped to try and make out the words, and as I stood in the cold, windowless hallway a strange sadness overcame me. I was overwhelmed by an incredible longing, an irresistible feeling of loss and nostalgia. I wanted to be home. I thought of being by a warm fire with the smell of my mother's cooking in the air, but the sadness deepened because somehow that wasn't it. That wasn't home. My knees began to quiver in the cold and emotion. I had never felt so lost and alone. I sat down heavily in the middle of the stairs and began to cry.

After several minutes I heard the kitchen door open and the sound of footsteps in the hall. I jumped to my feet, composed myself as best I could, and hurried down the rest of the steps. There in the hallway was Rose.

"Watch out for frostbite," he said as we passed each other.

He had started to open one of the hallway doors and I was almost back to the kitchen, when I turned and spoke to him.

"Mister Rose? Could I talk to you a minute?"

"Sure, sure." he said, reaching into his pocket and pulling out an enormous set of keys. He closed the door he had started to open and led me instead down the hallway to the room furthest from the kitchen. He flipped through his keys for the right one and unlocked the door.

"Come on in," he said.

This room was even more cluttered than the kitchen. A unmade cast-iron bed with sagging mattress was shoved into one corner with several pieces of clothing draped over it. Against one wall stood a pair of black steel filing cabinets, one of them with an open drawer. I glanced at the manila folders that were jammed in there and noticed that each had a person's name on it. Cardboard boxes full of newspaper and magazine clippings were pushed up against the walls, and the dresser and tables were covered with stacks of books and pamphlets. What appeared to be manuscript pages of a book he was writing were spread out on an old wooden desk.

He removed some papers from a couple of straight-back wooden chairs and placed them in the middle of the room facing each other. We sat down.

"Things are still a bit disorganized," he said without apology. "This used to be just my study, but we're running out of sleeping space so I moved my bedroom in here, too."

I felt a sudden surge of affection for this man who squeezed all his belongings into such a small place to make room for strangers.

"Do these people pay you rent?" I asked.

"Everybody chips in ten bucks for lights and heat," he grinned. "Such as it is."

He made small talk by telling me about some of the things in the room. The filing cabinets, he said, were filled with forty years of correspondence—every letter he had ever received, and carbon copies of every one he had written. Some were responses to ads he had placed in occult magazines or from people who had run across his book, and I learned that it was not unusual for him to correspond for years with people he had never met.

"I've turned up some real characters over the years," he said. "I guess that comes with the territory."

"What about the people who live here with you now?"

"Oh, they're all right, I guess. Some of them may be sincere. It's not my place to judge. They've come through the door for some reason. You can tell by the way things happen that it's no accident. But once they disappear, they seem to be gone forever. Not many stay in touch. Of course, everyone has to take off some day. That is, if they're ever going to have any sort of spiritual realization of their own." He smiled. "If they didn't leave, I'd have to kick 'em out."

He stopped talking. It was time for me to say what was on my mind.

"You know, Mister Rose, I don't know how to describe it exactly, but right before I came downstairs and ran into you in the hallway, I was overcome by some kind of powerful homesickness, or something. Almost out of nowhere. I just felt incredibly sad and alone."

He smiled warmly. "You miss little Davie," he said.

The childlike simplicity of his expression exactly matched my mood and I could feel the tears welling up again. "I'm afraid if I don't hang on I'll lose him forever," I said.

"Let him go," Rose said impassively. "He's a coward."

His voice was still warm and fatherly, but his words were like a slap in the face. I felt set up. My urge to cry disappeared completely.

"Nobody wants to give up his cozy illusions," he went on, "no matter how painful they are. Most people never do. They never even consider it. A few people, though—the lucky ones—have something happen to them that makes them start to grow up. They begin to see through the illusion just enough to get curious. So they look into it a little, then a little more, and they begin to see that this life isn't at all what it seems. After that, finding out the Truth becomes the only thing that matters."

"I don't know if I'm at that point," I said, still smarting at being called a coward.

"Only you would know," Rose said. "I'm here and talking for those that already find themselves on the path and are looking for help. I don't go out looking for converts. My own children, in fact, have no spiritual interest. There's nothing I can do about that, no matter how much I might wish it for them.

"A couple of years ago, for instance, my daughter Ruth was home from college on summer break. I'd just finished writing *The Albigen Papers*, and I hoped maybe it might stir something spiritual in her if she read it. But I had to give it to her at the right time and in the right way. One morning I came into the kitchen and she's at the sink, finishing up the breakfast dishes. Did you notice how low the sink is?"

I nodded.

"My mother was a tiny woman and my father put that sink in for her. So anyway, Ruth is standing there and I figure this might be a good time to ask her. So I gave her the manuscript and told her I wanted to get some feedback, to find out if it was worth trying to get the thing published. Which was also true. I did value her opinion—she's always been a bright girl, sensitive and level-headed. She said, 'Sure.'

"A few days later I come home from work and she's at the kitchen table with the manuscript open in front of her, staring straight ahead, like she's in a trance. I stood there for a minute but she didn't say anything so I just picked up manuscript and walked away.

"I figured eventually she'd tell me what was on her mind, but a couple of weeks went by and she still hadn't said anything about the book. So finally one day when we were alone I brought it up. 'By the way, Ruth,' I said, 'I never got a chance to talk to you about my book. What did you think?'

"I'll never forget the look on her face when she turned around, almost angry. She looked me in the eye and said, 'Daddy, I know you're God. But I've got games to play.'"

I didn't know what to say. Rose remained silent. He was looking in my direction, yet his eyes did not seem to be focused on me, but rather on a point somewhere behind me.

"I guess I'm in the same boat," I said finally. "I'm afraid that if I get involved in this work I'll never get a chance to experience all the things I want to do in life."

Rose's eyes re-focused on my face. "Every one of us has some game we feel compelled to play," he said, "especially when we're young. We think we're unique and important, and that God put us here to have lots of fun because he loves us so much. But it's a trap. Our lives are nothing more than a series of distractions.

"One of the most difficult things for people on a spiritual path to get away from is cowardice—allowing things to happen to them because 'God wants them to happen.' And while you're indulging in some fascination or another you're convinced, 'This is important, this is my destiny, this is the real me.' But after your appetite is sated, you look up and shake your head and wonder what is was that possessed you. Whole lives pass that way, moving from one distraction and disappointment to another, and people never wise up—until it's too late.

I stared at him blankly, once again at a loss for words. Rose didn't say anything for a moment either, then he stood up. "Well, we better get back to the kitchen before Augie caves in any more of my chairs," he said. "He has two to his credit already. That boy has the grace of a walrus."

I followed Rose down the unheated hallway, past the rooms he had abandoned in favor of strangers who would someday abandon him, and into the warm, vibrant kitchen where Augie was happily holding forth, laughing, rocking back on the old oak stool that creaked and groaned as if ready to break apart at any moment.

"...so the guy says, 'I don't have to leave. This is a public meeting and I can do whatever I want.' Mister Rose just looks at him and says, 'Oh, you're leaving all right. That much has been established. The only question is whether it's by the door or the window....'"

Chapter Five

The Path

I didn't see Rose again for a month. Every Thursday evening I showed up at the Pyramid Zen Society, but no Rose. The meetings were dry and lifeless without him. They began with Ray reciting almost word-for-word the same opening statement he gave the night of my second meeting. Then he'd try to moderate a discussion on some aspect of Rose's philosophy, or to lead us in confrontation, which he routinely described as "a questioning exercise designed to expose the falseness in our philosophy and behavior." It all seemed forced and contrived. Without Rose the meetings drifted and had no focus or real substance. Ray always said in his introduction that the purpose of the meetings was to clarify Rose's system. But for me, each meeting without Rose only confused me more and I began again to wonder whether I should be coming at all.

I felt I was at a turning point, and that I had come to the end of the "trial period" I had granted myself with Rose and his system. I sensed it was time to decide whether or not to commit to the kind of life that Rose embodied. In a strange way this angered me. One part of me was pulled towards the spiritual, but another part deeply resented having my life and plans so disrupted and devalued by this new turn of events.

One Thursday evening as I drove to the meeting these conflicts flooded me so completely I pulled the car over to the side of the road and sat staring blankly through the windshield, depressed and confused. I came close that night to turning my car around and never going back. Instead I sat there, listening to the engine idle, letting the time pass until I was sure I'd be late. Then I put the car in gear and drove slowly to the meeting.

Rose was there. No one had known he was coming, yet they were many more people than usual in the room that night. The meeting was in full stride as I made my way to a seat.

"It's true, I don't object to healing people occasionally," Rose was saying to a thin young man, "but that's not my primary function. I'm not interested in being a utility. I'm interested in solving once and forever the problem that will solve all other problems."

"Well, the reason I came here tonight was because Frank told me about some amazing things that have happened at your house."

"Oh, he did, did he?" Rose looked over at Frank, who had been with him almost from the beginning of the group. They exchanged smiles. In the last several weeks I'd come to know Frank, and look up to him. He was older than most of the other group members—almost thirty—and had been a pretty good football player in college.

"I just mentioned healing in passing," Frank said. "Mostly I was talking about *transmission*. Like when Jane went into that Experience with you during that rapport sitting."

"Transmission?" someone asked.

Rose pulled absently at his white goatee. "Yes, well, that's a whole other story. Transmission occurs when someone is leaning on the door and I open it up. You see, the thing is, yes, I can focus attention on people and cause a spark of life. Maybe even shake them into something. But I'm never sure whether that's a good idea or not. In a way that person becomes a spiritual slave to me. Their spiritual realization gets tied into mine. Whereas when they have their own Experience, I won't exist."

"But the healings. I mean, you *have* healed people, right?" the thin boy persisted. He looked pale and drained.

"People have been healed around me, yes. But I'm interested in seekers, not people looking for entertainment or rejuvenation. There's people who've come around who have dissipated their energy and life force in a very negative and self-indulgent lifestyle. They want me to patch up their fun machine for them so they can go out and dissipate some more. They have no intention of changing their lifestyle."

"But wouldn't using these powers bring more people into—"

Rose stopped him with a wave of his hand. "I'm not out to make a name for myself. I'm trying to get a message across, and all this other stuff might get in the way." He smiled. "Already people come down to Benwood to see how I live. Do I have a bathroom? Do I *need* a bathroom?"

The room exploded in laughter.

"Finding the Answer has nothing to do with healing, or reading minds, or making a splash," he went on, making an effortless transition to total seriousness. "In fact, the path to Truth is very simple. You make a commitment to the Truth, and whenever you come to a crossroads where you have to choose between the Truth and something else, you choose your commitment to Truth, that's all."

"But it was easy for you, Mister Rose," Frank said. "You were obsessed even as a child with finding the Answer. Most people don't have that kind of fire."

"Nothing's easy for anybody. There's no more God inside me than there is inside of you—if you care to look. You don't learn the Truth the way you learn algebra in high school. Christ didn't say he *found* the Truth, or that he *had* the Truth. He said, 'I *am* the Truth.' What we're talking about here is changing your *being*."

"But how does a person do that?" asked a respectful voice in the back of the room. "Change your being? I mean..."

"You work towards becoming the Truth the same way you work at anything. If you want to be a baseball player, you allow yourself to become intrigued with baseball, to become obsessed by baseball. You watch, you practice, you hang out with older players and try to pick up a few pointers. Eventually you grow into it. At some point you *become* a ballplayer.

"It's the same way with spiritual work. The laws are the same. You find ways to become more and more obsessed by the Truth. You live the small truths in all that you do, and eventually you become a more truthful creature. With hard work and luck you become a person capable of perceiving the Truth directly.

"The search itself changes you," Rose went on. "It transforms you. You start off by honestly acknowledging that you have a big problem: you don't know who you are, or where you came from, or where you're going after death. Most people spend their lives keeping themselves too distracted to think about this.

"But a few people get obsessed with *knowing*. Somewhere along the way they come to understand that the problem *must* be solved because there's something enormous at stake. They are the ones who get the answer. They keep feeding the problem into their mental computer—knowing the computer can't solve it, knowing that the only solution is a change of being."

"That kind of conviction is hard to come by," I said. I was actually startled by the sound of my own voice. I'd had no conscious forethought that I was going to speak. Rose looked in my direction.

"You can't just hope that some day you'll have conviction. You create conviction by *action*. Action *precedes* conviction. Most people wait to be inspired to do something with their lives, when what they really need is to just get moving in some small way in a positive direction. That action will then result in the inspiration to perform increasingly larger and more beneficial actions.

"You need to keep moving, to keep asking the questions. 'Who am I? Where did I come from? What happens to me when I die?' Keep banging your head against the wall. Make up your mind you're going to find the Truth regardless of what it takes, even if it costs you your life. You must be prepared to die for this, if necessary—then you'll get somewhere."

I spoke up again. "I mean, I don't understand how a person can *make* himself obsessed with something. You either are or you aren't, right?"

Rose took a drink of soda before answering, then set the can on the floor.

"The mistake people make is to wait for something to happen to them *before* they begin searching," he said. "They want the voice of God, or something, to tell them to get started. Or maybe they know they should be doing something but they procrastinate, hoping that tomorrow they'll have more conviction and be more determined. What they forget is there may *be* no tomorrow for them."

"But so much of this is out of our control," I said. "We're born with certain—"

"Right, right," he interrupted. "But you still have to work like it all depends on *you*." His words came more quickly and he began to punctuate them with pointing gestures in the air.

"You have to do everything you can yourself. Push your head from the inside, push it to the end of its capacity. Persist. Have faith in the process and in yourself, regardless of whether you go insane, drop dead, or whatever. Persist. Keep the computer going. Eventually, if you're lucky, your head explodes."

He paused for a moment, then softened his tone.

"That's one side of the equation—persistence. The one you have control over. The other side is *grace*. A person on the path has help. Once a person makes a commitment to the Truth—I mean truly demonstrates a sincere desire to find his Real Self at all cost—then this commitment will attract assistance and protection. Opportunities arise. Blocks are removed. Decisions may even be made for you."

My thoughts were incoherent and confused but I couldn't stop asking questions. "But who? What makes these decisions? I mean, where does this help come from?"

"I won't presume to name it. All I'm saying is that there are levels of intelligence that help other levels of intelligence. There is an interpenetration of dimensions. But you can't count on this help or get too secure in the knowledge that it's there. Just when you think you need it most, it will desert you and leave you to suffer the 'dark night of the soul,' as John of the Cross calls it. Because despair is necessary. Despair is part of the final formula for cracking the head. You have to maintain a state of *between-ness* the whole time. Because no matter how hard you push, in actuality, *you* can't change your being. You're being is changed for you."

"So what's a person supposed to be doing while—"

"You can't do it yourself but you have to act as though you can," Rose said, interrupting me. "Action is everything. Everyone has to plot his own road map out of ignorance, and this requires planning. You have to establish an internal 'Ways and Means Committee.' Call on all your faculties—the senses, logic, intuition, memory, emotions—to come up with a plan of action. Then take the first steps in the plan. Start with little things, like coming to these meetings regularly if your intuition tells you this is where you should be. Then build on it, take more action, plan your next steps. Follow the threads and clues you stumble on.

"It's difficult, but not complex. The path to Truth only seems complex because we have to navigate the complexities and interferences of the mind. As these interferences are removed, the path becomes simpler. That's why one of the first things you need to do is get your house in order. Get your life organized to the point where you can at least *think*. Take an honest look at your life to see what's holding you up. Maybe it's fear, or an appetite, or a habit that no one else would consider destructive—and maybe it *isn't* destructive, except to the *search*.

"Once you figure out what the blockages are, you start taking steps to remove them. Then, as each obsession falls away, you get more clarity and confidence. Not only that, you now have the use of the energy you used to burn up on those obsessions.

"Start to cultivate self-discipline. Become a person who can make a decision and carry it out. Set yourself a task and follow through with it. It doesn't have to be anything spectacular. I've advised people to just take a walk around the block every evening after dinner. Literally, just walk once around the block each night. Do that simple thing for one month and you'll have power. Power you can use to take the next step.

"But no, most people think that's too simple. That's not worthy of their great spiritual potential. They want to get right into the heavy work and do something big. The result is that they end up doing nothing.

"If you're honest with yourself—and you have to be honest with yourself if you're going to be a student of the Truth—you start by admitting that you don't know what the Truth is. Otherwise you wouldn't have to go out looking for it. And if you don't know what it is, you certainly don't know how to approach it."

Rose paused and slowly looked around the room.

"The common denominator among all seekers is ignorance," he said. People who think they already know the answer—or think they know *where* to find it or *how* to find it—aren't seekers. They're believers. As soon as you quit doubting and start believing, that's the end of the road as far as your search is concerned.

"If you want to find real answers, as opposed to just accepting what someone else tells you, then you've got to start digging. Christ said, '*Seek* and ye shall find,' not '*Believe* and ye shall find.' You can't start off presuming to know what you're going to stumble into. Believers do this. Believers postulate what the Truth is—what they *hope* it is, what they *want* it to be—and hang on to it for dear life. Seekers search for the Truth plain and simple—*whatever* it may turn out to be. Truth for Truth's sake.

"To end up at a state free of error, you have to start with zero convictions and work from there. Belief is no proof for belief. To believe is to weave. To *know*, is to know beyond a shadow of a doubt what *is*. Knowing means crossing over and back. Belief, and all our thinking processes, are merely visions. Because we do not think—we conjure."

"If you don't know what you're looking for, how do you know where to look?" I asked.

"That's exactly my point!" Rose said enthusiastically. "You can't approach it directly because you don't know what direction it's in. The only thing you can do is create a *reverse vector*—a movement away from ignorance. You approach the Truth by retreating from *un*-truth. You don't know what the final or Absolute Truth is, but you can see what *isn't* true all around you every day of your life. These untruths are what you're looking for, and what you've got to discard once you recognize them.

"Untruths?"

"Lies, inconsistencies, phoniness..." Rose said.

"Bullshit," someone called out.

There was an expectant silence as Rose looked for the speaker. "Was that an editorial comment?"

"No, no," stammered a young man, "I mean you have to get *rid* of the bullshit."

Rose smiled. "Right, right. A real seeker of Truth has to scrutinize his beliefs and actions to pick out the true from the false. For instance, a lot of you probably still believe in Santa Claus. Not the fat guy in the red suit, maybe. But your underlying belief is that the universe is run by a jolly, paternalistic creature who has your best interests at heart, and that all you have to do to get into heaven is to fall in step with the herd and hope for the best.

"Or maybe some habit or obsession is sapping your strength. Or you're scared—fear can paralyze a seeker. Some people face fear and take the next step, but others run away then tell themselves, 'Hell, I didn't want to go into those dark corners anyhow.'

"There's a million ways a man gets fooled, and he first has to get a perspective on these tricks he's been playing on himself before he can discover the nature of God, or the universe, or even the true inner nature of man. He's got to see untruth wherever it is, whether it's in his beliefs about life after death, or in the facade he holds up to the public.

"And once a man faces up to these illusions, the next step is to get rid of them, to dump them from his life and then look around for something that's less phony and more consistent. And as these barnacles fall away, he's automatically going to be headed in a more truthful direction. *That's* the path."

Rose paused and looked around the room. His gaze stopped on me. As if cued, I asked another question.

"But if you're right, and we can't know what's true, how can we know if your system is any good?"

"You *don't* know," Rose said emphatically. "And I don't expect or want anyone to merely accept that this system is good. Check everything out for yourself. In this group, *doubt* is sacred, not belief. A person should doubt everything except their ability to doubt. And that includes doubting me and everything I say. Don't take my word for anything. I may be nothing but an old hillbilly with one pant leg rolled higher than the other, drinking coffee out of a Mason jar."

Rose continued over the laughter.

"Look," Rose said, "you don't need me. Nobody needs me. All you need is your own inner determination. Maybe a few words or lines in a book will help you, maybe they won't. But if something you hear appeals to your intuition, check it out. Prove or disprove it for yourself. Because when you get into these matters the only thing you have to go by is your intuition. And the more perfected your intuition becomes, the better you are at discrimination."

"But if you can't recognize Truth when you see it, how can you recognize untruth?" someone asked.

"It's not that difficult. After awhile you get to know what garbage smells like and you just won't tramp in it. The biggest obstacle to Truth is ourselves. That's why you can't lay down a set of rules for how to go about this because different people have different obstacles standing between them and Enlightenment.

"But there are valid disciplines," Rose continued, "valid pursuits, that can be used by a serious seeker. Each will take you part of the way. There's philosophy, which tries to discover Truth. Science, which aims for Reality. And religion, which seeks to approach God. The fact is that when you find yourself—your final, absolute, eternally aware *Self*—you'll become all three: Truth, Reality, God. They are One."

"What about meditation, Mister Rose?" a young woman asked. "Will that help?"

"I don't like to use that word because you need hip boots to wade through some of the stuff they call meditation nowadays." Several people laughed. "Basically, wisdom comes during work, not meditation," Rose continued. However, I do believe a person should sit quietly at a set time each day for a half-hour or an hour."

"Like with a mantra?"

"No. That's a type of meditation I advise against. Repeating a sonorous sound or word isn't going to teach you about yourself. You need to challenge the mind during meditation, not put it to sleep. I don't recommend visualization, either—you know, where you conjure up peaceful scenes and repeat how happy and holy you are. That's just another form of autosuggestion. We're hypnotized enough by life as it is. We don't need to lay it on any thicker. We're not looking for peace and relaxation, we're looking for Truth, for the *ultimate answer*. Now that may sound like a tall order. But some people figure life's not worth living until they know *who's* living, and *why*.

"What kind of meditation do you recommend?" someone asked.

"To begin, start looking back at the people and events of your life, especially the traumas. Everybody has an unfinished agenda that needs cleaning up. It's beneficial to meditate on those people or situations that left you with a sense of injury. Times when you felt mistreated, events that left you feeling sorry for yourself, perhaps. I don't mean relive them or psychoanalyze them. Just go back and try to remember them, then see if you can observe them dispassionately.

If you stick with it for awhile, eventually you'll start seeing what a fathead you were, seeing what got you into trouble. And if you follow up on it, maybe you'll see that you're still making the same mistakes right now.

"As you mature, some of this takes place normally," Rose said with a smile. "I just recommend accelerating the process so it doesn't take you ninety years or ninety lifetimes to figure out what a fool you are and start making some adjustments."

A young woman with long blonde hair spoke up softly. "You seemed to intimate that there are also higher forms of meditation?"

"Oh yes. I wrote a little pamphlet about this—the boys here may have some copies at the table, I don't know. But, yes, once you've disciplined the body to sit quietly and have gained a familiarity with your thought processes, you can *observe the mind directly*. Watch your thoughts as they happen, as they come and go. This brings you into contact with a hidden faculty of the mind—the *observer*. This observer—that which *sees*—is a more real part of yourself, because the observer is not a part of this picture show we live."

Ted, a boy who had been coming for a couple weeks but had not met Rose yet, spoke up. "In traditional Zen there is a lot of emphasis on work with *koans*, you know, like unsolvable riddles that—"

"I don't give people koans," Rose said with a smile. "Your everyday life will give you all the *koans* you need to get enlightened."

"I mean, it seems like that's a system that has—"

"Zen is a system that takes into account the fact that most of the game is already fixed. Zen says it's a good idea to see things as they are rather than try to change things that cannot be changed. This is all true. Zen is a system I admire. But there's no rigid formula for finding the Truth. You can't get this stuff out of a cookbook. Each man's path is different. The only thing enlightened people have in common is what they find.

"I tell people to turn over every rock—read everything you can get your hands on, find teachers, talk to your fellows, compare notes. But I don't presume to prescribe specific practices. It's up to each person to find his own way. There's no ritual or discipline you can give out that will work for everybody. All you need is a tremendous hunger."

"You mean you don't have a system?" someone asked.

"Oh, we most definitely have a system. That's the whole reason we're here—to try and find ways and means to discover the unspeakable. But it's not some neatly packaged concept structure that piles one unproven postulation upon another. You've got to dig through this stuff yourself. It can't be handed to you."

"But there don't seem to be any specific disciplines or practices that you—"

"Those who teach disciplines," Rose interrupted, "unless the disciplines are for introspection or for dying, are teaching systems of orderly leisure, auto-hypnosis, or self deceit."

Rose sat with his hands on his knees, impassively waiting out a long silence. Finally, a professional-looking man in his thirties seated next to a well-dressed woman about the same age raised his hand.

"Mister Rose you continually prod people to work, and study, and make a *vector* of their lives, but in your book, *The Albigen Papers*, you wrote that Enlightenment is always an accident."

"Yes, that's true. Spiritual experiences cannot be envisioned beforehand," Rose said. "The spontaneity and utter surprise at what you find is what validates your experience. If you had a spiritual experience that followed your expectations—seeing Jesus, or whatever—you could never be sure that you didn't create the experience yourself to satisfy your own desires."

"But that's my point," the man continued. "If Enlightenment is indeed an accident, why should we try to work for it?"

"You have no choice," Rose replied, his voice rising. "You become what you *do*. If you *do* nothing, you *become* nothing. And so you work. Work without knowing why you're working. Without even understanding what you're working for. You just want an answer and you know it won't come if you surrender to lethargy and despair.

"It's true—the *Absolute Answer* comes as an accident. But it's an accident that is the result of work. Work that makes the sum and extent of your entire life your *prayer for the answer*. And if that prayer is persistent and sincere enough, maybe you'll develop into someone who becomes *accident prone*.

"But how do you—"

"By making Truth your God. By living and telling and seeking the truth in everything you do. By refusing to allow the least bit of falseness to creep into your life or your philosophy. Because if you rationalize even 'little' lies you become comfortable with lies and rationalizations. If you can't face small truths about yourself, you'll never develop the capacity to withstand the impact of *Absolute Truth*. You'd never survive it."

Rose paused and let the room stay silent for a moment before speaking again. "Truth is kind," he said finally. "If you're weak, it keeps it's distance. It won't reveal itself until you're strong enough to take it."

A tentative hand went up in the middle of he crowd.

"What exactly are you trying to do here tonight?" There was both respect and confusion in the young man's voice.

"Do? Nothing really. I'm just trying to find people whose heads are partly open, then pry them open a little more. I believe the only thing anyone does who has a genuine spiritual message—the only thing he *can* do—is to be there when someone is ready. When you feel you have to go out and convert people, that's just an ego talking. At the same time, if you've discovered something, there's an obligation to pass it on if you can.

"I know it sounds paradoxical, but if you have something to offer that you think could help somebody transcend his level, then you have to make yourself known. Because people looking for a higher level are blind on that level—they can't find *you*. But if you put yourself in their path these people might bump into you at the right moment. Then, perhaps, you might be able to be of some service.

"I have discovered. I don't know how many others can discover through the same procedure, but I feel compelled to make it known. So I draw diagrams and make noises as if it might make a difference. But in the end I know each man must find it for himself.

"When I was in my twenties I used to curse the darkness. Every place I looked on the path, it seemed, I found phonies and hucksters, even some people with truly bad intentions. It made me doubt the validity of what I was trying to do. I began to feel I was wasting the most valuable years of my life when I could be having fun getting drunk or raising a bunch of kids, or whatever having fun is supposed to be.

"The temptation was always there, naturally, but I kept putting it aside, hoping I'd find this thing called Truth someday. And as I fought my way through, I made a vow that if I ever found anything, I'd try to pass it on, if I ever found anybody that wanted help, I'd try to help them. That was my obligation.

"Looking back, I believe it may have been the final piece of the puzzle that propelled me into my Experience, and I encourage anyone on the path to make the same vow. I encourage the people who work with me to work with others as they go—to teach along the way. I think everyone in the group should teach. When people say to me, 'But

I don't know anything.' I say 'Nonsense.' You *do* know something. Something that people on the rung below you can use."

"What do you mean, 'the rung below you'?" someone asked.

"All human effort and success is pyramidal in form," Rose replied, "including spiritual. In finances, for instance, you've got massive amounts of people on the lower levels, then fewer and fewer as you go up, until at the top you have only a handful of billionaires. It's the same no matter how you slice up the population — by IQ, artistic ability, athletic ability, anything.

"It's the same with spiritual levels. The majority of people are on the lower levels, with fewer and fewer as you go up. I sometimes describe this as the spiritual ladder — a ladder where the rungs become smaller as you near the top. You've got to fight your way up the ladder, and every step of the way, you'll part company with more and more people. That's okay. That's good. This isn't a convoy where we move at the speed of the slowest vehicle and all arrive together. You are responsible for your own destiny. You are responsible for *saving your own soul*.

"People are always attacking me at my university lectures because they resent this idea. The popular notion now is that we're all entitled to an equal share, that nobody should be allowed to get too far ahead of the pack. But I don't believe in that kind of equality — where everybody stays at the bottom of the pyramid so that no one feels like a failure. I believe in climbing the pyramid as fast as you can, and in helping anyone who wants to climb with you."

"But aren't other people sometimes a hindrance to your own spiritual search?"

"Absolutely. That's why I emphasize what I call the 'Law of the Ladder.' What I tell people in the group is to work with your fellows, but to obey the Law of the Ladder.

"The Law of the Ladder says that you should work on only three rungs of the ladder, but work on all three at once. You learn from those on the rung above, teach those on the rung below, and join efforts with your fellows on the rung where you stand. If you reach two rungs above, you won't understand what the person is saying. If you reach two rungs below, you'll get crucified."

"But if a person isn't enlightened, how can he keep teaching from becoming just another ego trip?"

"Do like I do," Rose grinned. "Don't shave, don't wash. Wear dead-men's clothes."

There was scattered laughter.

"What about earning a living, though," I said. "What kind of job can you have that will let you be a spiritual teacher or student at the same time?"

"If you're sincere it doesn't matter. Some jobs leave you more time to think your own thoughts than others do, but it will be different for everyone."

"Does that mean a person can have material success and still be on a spiritual path?"

"Depends of what you're committed to. If you're committed to money, no. If you're committed to spiritual work, maybe. But a person can have only one major commitment in life. You can't do everything you want and still arrive at an ultimate answer. You can't let yourself get confused with too many ideas or too many drives. It divides your attention and drains you. A person needs every ounce of energy he can muster for the search. You're going to walk through death, and that takes some vitality."

"You mean if you're honest commitment is to spiritual work, then financial success won't hurt you?" I persisted.

"It doesn't have to. If a person wants to be successful in spiritual matters he should be a success on every level of his life. A man doesn't *achieve* success, whether it's spiritual or material. He *becomes* a success. And that requires getting into the habit of success—establishing a vector of success that can be applied in any direction he chooses."

"But doesn't material success just feed the ego?" someone asked.

"If you let it. The trick is to work dynamically towards your goals until somewhere along the way, if you're lucky, you realize that *you* do nothing in this life. You're just an observer of your destiny. After that, the ego disappears."

"But what's the point of doing anything if all you discover is that there's nothing to be done," I blurted out.

"Because you'll never find out anything unless you do, that's why." The intensity in Rose's reply bordered on irritation. "You've got people who can't wipe their own noses who think their laziness and incompetence is some sort of spiritual detachment. They want to jump over the material world without ever mastering it, and get right into Enlightenment. As a result they end up doing nothing on either the material or the spiritual plane. You have to extend your material being to the limit. Only then will you find out that you don't exist—at least not as you think you do. You've got to fatten up your head before you chop it off."

Rose paused for a moment to take a drink of his soda, then spoke more softly.

"You've got to somehow build up a tremendous ball of energy if you want to find the Answer, and that's not going to happen without a bit of ego. You use the ego, let it go along for the ride. Take on the world, tackle some projects, practice some ascetic disciplines—maybe perform a miracle or two if the opportunity presents itself. Success in these things will give you confidence and momentum—a *vector*—to use for the bigger task. And when the door opens to the Absolute, your *vector* is what takes you through it. The ego can't go.

"The point is," he said, "you don't have to give up the material world to embark on a spiritual search. If you're sincere and something lies in your way, you won't have to give it up. It will be taken from you."

"Is that supposed to be comforting?" Frank said. Everyone laughed.

"In a way, yes," Rose said. "It means you can do what thou wilt as long as you hold your head the right way."

"Between-ness," Frank said seriously.

"Yes, between-ness," Rose nodded. "Running between the raindrops. If you make your life a prayer, true prayer—one person continually asking one question—then all the rest is just details."

Chapter Six

The Farm

After the meeting that night I decided to postpone my "big decision" about getting into spiritual work and just start "getting my house in order," as Rose called it. I cleaned and organized everything I owned. I stopped drinking. I began trying to meditate. I kept a journal. I walked around the block at night.

Almost immediately I felt better, or at least better about myself. Besides a boost in energy and confidence, I discovered that the more control I had over small things, the less nervous I was about my life in general. I even started getting insights into situations and human behavior I'd previously thought were hopeless or inexplicable. In short, the small things were beginning to prove themselves in my life, and I began to look forward to Rose's next visit with great enthusiasm.

Again, however, several weeks passed without Rose showing up at a meeting. One night while Augie and I were putting up meeting posters around campus I asked him when Rose might be back.

"Hard to say. He's holed up at the farm writing a new book. He may not come out for awhile."

"The meetings are nothing without him," I said. "I feel like I need to see him."

Augie held a poster up to a telephone pole and slammed the staple hammer into it twice. "The road goes two ways, you know," he said.

"That almost sounds profound," I laughed.

"Yeah, well. I stole it from Mister Rose. He sometimes goes around asking people, 'What do you know for sure?' just to see what they'll say. People in the group mostly, but friends and neighbors, too. He told me once that with all the college kids and intellectuals he's asked, the only person who ever gave him a decent answer was an uneducated hillbilly farmer. When Rose asked him, 'What do you know for sure?' the farmer said, 'The road goes two ways, and it ends in the marble orchard.' Rose loves that story. He still calls graveyards marble orchards."

"Can people just drop by the farm to visit him?"

"It's better to call first. He's not always there."

"I'd feel funny calling him."

"All the more reason to do it."

"I don't know. Do you have his number on you?"

"Tell you what. I'm going down there on Friday to drive him to a lecture he's giving at Ohio State. You can come along if you want."

That sounded perfect and we made the arrangements. We were both in high spirits that night and we joked and laughed as we finished the posters. When Augie picked me up a few days later, however, he seemed agitated and his conversation was curt, much like it was the day he picked me up to go to Benwood. I waited for him to loosen up, but the longer we rode the more irritated he became. I sensed his displeasure was somehow connected with his feelings about the farm. I brought up the subject a couple of times, but he didn't respond and I didn't push it.

We took the same exit off the interstate as before but instead of proceeding straight up the hill we made a quick left at the traffic light and headed away from town. Augie's mood grew increasingly sour with the changing scenery and I realized that he just didn't like being in the country. He maintained a steady monologue of complaint about everything we passed. To him, the rocky trout stream that hugged the road was just another inconvenience, a flood hazard every spring. The winding, unpredictable roads concealed a drunken hillbilly in a pick-up truck around each bend. He pointed out every shack, every junker, every beached school bus and overgrown outhouse as if they vindicated his displeasure and sour mood. I gradually tuned him out.

The road grew narrower and more bumpy until the pavement disappeared entirely, giving way to a rutted dirt roadway that wound its way up a steep, rocky mountainside. The road made a ninety-degree turn at the peak of the ridge, opening up a spectacular view of the river and valley below. Augie had sunk into complete silence, so I knew we must be getting close. A little farther up the road we came to a collection of rustic farm buildings and Augie pulled into a dirt parking area nearby. There were two other vehicles parked there.

"Looks like Rose is here, all right," Augie said. "That's his car—the black Olds."

I looked around at the surroundings. Remembering Rose's house in Benwood, I had prepared myself for something less than a picture-postcard hideaway. Even so, I was stunned and disappointed.

The small, unassuming farmhouse was strictly functional and badly in need of paint. A foreboding, seven-foot high fence of sharpened locust logs ran along the road in front of the house, giving the effect of a stockade or fortification. Several small sheds built from cast-off lumber and painted an unusual shade of green surrounded the house, and an old blue school bus sat rusting in the weeds a few yards from where we pulled in. Augie kept the motor running.

"You coming in?" I asked hopefully.

"Like to, but I'm running late. I've got to pick up some stuff in town. Tell Mister Rose I'll be back out in a few hours."

I got out and watched his white van bump and rattle down the dirt road until it was out of sight, leaving me standing alone in an almost eerie silence. I looked around. Besides the house and outbuildings there were several barns of various sizes and a rusty house trailer. After a minute or so I headed for the house and knocked on the front door. No one came. After another try I walked around to the back porch. There was a screen door, but the interior door was open to the kitchen. I peered inside.

"Anybody home?" No answer. I walked out of the yard again and looked around at the farm. The place seemed deserted, but I could hear the braying of a goat coming from the hillside across the road from the house. There were other barns and outbuildings on the hill that looked like they were part of the Rose farm, so for lack of anything better to do I headed in that direction.

Eventually, I found the source of the braying. Near the edge of a clearing a man was struggling to free a goat from some kind of entanglement. As I approached I could see that the goat, apparently staked out to graze, had managed to wind her chain around a small sapling until only a few links separated her from strangulation. As the man struggled to free her the goat did everything she could to stay tangled. I watched for a minute as he tried to pull the goat in the opposite direction of her entanglement. The goat sat down. Using all his strength the man got the goat to her feet and tried to chase her around the tree. The goat put her horns against his knees and stood firm.

"Can I help?" I asked as I cautiously approached.

"Yeah, hold her collar," he said, as if he'd known I was there all along.

He was in his late twenties, tall and wiry, with reddish hair and a certain frenetic look about him, as if he was running twice as fast on the inside as he was on the outside. His clothes had dirt crusted on them, and the butt of a pistol protruded from the back pocket of his jeans.

"Augie said he was dropping somebody off here today," he said.

"Yeah. I'm Dave."

He glanced up at me for a moment. "Larry," he said, not offering his hand. Then he gestured towards the goat with his chin. I gingerly took hold of what looked like a dog collar. The goat's hair was rough, hot, and uncomfortable to the touch.

Larry glanced at my tentative grip and shook his head. "You better hold her tighter than that or we'll be chasing her all over the farm."

I grabbed the collar with both hands and held on while Larry unhooked the chain. Amazingly, the goat stood passively in my grasp as Larry unwound the chain from the sapling. Then, forcefully and unexpectedly, Larry took hold of the goat's collar and started pulling her away from the tree. The goat bellowed loudly as he dragged her about twenty feet away then reattached the chain to her collar.

"There's a couple more in the same mess," he said. I followed him to the next entangled goat and we repeated the procedure.

"They're mad because they're staked out, and this is their way of getting even," he said as he unwound the chain from a tree stump.

"How come they're not running free?"

"They been getting into the cornfields. They're the dumbest animals in the world until it comes to finding a hole in the fence. Then they turn into goddamn geniuses."

"Cornfields? What else do you grow on this farm?"

"They're not our fields. They belong to the Krishnas'."

We began untangling a third goat.

"Krishnas? Hare Krishnas?"

"Yep." He gave the goat a gratuitous yank. "They've got us surrounded."

I looked around. All I saw were trees and what to me looked like wilderness. I could see that Larry was getting a kick out of my confusion.

"Hundreds of them. Thousands of acres. Rose's farm is the only piece of land on this ridge they don't own." He gave me an ominous grin. "And they want this land *bad*."

We finished untangling the last goat then stood for a moment in silence. I looked into the dense forest that covered the hillsides in all directions, and tried to envision hundreds of orange-robed devotees pressing in on us. It was too incongruous. I couldn't bring forth the image even in imagination.

"Well, are they friendly at least? Spiritual brothers of sorts?"

Larry patted the pistol in his back pocket. "I don't carry this for squirrels."

It was an unexpected answer. "A gun? Because of some Hare Krishna's?" I said.

"This bunch around here are a little different."

As if to punctuate our conversation, a rifle shot suddenly rang out. I flinched and involuntarily ducked even though it was obvious the shot was not in our immediate vicinity. Larry got a big laugh out of it.

"That's just Phil. Raccoons have been getting into the garden."

"Thought for sure it sounded like a Krishna rifle," I joked nervously. Larry looked at me quizzically as if trying to decide if I was serious.

"Is Mister Rose around?" I said.

"Yeah. Down at the spring, I think." He pointed vaguely in the direction of the house. There's a path on the other side of the house. Just follow it."

"Thanks." I walked back down the hillside. When I got to the rear of the house I noticed someone kneeling by the garden fence with a rifle slung over his shoulder.

"Hello," I yelled from a safe distance. "Anybody home?"

A young man with a thin face looked up.

"Just me," he said, then bent back to his work. As I approached I saw he was skinning a raccoon. It was my first exposure to the insides of an animal.

"You must be Phil," I said.

"One shot, forty yards," he said, pointing to the wound with the tip of his knife.

"What are you going to do with him?"

"Hang the hide on the fence. I've been reading where it'll keep the other raccoons out of the garden."

As he spoke he slid his knife under one edge of the skin and started peeling. I felt suddenly queasy and turned away, pretending to take in more of the surroundings.

"Mister Rose around?"

Phil looked me over before answering, as if uncertain about my capacity for tramping around the farm. Finally he pointed to an overgrown path leading away from the garden towards some woods.

"Yeah, down that way, at the spring. You'll see him."

As I started out he called after me. "Watch out for snakes," he said with a laugh.

The path took me through an old pasture that separated the house from the woods. It was overgrown with saplings and prickly weeds that seemed to get more dense as I neared the trees. At the edge of the field was a wire fence strung between crooked locust posts, and a wooden gate made of discarded pallets. On the other side of the gate the path widened into what appeared to be an old logging road that went deep into the woods.

I walked a few yards and heard the sound of running water coming from the other side of a steep embankment. I looked over the edge and saw the spring, flowing through a steel pipe that protruded from a somewhat lopsided cement bunker. A steady stream of clear water poured from the pipe into an old porcelain bathtub fringed with algae. Bars of soap and shampoo bottles were lined up on cinder blocks next to the tub, and several frayed towels hung on nearby branches. Mister Rose, however, was nowhere around.

I was hot and sweaty, probably more from nervousness than from my short walk, so I climbed down to the spring and stuck my head into the overflowing tub without first testing the water. My heart nearly stopped. I would never have believed water could be that cold without becoming ice.

I hurriedly dried my hair on one of the towels then climbed back up the embankment and continued down the logging road, which became increasingly narrow until it was little more than a deer run. When it finally disappeared I sat down on the edge of a steep hillside and stared at the valley below.

A break in the trees provided me a clear view of a beautiful, sprawling farm that occupied the whole valley. A wide creek wound through flat green fields where herds of black and white cattle grazed in the afternoon sun. With its large, freshly painted buildings, contented livestock, lush pastures and well-maintained fences, the neighbor's farm in the valley represented everything the Rose farm was not. Suddenly, I understood Augie's aversion to this place. Like Rose's house, his car, his clothes—like everything that surrounded him—Rose's farm was stark, austere, comfortless.

Suddenly, there was a voice not ten feet behind me.

"Well, if it isn't little Davie."

I was so startled I literally jumped straight to my feet from a sitting position. "Mister Rose," I stammered, my heart pounding. "I didn't hear you."

"I thought I'd see how close I could get without you coming out of your coma," he said.

"Larry said you were at the spring. I came down looking for you."

"Yeah, the spring house always needs repairing," he said with a wide grin. "Augie built it." We both laughed and I began to feel more comfortable. We made small talk for a few minutes, then he started walking deeper into the woods. I fell in step beside him. As we walked he spoke about the land. He told me when the logging road was cut, how far his property extended in each direction, and where to look if I wanted to see deer. We skirted the edge of a steep ridge then descended a gradual slope and crossed a small stream. On the other side was a large clearing. As we emerged from the trees I noticed quite a few junked cars and trucks rusting in the weeds.

"This here's the racetrack," Rose said.

I laughed at what I assumed was a euphemism for the farm junkyard, but he continued to explain.

"I had a deal with a few guys awhile back to have a racetrack built here on my land. This is as far as it got before things went sour."

As I looked around I saw that there was a distinct oval track around the perimeter of the field where the weeds were shorter and no saplings had yet grown back.

"In exchange for using my land I had the rights to all the concessions in the place. It would've been noisy on race days, but I was always looking for ways to support the family."

We continued our walk, eventually crossing the dirt road and climbing the hill towards where Larry and I had freed the goats. We picked up another logging road that wound through more dense woods, and as we walked Rose talked about everything we passed — the goats, the gates that needed repair, the budding plants and trees.

"This here looks like moss, but it's actually patches of tiny evergreens," he said, bending to stroke a ground-hugging plant.

"I'm glad to get a chance to talk to you today, Mister Rose," I said. "Some things have been on my mind."

"Yeah?"

"It's nothing I can put my finger on, really. I guess I'm just confused about what I should be doing. I don't know how a person on a spiritual path should act."

"One of the worst egos you can have is to get on a spiritual path and think you're a spiritual person. A person on a true spiritual path never knows how to act. He just *acts*. That's the reason I don't act the way people think a spiritual person should. They'd try to copy me, and when they got so's they could imitate my actions they'd think they were spiritual." Then he laughed. "They try it anyway, but I keep 'em guessing."

"I guess the main thing that's bothering me," I said, "is whether to come to the Intensive this summer." Periodically, Rose held "Intensives" at the farm, and the one planned for that summer was the talk of the group — a chance to live and work with him every day, not just once or twice a month at meetings. Everyone, it seemed, was going but me.

"My problem is that I have to earn enough money this summer to pay for law school in the fall. I don't see how I can do both."

"Well, sometimes it does seem like everything's working against you, that's true." Rose spoke reflectively, almost to himself. "Back when I was in my late twenties, for instance, I couldn't get anything to go right. All the time and effort I'd put into the search, and I had nothing to show for it. Instead of rewarding me for what I thought was a spiritual lifestyle, God seemed to be punishing me. Other people had money, security, families, and all I had was a bald head and rotten teeth."

I didn't catch the meaning of his example. "I mean, I wonder whether going to law school is such a good idea after all," I said. "It seems like a law career is incompatible with spiritual work."

"Stick with it," he said firmly. "We need one honest lawyer in the world. Besides, you're not cut out to be a wood-chopping monk. That's not your path."

I was both intrigued and unsettled by the certainty in his voice.

"Maybe I'm fooling myself, Mister Rose, but I feel like I want to find some answers. Maybe not as badly as you did, but badly enough that I don't want a career to get in the way."

"You don't know what might get in the way and what might cause a breakthrough. You never know what a person's destiny is, or how that destiny might play out. Like when I wanted to get married. If I'd have found a wife when I was looking for one, I feel certain I never would have had my Experience.

"A couple years afterwards, though, I ran into a woman who needed a husband. She was pregnant and the baby's father wouldn't marry her. I said I would, so we got married. Funny thing is, I'd seen this woman in a dream, years before. In the dream she was walking down the road towards my farmhouse in a red dress. I didn't know her—never seen her before—but when I woke up I said to myself, 'That's the woman I'm going to marry.' Incidentally, when I met her later, she had on the same red dress from the dream."

He talked for a few more minutes about dreams, and speculated about their source and the validity of the information that came through them. I felt he wasn't answering my questions, or if he was, I was missing his point.

"I guess what I want to know is, do you think I should come to the farm for the Intensive and not worry about work and school?"

"There is no way to predict the interweavings of destiny. You do what you feel is right then accept the consequences. My father shot and killed a man because he thought it was the right thing to do. In a strange way, this may have been a contributing factor to my spiritual vector and my eventual Experience."

"Your father killed a man?"

"A man named William Porter. Killed him because he pushed my mother off the sidewalk. He didn't kill him because he was angry, or to prove he was a tough guy. He did it because his wife was pregnant, and he believed that a man has an obligation to protect his family.

"He didn't even try to get away with it. Walked straight to the police station and turned himself in. The prosecutor wanted to make an example of him, but the jury only convicted him of second degree murder. He was sentenced to nine years. The day after he was sentenced, my mother went to Charleston and camped out on the governor's steps. Literally camped out there, day and night, refusing to leave until the governor gave my father a pardon. She was pregnant with me at the time and it was the middle of winter, but she wouldn't budge. She stayed on those steps for two and a half months in the cold and snow and was prepared to die there if she had to. Eventually they caved in. The governor didn't want a frozen pregnant woman on his hands. I've still got a copy of that pardon around somewhere.

"Later in his life my father sometimes said that each of his sons reflected the mood of our mother as she carried us—and all four of us were different. A lot of the mountain people around here believe this—that a child's character is formed in the womb. I believe it, too, to a certain extent. In my case, I believe I was marked by two things: the fact that my mother was forced by circumstances to be celibate while she carried me, and the iron determination she had as she sat on those steps in the snow."

Chapter Seven

After the Absolute

When Rose and I arrived back at the farmhouse Augie's van was there, along with an orange Volkswagen. Augie and four guys I didn't know were standing around the parking area. Rose asked Augie if he'd picked up everything he was supposed to for the lecture and they discussed the details. As it turns out Augie had forgotten something. Rose became irritated and we all gave him plenty of room as he transferred a couple of boxes of books from the Volkswagen into the van. When Rose got into the van himself, everyone opted for the other car except Augie and me.

"Let's go," Rose said impatiently.

Rose sat in a lawn chair in the passenger seat area, while I searched through the rubble in the back for a place to sit. Rose watched me struggle with the clutter.

"Christ, Augie. Why the hell didn't you clear some of this junk out of here?" he grumbled. "We might've needed to take more people."

Augie offered a weak explanation, which Rose summarily dismissed.

"Augie's the kind of guy who'd throw people out of a lifeboat to make sure he had room to stretch out," Rose said, turning to me without smiling. "It don't occur to him people might need a spot to sit in his van."

I arranged some carpet foam into a fairly stable seat for myself and was glad to be in the back out of the line of fire. After a few miles, though, Rose seemed to ease up.

"I used to hitchhike this route a lot when I was a kid," he said. "Not this interstate, of course. Old Route 40. But it ran through the same towns. This was during the depression. We didn't have any money for entertainment so sometimes we'd stick our thumbs out just to go somewhere. If you were lucky you'd pick up a meal along the way. Otherwise you might not eat for days.

"We never really thought of ourselves as poor, though. Back then, everybody was starving. Going hungry was a way of life. In college I lived on a quarter a day. A candy bar and a quart of milk. That's what I ate for two years at West Liberty."

"You didn't finish?" I asked.

"No, even on a quarter a day my money ran out. It was probably just as well. Time to move on. I went there to study chemistry and physics—as a reaction to the brainwashing I got in the seminary. I'd had a bellyful of faith, so I went looking for some scientific proof about God and existence, that sort of thing. I thought if you could peer inside an atom you might find the secrets of the universe in there. Later, of course, I saw that science was just another endless tangent.

"So by twenty-one years of age I was burned out on religion and science. It was traumatic in a way, but I'd come to realize that if a man is ever going to grasp anything it won't be by learning. His *being* has to change. You are what you do, not what you know. A man never learns, he *becomes*. To become, you must find ways and means to change your entire *state-of-mind*. This in turn will lead to a change of being.

"Anyhow, that's when I started experimenting with yoga and celibacy and meditation. I made my body a laboratory. I traveled around the country looking for people who knew about other ways a person might change his being and *become* something more than he is. I also spent a lot of time alone out on my back farm. Solitude is beautiful."

"You have two farms?" I asked.

"Used to. I gave a ninety-nine year lease on the back farm to a couple of guys who said they wanted to start a non-denominational spiritual community. Turns out they were Krishnites. As soon as they got the papers signed they started wearing bed sheets and chanting gibberish. We don't get along too good now."

"You know, Mister Rose," Augie said tentatively, "I've always wondered how that could happen to you, letting the Krishna's get your farm like that. I mean, you're an enlightened man..."

Rose squinted at him like the answer should be obvious. "I was duped," he said. Augie glanced over at him then the two of them broke into uproarious laughter.

Rose moved from one story to another and the miles passed quickly. When we reached the outskirts of Columbus he asked what time it was. Augie told him we still had about three hours before the lecture.

"Let's get something to eat, then," Rose said.

Augie took the next exit and pulled into a fast food restaurant, the orange VW close behind. As we all got out there was joking and small talk, but after listening to Rose's stories in the intimate atmosphere of the van I found myself resenting the presence of the others. The feeling surprised and embarrassed me and I held back as we walked to the restaurant, waiting for the feeling to pass. Augie drifted back from Rose's side to join me.

"I know how you feel," he said softly. "But no matter how close you get, you can never stake a claim to him."

The restaurant patrons stared at us as we walked in—six young men circling respectfully around a sixty-year-old man in a bright orange hunting cap. Knowing we had plenty of time we ate slowly and lingered awhile afterwards, talking over coffee.

The girls behind the counter could not take their eyes off of Rose. They seemed to strain to hear every word, blushing a little at his ribald humor and whispering to each other when the conversation drifted into more esoteric matters. One of them went into the back and returned with the manager, who then also stood listening, trying unsuccessfully to be unobtrusive about it. Rose didn't seem to notice, but later, as we filed past the counter on our way out, he waved goodbye to the manager.

"These are my six illegitimate sons," Rose explained to him. "It took a lot of work and persistence, but I was finally able to get them all furloughed from the penitentiary so their mother could see them one last time before she died."

A couple of hours later, Rose stood in front of a hundred or so people in a large room at Ohio State University's Student Center. The crowd looked like the same eclectic mix of people who attended the Pittsburgh meetings. Rose had asked me to handle the book sales, which was an unexpected honor, and I sat proudly at a card table in the back of the room with a dozen copies of *The Albigen Papers* stacked neatly before me.

His first few words were drowned out by the screeching of the microphone, which he then took off, asking loudly, "Can you hear?" There were nods and affirmatives from the back, so he set the mike aside and started again.

His talk began slowly, almost awkwardly. He shuffled his notes and fumbled for words. I knew he wasn't nervous, and I wondered why he didn't just let loose with an effortless stream of articulate thought like he did at the meetings or in his house, or everywhere I had ever heard him speak. Augie, who had remained on stage after introducing Rose, fidgeted in his folding metal chair.

And then suddenly his tempo changed and the mood shifted. It was almost as if another person took over inside him.

"I have the sense that time is short," Rose said. "We only have a couple of hours together and I want to answer as many of your questions as possible. So even though I have some notes prepared, I want you to ask questions. Don't be afraid to interrupt me if you don't understand something or if you want me to elaborate.

"Now, even though I want to encourage a dialogue, we need to set some ground rules. And the main thing is that I don't want to argue with you. You can't argue people into the Truth. If we disagree, that's fine, that's what we're here for, to sort out the true from the false. But I won't stand here while you throw loaded questions at me in order to prove that you're smarter than me. If you need to believe that, fine. I'll admit it up front—you're all smarter than me." There was some nervous chuckling, and Rose briefly smiled, too. Then he unzipped a blue plastic folder and removed a handful of papers.

"While I was waiting for Augie to introduce me I was talking with somebody in the audience and he asked me if my talk was going to be about my philosophy. I told him no. Because my life isn't about philosophy. It's an experiential story of discovery.

"I'm not saying that if you do everything I did there's any assurance you'll discover something, too. In fact, I actively discourage people from imitation. You need to discover the underlying conditions that are conducive to an Experience, not try to duplicate the surface mannerisms or characteristics of a teacher.

"But I have read about people who've had spiritual experiences similar to mine—even met a few others personally—and I've noticed some common denominators in our lives. Regardless of geography. People who have experienced this knowledge have come from all parts of the world, and all times in history. You don't have to go to India or Tibet to find the Truth. You start from wherever you are, right now.

"Anyhow, I've come to believe there's three basic things a person must have, or cultivate in himself, in order to have any hope of success in these matters—to have any hope of *becoming*.

"First, You need to want the Truth more than anything else. Not at first maybe—you might start with just a mild curiosity. But eventually, if anything is going to crack for you, you'll need a tremendous hunger for the Truth.

"There's a story of the student who asked a Zen master what it took to reach Enlightenment. The master led him into a nearby lake until they were chest deep in water, then he grabbed the student and held his head under water. At first the student didn't resist because it was the master and he figured there must be a good reason for it. But as he started to run out of air he began to struggle more and more until eventually he was fighting with everything he had to get free. Finally the master let him up and the student gasped and coughed and almost collapsed. When he got control of himself again he asked the master why he had held him under. The master said, "When you want the Truth as much as you wanted air just now, there's no way you can miss it."

There was scattered laughter in the audience, but Rose did not smile or pause.

"Second," he continued, "you need energy. You need to become dynamic enough to do the digging and work it takes—finding the books, the teachers, the methods, and *acting on* the things you discover along the way. This requires a lot of energy, so you'll need to conserve what you have and use it for this purpose.

"And third, it takes commitment—a simple pledge to yourself and any God who might be listening. These are the three things. Without these, all philosophies are empty words."

Rose had yet to look at his notes. He seemed to be taking his cues from the mood of the room.

"There are no guarantees in this line of work, this business of *becoming*," he said. "Anyone who tells you otherwise has something he's trying to sell. The only thing I, or anyone else who's been down this road, can do is give you the benefit of his own experiences."

So Rose proceeded to do just that, recounting for the audience the stages of his life's search—the time of faith in the seminary, the pursuit of logic and science in college, the years of meditation and ascetic disciplines.

"Then," he said, "at thirty years of age I had an experience that came about as a result of *none* of these factors."

Rose then told the story of his Enlightenment experience in much the same way he told it in his kitchen in Benwood that first day I was there. Yet for some reason, that night at the lecture, it had a much greater impact on me. At one point I even had the sensation of being physically touched, but when I turned around there was no one near me. When I looked up at Rose again he was staring at me as he spoke. Without warning the hair bristled on the back of my neck and a cold chill shot through me. Rose then looked away and continued describing what it was like to become the Absolute. When he finished there was a long silence, during which he got a glass of water from the table behind him and took a drink. Finally, a man about Rose's age raised his hand.

"Would you say, then, that you found God in your Experience?"

"You become God, yes," Rose said matter-of-factly. "Although I hesitate to use that word because it comes with a long history of childish connotations. We're not talking about a big guy with white whiskers keeping tabs on how many rules we break."

"I think of God as more of a 'Universal Mind,'" the man continued quietly.

"Well, perhaps," Rose said. "But the Absolute is beyond Universal Mind. Mind is still a dimension. You discover this by losing your own individual mind. Then you realize—because *Mind* is still there—that what you had all your life was not the *individual* mind you thought you had, but merely contact with an undifferentiated Mind *dimension*.

"So, yes, it's accurate to say I found God, or *became* God, in the experience. But it's also accurate to say I found nothing. There was no one there but me. You command creation, and yet you're not operating under the illusion that you can change anything."

A tall man who had been taking notes throughout the talk raised his hand.

"Then you encountered no other intelligences during your Experience?"

"I didn't see anybody there but me. And yet, I sensed that something was helping me, maybe even guiding me—something that was just outside the picture. In fact, I sometimes think the whole experience was orchestrated for the purpose of showing me that Richard Rose the body doesn't exist."

"So you had help?" another man asked.

"Yes. I believe the whole experience was engineered. I just never got a good look at who or what was helping me. It was benevolent help, of course, but not protective. If you're going to visit the Totality and the Void, your Holy Guardian Angel can't tell you beforehand that everything will be all right, that he'll be right there with you. No. You have to die like a dog. Die without hope. Only then can you make the personal discovery that through it all *you are still observing*—'I'm still here!' It wasn't until I returned that I realized something had created the Experience, even the physical conditions preceding it."

"But aren't there other systems that can bring you to the Truth without all this disaster?"

"To know death properly, a person must die."

"Then why would anyone want to pursue something like that, I mean, if they knew it meant they had to die to get there?"

"*Who* dies? *What* dies?" Rose asked, not altogether rhetorically. "Sometimes you have to plow under a city to build something more beautiful."

The room stayed silent.

"I know. Nobody looks for death," Rose continued. "I wasn't looking for death. I didn't want to find Nothingness. In fact, I always wanted to assert my individuality to the greatest degree of it's intensity."

I could hear a young woman's voice from the front row. "The whole experience doesn't sound very pleasant."

"Who said it would be?"

"I mean, its not the type of spiritual experiences I've been reading about."

"Then you're reading about lesser experiences. Enlightenment is the death of the mind. *Death*. You think you are dying—completely and forever. And it's good to think that because it kills the ego. When a person feels himself dying he immediately drops all his egos.

"It has to be this way. You must go through death with no hope of survival. Because you have to be truthful with yourself—all those tales about life after death could be fiction. But when you die honestly, you die with absolute despair. And that absolute despair removes the last ego you've got left—the spiritual ego that believes the *individual* mind is immortal.

"But then something amazing happens. After you die, you find yourself still here, observing this mess. And that observing is the secret of immortality. In fact, the only thing I think is valuable to know is that when you die, *the Observer still lives*.

"What I found in the Experience is that the soul of man is God. Every human being has the potential to discover this—to discover his essence, his soul. And in the act of discovery one becomes what he has discovered. If we were nothing more than the projected illusion we call 'me,' at death we would go out like a candle."

A student sitting on the steps in the aisle raised his hand.

"Where did the soul of man come from?" he asked.

"Does it have to come from something? Can't it just be? It *is*."

"If the soul of man can just be, why can't we just be? Why all this effort?"

"Because we are not the soul of man," Rose said, suddenly animated. "*We are not the soul of man!* We are shadows on the wall of Plato's cave. Each individual on this planet has the potential to find his soul, to *become* a soul. But you are not a soul until you discover yourself, your True Self. And yet it is also accurate to say that what you are *is* a soul. You don't *have* a soul, you *are* a soul. What you *have* is a projected body-mind unit that operates in the vicinity of the soul that is observing your fictional life.

"But you will not gain immortality by listening to me or anyone else try to explain this, or by believing me or anyone else. The only immortality possible is to become fully identified with the soul — the Observer, your True Self — before your body dies. Then you will not die with the body. In traditional Zen this is expressed with the saying, 'If you die before you die, then when you die you will not die.'"

"But you said you found Nothingness."

"Yes, but a person can't conceive of Nothingness. In the Experience, you don't *think* of Nothingness. Nothingness descends upon you."

"Isn't that oblivion?"

"Nothingness is not oblivion. I don't think anyone really finds oblivion at death. Certain people — purely instinctive people who are living a basic animal existence — might descend into blackness for a period. But for how long, I don't know."

"Death is different for each person, then?"

"Absolutely. If everyone found the same thing at death — if your actions on earth had no effect on your situation after death — then there wouldn't be much point in me talking."

"So what will it be like for *you*?"

Rose smiled. "My life is no longer tied to this planet. This place is a stage, and when you leave, you turn out the lights."

There was a long pause before the next question.

"Don't you believe in reincarnation, Mister Rose?" The speaker was an attractive middle-aged woman.

"I don't believe it or disbelieve it. I've got no proof either way. I may have been here before, but I have no memory of it. What I've noticed, though, is that the people who push reincarnation the hardest are generally using it as an excuse to keep from putting out any spiritual effort in *this* lifetime.

"I will say that as an explanation for human suffering and the inequities you see in society, reincarnation is a more easily digestible system to the human intellect than the concept of 'one chance then heaven or hell forever.' But just because it's more digestible doesn't mean it's true. In fact, the more palatable an explanation for things is, the more likelihood it's been created out of the wishful mind of man.

"Besides," he added, turning back to the woman who asked the question, "if people do come back, it's only because they don't realize they could just stay dead and be a lot better off. In their ignorance they feel somehow compelled to continue to play the game, to go back on stage."

A young man directly in front of me raised his hand and Rose nodded in his direction.

"What *is* it like to come back, Mister Rose?" he asked. "Is the world different, or do you leave the Experience behind?"

"The world is never the same again. For me now, it's like I'm an insane man watching all this. Of course that's a very liberating state to be in," he said with a grin. "An insane man is free to do all sorts of insane things."

The laughter provided a welcome break from the seriousness. The whole room seemed to loosen up, including Rose.

"It was pretty rough at first, though. The night I came back I couldn't stop weeping. I just wandered the streets crying uncontrollably, looking for a bridge high enough to jump off of. Seriously. I didn't want to live. I couldn't stand the thought of being back here in the nightmare. The only reason I didn't jump is the rivers are shallow out there and I was afraid I'd just get stuck in the mud.

"Then I passed a church and that gave me hope. I figured that priests spend their lives looking, maybe one of them has read something about what just happened to me. So I knocked on the door. This blob of a priest with an enormous gut answers and he looks at me like I'm some kind of worm. I knew he wasn't going to be any help, so I asked him, 'Are there any older priests around?' There I am, standing on the church steps with tears streaming down my cheeks and he doesn't even invite me in. He just scowls at me and says, 'How long has it been since you've been to confession.'

"And I thought, 'Where's my gun?'" Rose continued talking through the laughter. "Really. I wanted to shoot the bastard. But the anger was good. It helped bring me out of it. It helped me stop weeping.

"Gradually, the worst of the trauma passed and I started drifting back into life again. But I still felt terribly out of place in a world that I knew without a shadow of a doubt was an illusion—having just visited the real place. For several weeks people were transparent to me. I mean literally transparent—I could see right through their bodies.

"So I figured I'd better head back home, because I still wasn't too stable. I had an old friend living in Alliance, Ohio, and he got me a job at the place he was working. That's when everything became beautiful to me. Hills were once more hills, valleys once more valleys. Children looked like baby dolls. The starkness of the Absolute I had visited now made life and motion appear as beauty to me. Those months following my Experience were the happiest of my life, except maybe for the years of peace and bliss I had in my twenties when I was living a very ascetic lifestyle.

"Every day I'd come back to my room after work and sit down in front of the typewriter. I'd given up on trying to talk about the Experience—you just can't describe an Absolute condition using relative terms—but I had hoped to write a book of poetry and at least try to capture the beauty of the illusion I'd been forced to come back to. Most of it I tore up as soon as I wrote it. But then one day something came over me and I was able to write about my Experience. That's when I wrote 'The Three Books of the Absolute.'

"It was like automatic writing," Rose continued. "The words just appeared on the page."

A hand was raised near the front of the room. "Do you think your years of asceticism brought about your Experience?"

"Not really. It was like a period of adolescence on the way to adulthood. Necessary, but not directly causal. However, I do think that all that experimentation, investigation, and especially conservation of my energy, was definitely part of the preparation for my Experience."

"What's the other part?"

"The main preparation for Enlightenment is trauma. But you don't need to engage in any special disciplines to induce it. Your life will give you plenty of trauma whether you're on a spiritual path or not. Indulge in it while you can. You'll have plenty of peace in the marble orchard—maybe." Rose laughed in a way that made me uneasy.

"What I mean is," he continued, "you have to go through these traumas in life—now, while you're on Earth—in order to improve your situation after death. Everyone may be immortal, but we don't all go to the same place when we die. Awareness may not terminate for anyone, but you can't expect to advance into a dimension that you haven't mentally *vaccinated* yourself to beforehand. If the average mind—with its convictions and limitations—landed in an Absolute dimension, it would think it was either in oblivion or hell."

"Will a person who's been doing spiritual practices, like meditating regularly, get a foreshadowing of what you finally experienced?"

"No. This does not accrue gradually. It happens suddenly and is never anything like you might imagine beforehand. I always thought a spiritual experience would be sheer beauty. I had visions of reaching some beautiful fields of flowers or God knows what. And the fact that I found something so utterly devastating and contrary to my desires convinced me that the experience was genuine, and not the product of wishful thinking.

"It's the effort you put forth—the *vector* you create—that propels you into this, not an accumulation of knowledge. You're engaged in a relentless pursuit of Truth, yes, but even in the midst of it you suspect that you are incapable of perceiving the Truth. So you engage in the obsessive pursuit of a goal while simultaneously believing you will never be successful.

"*You live this!* A person on the spiritual path lives this every moment of every day of his life. You push and push and push without hope. And then, no words or logic can explain what finally happens. It's an explosion. Your *being* changes."

"But doesn't the wisdom you acquire on your search coalesce in Enlightenment?"

"No," Rose said flatly. "That is not the path. You can't acquire wisdom because you don't know what it is. The path is *subtractive*. You keep sorting through the garbage pile to see if something real lies underneath it. And after you get done subtracting everything, what's left is an Absolute condition. That's what's real, not the little bits and pieces you set aside because you thought they were true along the way. *You don't know anything until you know Everything.*"

"Do you think other people have had the same type of experience you did?"

"Oh yes, I know that now. But after my Experience I felt completely isolated. It wasn't until years later that I found out about other spiritual incidents. I was in Steubenville, Ohio—we had a little group that met there—and after one of the meetings a woman handed me a copy of Richard Bucke's *Cosmic Consciousness*." When I read it I knew I wasn't alone.

"But cosmic consciousness isn't the final experience," Rose continued. "The people in Bucke's book describe an experience where they understand the harmonious interworkings of everything in the universe. They see lights and experience bliss, and so on. This is wonderful. But experiencing the Absolute goes beyond all that. In the Absolute there is no bliss or sorrow."

Rose reached into his old black "satchel," as he called it, and rooted around for something. After a few moments he pulled out a copy *The Albigen Papers*.

"As I said, the closest I ever came to describing this was when I wrote 'The Three Books of the Absolute.' I'd tried several times before that to write about my Experience, but gave up. There was just no way to do it. Words and language exist in one dimension, so to speak, and the Experience in another—a dimension without words, a dimension that can't even be imagined in dimensions where words exist. And so, there was just no way.

"But one day this poem, or whatever it is, just came to me, complete, all at once. I could hear it and feel it and all I did was get it down as fast as I could. Once I'd finished I never went back and changed anything. I just published it as it came to me. Anyway, it's here in the back of this book. It's rather long and I don't want to put you through the whole thing, but I thought maybe I'd read the last few lines to you."

Rose patted his pockets and looked around the podium for his glasses. He found them in an inside coat pocket and put them on, then flipped through the book until he found the spot he was looking for. He stared at the words for several moments before speaking and by the time he began to read the room was impossibly silent.

"...And soon I see, looking ahead, that all my joys are not, that all my love is not, that all my being is not.

And I see that all Knowing is not. And the eminent I-ness melts into the embraces of oblivion.

It melts into the embraces of oblivion like a charmed lover, fighting the spell and languishing into it.

And now I breathe Space and walk in Emptiness. My soul freezes in the void and my thoughts melt into an indestructible blackness.

My consciousness struggles voiceless to articulate and it screams into the abysses of itself. Yet there is no echo.
All that remains is All.

My spark of life falls through the canyons of the universe, and my soul cannot weep for its loss....for lamentation and sorrow are things apart.

All that remains is All.

The universes pass like a fitful vision.
The darkness and the void are part of the Unknowing....
Nothing is everywhere....
Death shall exist forever....
All that remains is All."

Chapter Eight

The Intensive

The Intensive at the farm started in early June. I had decided to work half the summer then join the Intensive in mid-July, but I called Rose to ask if I could come down on weekends until then.

"No," he said harshly. "The farm is off limits to everyone who isn't taking part in the Intensive. I don't want commuters swooping in and making off with the honey."

When I finally arrived at the farm, I was stunned by all the cars and activity. Two months before I had visited a farm that, although desolate and austere, was also intimate and private. Now the parking area was jammed with old vans and brightly painted cars, and a cluster of tents dotted the hillside across the road. Inside the yard small groups of young men, many with long hair and full beards, sat on the porch or lounged beneath the giant sycamore tree in the side yard. I felt suddenly like an outsider. The two group members I knew best—Leigh and Augie—were not at the Intensive. Leigh had been much less involved with the Pittsburgh group lately, and Augie was off trying to start new groups.

I greeted the few people I knew and was introduced to some of those I didn't. No one was actually unfriendly, but their aloofness made it clear they considered me a latecomer with plenty of dues to pay before I would be one of them. In an attempt to make conversation I asked one of the guys I knew what they'd been doing so far.

"Digging," he said, and everybody laughed. I smiled and nodded my head, but didn't pursue it.

"Where's Mister Rose?" I asked. "I guess I should check in or something."

"Inside. If you need a bellhop, just ring." They all laughed again. I excused myself and headed for the house. As I opened the screen door and walked into the small kitchen I could hear Rose's voice coming from the narrow dining area to the right.

"How could you come down here without any food? What did you think this was, some kind of commune?" Rose was leaning against an ancient refrigerator, facing a gaunt youth who had his back pressed tightly against a metal cabinet.

"Well, yeah, I assumed it was." There was some subdued chuckling among the guys seated at the long wooden table that filled the room. "I figured that's what a Zen retreat was all about."

"Spare me," Rose said comically, but with enough irritation that nobody laughed. "I'd burn this place to the ground first. As soon as you take away individuality, the whole group automatically sinks to the level of the lowest common denominator. Is Phil in here?"

He looked around the room. Seeing me, he paused to say hello, then continued.

"Well anyway, when Phil and his girlfriend pulled in last summer, there were already a few people living here—Augie, Frank and his wife, and..." He turned to someone at the table. "What was that speed freak's name?"

"Rick," someone said.

"Right. Rick. So their first night here Phil says, 'Let's make a stew. We can all throw something into the pot.' Everyone thought that was wonderful. That's sharing. That's spiritual. So Frank had some rice and potatoes, Augie had a piece of chuck roast—he always has meat. That boy could eat the rear end of a cow in one sitting. I forget what the speed freak had. But when it comes to Phil's turn, he reaches into this filthy knapsack and pulls out a rotten onion and a scraggly carrot. That was his contribution to the stew.

"And that," Rose said with finality, "was our one and only experiment with communal living. Nobody's going to take advantage of anybody else on this farm as long as I'm alive."

But the skinny kid hung in. "Don't you think that if you had more patience with these people they would have made the adjustments to live together equitably and in harmony? I mean communally?"

"Patience?" Rose said, his voice rising. "You don't think I've got patience? If I had any sense I would have boarded up this place long ago. You wouldn't believe the stunts people have pulled out here."

And he proceeded to itemize. It was not a short list. Somebody destroyed his new rototiller trying to make a rocky, dried-up creek bed into a garden. Two others once threw knives all day at the huge, ancient sycamore in the yard and almost killed it. Somebody else cut the seat out of one of Rose's antique cane-bottomed chairs to use as an outhouse fixture. And on and on. The guys at the table were falling all over themselves in laughter.

I was enjoying it, too, but I couldn't stop thinking of the car full of gear that I had to haul out to the woods and set up before nightfall. I kept waiting for a chance to exit politely but it seemed there was always one more bonehead to be roasted. Eventually I gave up and headed towards the door.

Rose stopped in mid-story. "Don't mind Dave Gold," he said, loud enough to be sure I heard him. "He's not really unfriendly. He's just worn out from doing his goofoo bird imitation in Pittsburgh all summer."

"Goofoo bird?" someone asked.

"The goofoo bird is so confused it flies around in circles that get smaller and smaller until he finally runs his beak up his ass and disappears."

Everyone howled with laughter and I could feel my face flush as I hustled to my car. I stood for a moment, slightly disoriented, staring into the trunk full of gear I brought. Suddenly there was a voice behind me.

"Need any help?"

I turned to see two guys approaching.

"Sure," I said. "Thanks."

"We figured it'd be tough carrying all that stuff alone with your beak up your ass." one said with a grin. He had a bulldog build like Rose's and long hair that was thinning on top. "I'm Al," he said as we shook hands.

"Rob," said the other.

We grabbed what we could from my car and headed in the direction of the spring to find a campsite. A dark blue pup tent occupied the spot I had hoped to get—a flat, grassy area I had noticed on my first visit to the farm. But about a hundred yards farther down the trail we found another level clearing that was big enough for a campsite. Al and Rob helped me set up my tent, then we made another trip to the car for the rest of my gear and supplies. As we worked I got to know and like them very much. I asked Al how he met Rose.

"Went to one of his lectures at Kent State. I was a psychology major with a minor in Eastern Religions, and I thought I was something of an expert on Zen. Rose's lecture was nothing like I'd read about or heard in class so I figured he was a phony.

"When the time came for questions I threw everything I could at him. Hui-Neng, Ramana Maharshi, *The Tibetan Book of the Dead*. I quoted whatever I could think of. He waited until I was done then pointed at me and said, 'The first thing *you* have to do before you study Zen is get your head free of dope.' Just cut through all my bull and nailed me. I guess that's why I stuck around."

"Yeah, he saw through me pretty good, too," Rob said. He was a soft-spoken man who appeared a few years older than most of the others. He wore wire-rimmed glasses and looked like he spent a lot of time in libraries.

"I'd been reading self-help books and attending encounter groups, sensitivity sessions, stuff like that—anything I thought might help me overcome my shyness and feelings of inferiority. The first Pyramid Zen meeting I went to Rose was there, and afterwards we all went out for a hamburger. I was sitting at Rose's table telling everybody about this radical new therapy I was involved in that was guaranteed to bring people out of their shells.

"Rose looked up from his burger and said, 'Don't waste your time. You want to cure yourself? It's simple. Just hunt up the meanest looking cop you can find and punch him. You may get your head caved in, but you'll never again live in fear.'"

I laughed. "Did you take his advice?"

"I haven't found a cop mean enough to suit me yet," Rob grinned.

After a few more minutes they went back up to the house. I stayed to unpack and get settled in. By the time I finished it was dusk and a heavy mist was settling on the valley below. I stood for awhile watching it thicken and creep up the mountainside towards me.

Sounds of the evening milking at the dairy farm in the valley drifted up the mountain with great clarity, even though the farm was at least a mile away. The clanging buckets and lowing cows, even the farmer's gentle patter, seemed as close as the gathering mist.

Then, all at once I felt incredibly lonely and homesick again, just as I had during my first visit to Rose's house in Benwood. I sat down under the weight of it and the mood washed over me in great waves of sadness. I couldn't believe that these recurring feelings were simply the result of immaturity, or that I actually missed my home in Pittsburgh after being gone only six hours. It had to be Rose.

Somehow being close to him filled me with a nameless sense of loss. Was it something I was going to lose? Or something I long ago lost that he was calling me back to? After awhile the sounds of milking disappeared and I sat in silence as darkness closed in. Suddenly the screech of a large bird startled me from my thoughts. I grabbed a flashlight from my tent and hurried up to the farmhouse, hungry for company.

As I climbed the porch steps I was puzzled by the silence of the house. I opened the creaky screen door and walked softly through the vacant kitchen. Sounds of slight movements were coming from the main room around the corner, so I stepped through the alcove and looked in.

The room was packed. Rose and fifteen or twenty people were sitting in attentive silence. Rose sat perfectly erect, expressionless, his pale blue eyes glancing slowly around the room. I moved as quietly as I could just inside the doorway and found a place to stand. After a minute or so I began to feel what I can only describe as an energy that seemed to be both outside me and inside me at the same time. It was a purposeful, perhaps intelligent, force that pervaded the room but seemed to emanate from Rose.

"I know what each of you is thinking," Rose said suddenly.

He turned to a rugged-looking blond boy who appeared to still be in his teens.

"For instance, Eric here's thinking that if his girlfriend showed up tomorrow, he'd leave this place in a minute." His voice sounded slightly different to me. More resonant, perhaps.

Eric shuffled his feet and nodded his head with an embarrassed grin. "I could actually see her driving up in her old blue Toyota." He stroked his sparsely-bearded chin. "I suppose that would be a big mistake, huh?"

"I don't guess destinies. Who knows what a person might have to go through to finally crack his head? But I will say this. Once a person steps on this path he will always be tempted, always challenged. And unless you have an unshakable commitment to this work you'll get side-tracked by everything that comes along. So if you're serious, you have no choice but to make a vow to yourself and whatever God might be listening that you want nothing out of this life except the Truth. Then you'll get somewhere.

"And you, Paul," he said, turning to a heavy-set fellow with round, wire rimmed glasses. "As soon as the energy picked up, you thought you were going to be overwhelmed. You were afraid you'd get lost in it and never find your way back out."

A long silence followed. "You're right," Paul said finally. "I blew it. I was scared."

Rose's voice was reassuring. "Fear is nothing to be ashamed of. Everything has to live in fear. If something's afraid, it will rise to the occasion."

"You don't seem be afraid of anything."

"Believe me," Rose said, "no one embarks on a serious spiritual search without a healthy fear of death. Of course, it also takes a bit of courage to go out looking for death before your time, so there's a paradox involved."

He moved on. "Now Dan here, he's wondering whether or not he can risk dropping that rooster ego he's been carrying all these years."

Dan, who was built like a fireplug and had the face of a boxer, didn't flinch. "That's about right. What do you think? Should I?"

"That's the wrong way of looking at it. You can't set out to drop an ego intentionally. Too many other egos will rush to its aid. The only thing you can do is keep working, keep focusing your vector until you have a breakthrough that leaves the ego behind.

"And then there's little Davie," he said, glancing over at me. "He feels like he just missed the last stagecoach out of Dodge."

Everyone looked my way as if noticing for the first time I was there. I had been thinking of myself, as usual. Thinking of the sadness and longing that seemed to fill me when I was around Rose.

"Mister Rose, how can a person keep from being overwhelmed by moods?" I said.

"Walk, don't wobble," he said quickly, almost before I'd finished speaking. "A sane man walks straight all the time." It sounded like an enigmatic fortune cookie, but I nodded my head anyway, as if I understood. He smiled at me, knowing I didn't have a clue, then softened his tone.

"Moods are the message medium of dreamland," he said, looking straight at me." They're like colored glass through which we view the world. It's through moods that more permanent states of mind are created. I maintain there's only three basic moods: Fear, Seduction, and Nostalgia. Ninety percent of what people do in this dream world can be traced to the nostalgic mood. Nostalgia is the language of the soul. It 's the inner man trying to get through the earth man's paradigm, trying to communicate with him."

I was caught off guard by the unexpected nature of his explanation and by the way he looked at me as he spoke. When he stopped talking I realized I had taken in almost nothing of what he said. I started to ask him to elaborate, but he had moved on to the boy on my right, a teenager who had apparently been brooding over his parents.

"No one should hate his parents," Rose told him. "They sacrificed their spiritual future for you. They hatched you, then instead of reading or meditating, they spent twenty years working and worrying like hell so that you would survive and have the opportunity to be in this room tonight, if you were so inclined."

And on he went around the room. Somehow he held all our minds in his mind, finding just the right words, expression, and tone to let us know not only what we were thinking, but why we were thinking it. After awhile, people started to drift in and out, grabbing an apple or fixing a peanut butter sandwich. Rose didn't seem to mind. As long as there were people in the room he continued talking.

Gradually, the crowd grew smaller as people left without coming back. Rose ended the meeting by asking what time it was and remarking on the lateness of the hour. At that, everyone headed for the kitchen and started pulling food and snacks from their personal stashes. It was probably just my newness to the Intensive, but I wasn't hungry or in the mood for conversation. I left without saying anything and made my way back to my tent. All I wanted at that moment was to be alone and think about what had just taken place at the meeting. Minutes after I crawled into my sleeping bag, however, I was asleep.

The next morning I awoke to the sound of a loud engine in the distance. I was conscious that I'd been hearing it for some time, and that the sound had incorporated itself into my dreams. It took me a minute to figure out where I was. The noise seemed to be coming from the direction of the farmhouse so I dressed hurriedly and ran to see what I was missing.

As I approached the yard I could see several guys standing around an enormous railroad tie, probably twelve feet long and eighteen inches square. It had apparently been dragged to it's present location by the hulking black truck that was still idling nearby. Dan was unhooking the chain and several others stood staring at the tie like it was a dead body.

"What are you gonna do with that?" I said.

Dan looked up. "Mister Rose wants it loaded onto that truck," he said, pointing to an old stake-body parked a few yards away. "But I don't know. It's a monster."

"There's six of us now," I said, anxious to be a part of something.

Dan finished unhooking the chain then reached inside the truck and shut off the engine. "All right," he said. "Let's do it."

We lined ourselves up evenly along the sides of the tie then squatted down and gave a mighty, noisy heave. Nothing happened.

"Get on the ends," someone said.

We quickly arranged ourselves three to an end and gave it all we had. The tie stayed put.

"We need ropes," Larry said, turning away and heading for a nearby shed. In a few minutes he returned with three thick lengths, which we ran under the tie at evenly spaced locations. Each of us bent to grab an end and got ready to try again.

"There's no way you're gonna hoist that post onto the truck with ropes," said a familiar voice. Rose was standing several yards away with a milk crate full of what looked like engine parts on his shoulder.

We looked at each other with disgust and determination. How long had he been watching? Nobody wanted to fail in front of Rose.

"Come on, ladies," Dan said, almost under his breath. "Let's give it our best shot. Ready? One, two..."

On "Three!" we heaved and grunted until the veins in our foreheads bulged. The tie never moved.

Rose put down the milk crate and walked over to us. "See if you can get one end of her off the ground, will you?" he said.

All six of us crowded around one end and after a false start or two were finally able to raise one end five feet in the air. Without a word Rose ducked under the middle of the enormous tie and stood up, taking the full weight of it on his shoulder.

"Now," he said, "get the damn thing balanced."

We scurried like squirrels for positions, bumping into each other, shouting orders, no one wanting to be solely responsible for the crushing of the Master.

We must have looked like the keystone cops to Rose. "Hell, just get out of the way," he said finally, and with an incredible display of strength and speed, raced to the stake body and threw the tie onto the truck bed. The heavy springs heaved and groaned under it's massive weight.

"I hate to see anything die slow," he said.

We just stood there, staring at the tie and then each other.

"Mister Rose," Dan said, "how the hell'd you do that? Did you use between-ness on that thing, or what?"

Rose pulled a white handkerchief from his pocket and wiped his brow.

 "Yeah, I got in between a bunch of deadheads and lifted the post onto the truck."

We all laughed, except Phil, who was still too stunned. "I can't believe it," he said. "That thing is huge!"

"The power wagon even had trouble dragging it up from the racetrack," Dan said, gesturing to the rusty black vehicle that had woke me up. It looked like a tow truck from the 1950's. On the battered doors were painted the words "Farm Use," and there were several bullet holes in the body, including one that had turned the windshield into an intricate spider web of cracks.

"The engine's about shot on that thing," Rose said. "Doesn't have much compression anymore."

"Looks like somebody's been using it for target practice," I said.

"Yeah, it took some hits during the shootout," Rose said.

"Shootout?" I was not sure I'd heard correctly.

"We had a little trouble out here a few years back when I was first trying to get a group started. I had some real weirdoes staying out here. Dopeheads, hippies." He looked around at our faces.

"You was here that time, wasn't you, Pete?"

Pete, a tall boy with close-cropped hair, nodded. "Yeah, I'm the only one left from those days. The locals had never seen anything like us, I guess. It made them nervous."

"The locals didn't know what was going on out here," Rose went on, "but whatever it was they aimed to put a stop to it. One night a couple carloads of hillbillies pulled up in front of the house at about two in the morning and started shooting up the place. Bullets were coming through the windows and the walls."

Rose shook his head at the memory and wiped his brow again.

"Inside was a real circus," he went on. "We grabbed my hunting rifles and returned fire. These hippies on my place were always preaching peace and love, but when the shooting started they could really handle the rifles. This one speed freak, what was his name?"

"Rick," Pete said.

"Right, right. He was loading and firing a single-shot rifle so fast it sounded like a machine gun."

"Anybody hurt?" I asked.

"Nobody inside the house. One of the boys in the cars got shot. I got arrested for it even though the hillbillies attacked my place and fired on us first."

"But a man's got a right to defend his property," I said.

"It was a young kid who got hit in the car. He came from one of the bigger clans in the valley, and I guess the cops figured they had to arrest somebody. They put me in handcuffs and shoved me in the back of a cruiser. My son was living out here at the time, you know. He was about twelve then. A bullet ripped through the trailer where he was sleeping about a foot above his head. If something would have happened to him, there would've been real trouble, believe me."

"What happened after your arrest?" I asked.

"I posted bail and came back out to the farm. But as I sat there in the farmhouse it hit me: this could be the end of it. I could lose the farm, my family, the group, everything. And even though I can never forget this world isn't real, once it starts affecting you like it *is* real, then you have no choice but to react.

"So I made up my mind to fight—to protect my farm, my family, my work. To die or kill somebody if I had to. Because even though the group was just a bunch of potheads, at least it was a start. If I let the hillbillies scare them off then the serious people who might come in the next wave would have no place to settle. Besides, I'd made up my mind early in life that no matter what happened to me I'd never give in to fear.

"I've been asked why I did this, why I took up a gun to protect my farm. Well, I did it because those people were struggling for purity, struggling to become as little children. And you've got to protect that struggling, just like you'd protect a little child."

We stood there in silence for a moment, then Rose looked at our wrists. "Anybody got a watch? It's almost eight, isn't it?"

With that, everyone began to drift off and Rose walked into the house. I noticed several people starting up the hill across the road and decided to follow. When I caught up to them I fell in step with Phil.

"Where we going?" I asked him.

"The pit."

"The pit?"

"You'll see."

"See what? What's the daily schedule?"

"There's no schedule. The only planned activity is the evening meeting."

"Well, eight o'clock must mean something," I said.

"If you volunteered for physical work that's when it starts," he said. "Ends at noon. Everybody else spends the day pretty much as they please."

"What's Mister Rose going to do now?"

"Eat breakfast. Maybe go into town and check his mail."

The "pit" turned out to be an enormous hole in the earth, probably eighty by forty feet, and five or six feet deep. Around the perimeter was a cement foundation, with brick pillars begun at the corners. Everyone grabbed a pick or shovel and began working.

"What's all this?" I asked Phil.

"It *will* be a group community building someday," Phil said with a straight face, "Right now it's a hole."

I was truly amazed. "You did this with picks and shovels?"

Phil grinned at me then picked up a shovel and jumped in. For awhile I just stood and watched. There were nine or ten men in the pit and they worked like they'd been together for some time. The pickers broke up the hillside and the shovelers loaded the loosened rocks and dirt into a wheelbarrow. Then Dale, the biggest of the crew, stepped between the handles, while two others grabbed ropes looped through the front of the wheelbarrow.

"Mules!" Dale yelled. The two front men pulled while Dale lifted and pushed. The wheelbarrow picked up speed, until they were practically running up the wobbly planks that led out of the pit. Once on level ground, Dale took the load another twenty yards and dumped it over the steep hillside with a triumphant shout.

It looked like good, clean, dirty work, so with a shrug I jumped in. Soon I was swinging a pick and taking my shifts as a mule. The first few minutes were exhausting, even overwhelming, but once I got a second wind I began to enjoy it.

By noon I was exhausted but happy. I felt I'd given a decent account of myself and the others no longer seemed like intimidating strangers. We all washed up at the spring, then I returned to my campsite for lunch. Afterwards I hustled back up to the farmhouse for whatever was next on the agenda. But Phil was right. There was no agenda. Everyone had their own routines and were either busying themselves with some small tasks, or had gone off by themselves to read or meditate.

I was too tired for physical activity and too listless to sit still for any mental work. The campsite proved to be an impossible place to do anything. The heat inside the tent was as unbearable as the bugs were outside. Around mid-afternoon I wandered back up to the farmhouse and saw that Rose's van had returned. When I was unable to locate him in the house or yard, I asked Phil where he was.

"Same place he is every day at this time. Up in the pit, laying bricks."

"Is it okay to go up there while he's working?"

He gave me his by now familiar look of slightly irritated condescension. "I guess so. As long as you don't get in the way."

When I reached the top of the hill, I realized why the pick and shovel work was a morning job. The late afternoon sun was hot and merciless in the shadeless pit. Rose was standing on a step ladder over one of the pillars, carefully laying bricks. Two guys from Ohio — Art and Sandy — were cleaning and hauling used bricks from a mammoth pile about thirty feet from the pit. Frank, from the Pittsburgh group, was mixing cement with a hoe in a large, encrusted mortar box. The three young men were sweating profusely in their shorts and t-shirts, yet Rose seemed cool and dry in long pants, long-sleeve shirt, and a wide straw hat.

I watched him lay brick after brick with his thick, sunburned hands. Were it not for Rose's methodically slow pace and the clumsiness of his helpers, they could have been mistaken for a father-and-sons contracting team laying bricks anywhere on earth. There was no philosophy, no confrontation, no Zen. What talk there was between them was brief and direct, and concerned only bricks and mortar, strings and levels.

My initial impulse was to offer my help, but then I thought better of it. In spite of their silence and attention to the task at hand, something else seemed to be taking place between them. Something I wasn't sure I should interrupt. I turned and walked away, content to wait until the evening meeting to spend some time with Rose.

But when I returned from my tent after dinner, Rose's van was gone. I learned to my surprise that Rose rarely stuck around for evening meetings, although there was considerable disagreement in the group as to whether he was purposely leaving us to our own devices, or simply had more important commitments in town.

The evening meetings turned out to be mostly confrontation sessions, and whether it was because we had become so "intense," or simply because we were eighteen roosters cooped up without any hens, the sessions were harsh and sometimes even brutal. No one hesitated to tell you what was wrong with you, and if your feelings got hurt, that was just another ego you'd get confronted about. I was constantly amazed that there were no hard feelings afterwards. In the mornings guys who had been at each other's throats the night before worked side by side in the pit, joking, trading barbs and stories.

A recurrent topic of conversation in the pit was Rose, and I noticed that as soon as someone mentioned his name or started recounting an incident all other conversation stopped. As well as Rose seemed to know each of us, none of us seemed to have even the vaguest appreciation of who or what he was. Every new story from someone else was like a clue, a piece of a puzzle, and although no one said it outright, I think we all sensed that no individual could ever solve him. Only by chipping in our little pieces would the puzzle come together.

One day we were talking about how lucky we were to meet Rose, and offering our theories as to why he seemed to take such a special interest in us. Craig, a sturdy, jovial boy who had lived for awhile in South America, suggested we had earned our way here by some past actions, or karma. Someone else said it was destiny. I said I thought that Rose saw something inside each of us, some great hidden potential. Each of our theories had the common thread that we were somehow "chosen."

Dan, swinging his pick with both grace and power, had a minority view.

"Bullshit. You're just here, that's all." We waited, but Dan was a man of few words.

Finally Rob asked, "Do you want to explain that?"

Dan kept swinging as he talked, spitting out phrases on the downstroke. "November TAT meeting. Last year. We were all sitting in the room off by the kitchen. Rapport. Energy. Lots of juice — the place was humming."

"I remember," said Scott, a quiet engineering student from Carnegie Mellon. "The time with Bob Martin, right?"

"You got it," Dan said, still swinging. "Bob's an old friend of Rose's. An alcoholic. He's a royal pain when he's drunk, but impossible to be around when he's sober."

"In his own way, Bob's an incredible guy, though," Scott said. "Literally a genius at math, physics. He knew Einstein personally. He's also read more esoteric philosophy than anyone on earth. That's how he and Rose got hooked up. The trouble with Bob, though, is he can't live what he knows. Alcohol and women are his life." Scott stopped talking and looked to Dan, remembering, perhaps, that it was Dan's story.

Dan swung the pick in silence a few times as if considering whether to go on. Then he stopped and leaned forward on the handle, catching his breath.

"Bob begged Rose to help him that day. Said he'd taken the cure, been to AA, tried everything but just couldn't stay on the wagon. Rose just looks at him a minute then stands up and puts his hand on Bob's head. He holds it there for about ten seconds then jerks it away like he was attacked by something. And when his hand came off it was like all the demons in Hell flew out of Bob's head."

We all looked to Scott, as if expecting a more traditional explanation.

"That's about right," Scott said, nodding thoughtfully. "I remember it was a real still day. There wasn't any breeze outside at all, but suddenly a rush of wind blew a backdraft through the wood stove, scattering ashes all over the floor. Mister Rose's face got red. Beet red, redder than I've ever seen it. Veins were popping out on his head, and even though it's cold he starts sweating like crazy. I seriously thought he was going to have a heart attack. And meanwhile Bob is literally beaming—happier than I've ever seen him. Like he's just been set free."

Dan picked up the story again. "After a minute or so Mister Rose walks out to the dining room and a few seconds later I follow him because, like Scott says, I think he might keel over and have the 'big one.' There was Rose sitting at the table, crying. Any you guys seen Rose cry?"

No one had. I couldn't even imagine it.

"Me either. I'm real concerned and I say to him, 'Mister Rose, he ain't worth it.' Rose just looks up at me with tears running down his face—not even trying to wipe 'em away—and says, 'Who am I to say?'"

We all stood in motionless silence for a few moments, then Dan grabbed his pick and went back to work.

"So don't go pinning medals on each other just because Mister Rose lets you hang around," he said between swings. "He works with whoever comes through the door. He's willing to fight and die for us, yeah, but not because we're special. It's because were *here*, that's all. When we get scared or bored and go back to our games, he'll dedicate his life to teaching whoever comes along next."

Chapter Nine

Happiness

As the weeks wore on at the Intensive I settled into a comfortable routine. Working in the pit was good exercise and my strength and stamina seemed to increase daily. Afternoons I'd take a book down to Big Wheeling Creek and sit on the bank to read and think until I got restless, then take a swim or poke around the rocks looking for crayfish. As I got to know and trust the others at the farm, the evening meetings and confrontation sessions became less intimidating, and I looked upon them more as a challenge than a threat. I even began to look forward to them. In fact I found myself enjoying most everything about the Intensive, including the fact that I didn't see much of Rose. Then everything changed.

We'd gone a week without rain and the pit had become an unforgiving place of heat and dust. For several days we'd been battling a vein of solid rock and the hours passed slowly. Each day when noon finally arrived and we stood to survey our labors, it looked as if we'd never come. After nearly a week of this our spirits had dropped considerably. One day as we dragged past the farmhouse at noon on our way to wash at the spring, we were surprised to see Rose sitting on the porch. Rose's schedule that summer, like most everything else about him, was unpredictable. Still, it was unusual for him to come out to the farm before bricklaying time. For a moment he looked like any other farmer in these hills, rocking on his glider in a wide straw hat, gazing out at his land.

"You look like Arabian grave diggers," he said loudly as we headed towards him, our shirtless bodies caked with a thin layer of mud from the dust and sweat. "If there is such a thing."

"You figuring to start laying bricks a little early today, Mister Rose?" said Dan.

"No bricks today," Rose said. "I've got other plans—for all of us." He grinned mysteriously and we waited for him to elaborate. Instead he leaned back and cut his chin towards the road.

"Eric just took off about ten minutes ago," he said. "Some girl pulled up in a broken down car and honked her horn. He come running down the hill. They talked for a minute, then he hopped in and left. He won't be back."

I looked over to the edge of the field across from the house. Eric's bright blue tent was still among the trees.

"His tent's still here," I said.

"Yeah, he left everything, Rose said. "But he won't be back." The finality in his voice gave me chills. It was as if he were talking about someone who had just died.

"Why do you think he left, Mister Rose?" Rob asked.

Rose looked at him and shook his head in mock disbelief at such a naive question. "The same reason ordinary men do anything in this life," Rose said. "Sex. A girl honked her horn for him and he came running, that's all. Like a good little dog."

Rose gave a gleeful chuckle and patted an old black briefcase on the seat beside him. "The worst of it is, though, he'll never know the secret of what's in this satchel. Spread the word will you Phil? Everyone meet in the farmhouse at two o'clock."

After washing up I made lunch at my campsite. Two thoughts kept going through my mind. One was an excited curiosity about what was in Rose's satchel. The other was an obsessive reverie on the same thing that had taken Eric from the farm. If a girl had come by and honked for me at that moment, I may not have gone with her, but I would have been sorely tempted.

At two o'clock we all gathered in the living room and tittered excitedly like adolescents at a junior high dance. When Rose walked in the room fell silent. He sat down in his customary chair and laid his briefcase on the ottoman in front of him.

"For those of you who haven't heard," he said, clicking the brass catches one at a time, "this thing's filled with dynamite. I've been thinking about it, and the only way any of you people are going to get enlightened is if I blow us all into the Absolute at the same time." Everyone laughed nervously.

An hour later, however, many of us wished he hadn't been kidding. At least we would have died quickly. His satchel contained mimeographed sheets innocently entitled, "The Numbers," along with a cassette player and a half-dozen tapes.

He paired us off and gave each pair a copy of The Numbers, which was a set of six pages of mathematical problems. One person was to read the problems aloud and his partner was to add the numbers in his head. After an hour, we'd switch roles. It sounded innocent enough and everyone plunged into it in high spirits. Soon the room was filled with the sound of verbal math.

My partner, Mark, was holding the papers, so I shrugged to indicate I'd take first crack at it. Mark started firing. The first page was relatively easy, adding up pairs of two digit numbers. The second page was a little harder, requiring carry-overs from one column to another. Still, it was a manageable challenge, almost fun. But the problems continued to get harder—three digit numbers, three digit with carry-over—and the noise in the room increased with the frustration level. Then just as everyone was reaching the breaking point Rose turned on the cassette player and a tape of one of his lectures blared above the cacophony.

By two-thirty the room was a sweatbox. Adding columns of numbers in your head is hard enough without seventeen other people shouting numbers at the same time, while a tape of Rose explaining the difference between the Manifested Mind and the Unmanifested Mind plays loudly in the background.

With each new problem I thought of quitting, but Mark kept shouting numbers. When I looked around everyone else was pushing on, so I did too. Sometimes my mind went blank. At other times, answers came immediately, intuitively, without having to work through the individual math. Sometimes Rose's taped voice was just white noise, an irritating blur, but then I'd finish off a page of numbers and realize I could remember every word he said.

When my hour was over I was drained and I looked at Mark with true sympathy for what he was about to endure. When the two hours were finally up Rose announced that we would be doing this everyday at two o'clock from now on. Class dismissed.

I shuffled towards the creek in the late afternoon heat, tired and frustrated. Just when I felt I was settling into the rhythm of the farm and getting my head on straight, Rose shook everything up with this numbers routine. I was especially annoyed because tonight was my turn to chair the evening meeting. I'd spent hours planning for it, thinking up questions for each person and anticipating their answers, eager to show off my fledgling cross-examination skills. Now I felt sure the meeting would be a dud. After "The Numbers," who could think, let alone confront?

When I came out of the woods for the evening meeting I saw that Rose's van was still in the parking area, and I became even more despondent. Not only would my meeting flop, Rose would be there to see it happen. Inside, the farmhouse was alive with noise and energy. Rose was sitting at the dining room table, reading from some handwritten notes and peppering his listeners with one question after another. It turned out they were part of a lecture he was working on entitled, "The Lecture of Questions." The whole lecture was to be a litany of provocative questions, or *koans*.

"Does a man enjoy or is he consumed?" Rose intoned, his dime-store reading glasses perched on the end of his nose.

"Do you have possessions, or are you possessed by them?

"Does a man own a house, or does the house own him?

"Does a man have power, or is he overpowered?

"What is sin?

"Is it a sin to eat meat?

"Are the animals our brothers?

"Do animals sin when they eat other animals?

"Is it wrong to kill except for food?

"If so, do we do wrong by not eating the people we kill?"

Some of those present seemed lost in thought, as if pondering something three or four questions back. Others were excited, even agitated, asking Rose questions about his questions, or arguing about them with each other. I tried to hide my annoyance. Rose had pre-empted my evening in the limelight. Or so I thought.

"It's after seven, if you want to have a meeting," he said.

His comment was close enough to a directive that people grudgingly left the table and filed into the living room. I was still worried that Rose would join us and overwhelm the meeting, but he remained in the dining room.

I began with a quote from Ouspensky's *The Fourth Way*. With everyone still fired up from Rose's questions the meeting took off quickly, and soon became a heated confrontation session. Most of the confrontation focused on Jack, who had angered a few people recently, and who had enough quirks to fill a month of meetings.

Jack was hot-tempered and emotional, and always appeared as if he was on the verge of breaking into something — laughter, tears, uncontrollable rage — you could never be quite sure which. Everyone took turns throwing tough comments and questions at him. I sat back smugly, pleased that "my" meeting had turned out so well. Then Rose's short, imposing figure appeared in the doorway.

"Maybe it's none of my business," he said quietly, "but this is all bullshit. Completely useless." The room fell silent. "I've told you people before, if confrontation is too direct the person will just get angry, not have any realizations." Then he disappeared back into the dining room.

Technically, it was still my meeting. But the fire was out and there was no getting it lit again. One by one people filed out, until Rose once more had a quorum in the dining room. He told us he would be staying at the farm full time now, until his lecture was completed. Then he began reading from his notes again.

"What are you doing for certain and what is done to you?

"Do we think or imagine that we think?

"Does a tree create wind by waving its branches?

"If we observe our thoughts, who is looking?

"Is there a soul? Did it exist before the body or must it be developed, grown, or evolved?

"Can a man become?

"How shall he know what he should become?"

The next morning the pit was jammed. The veterans wondered aloud at this sudden recognition of the spiritual benefits of pick and shovel work by those who formerly thought it beneath them, but were grateful for the new blood. We now had enough bodies for two full shifts of shovelers and pickers, and a good-natured competition sprang up between the two crews. There was joking and ribbing and the morning flew by.

Just before noon I noticed that everyone had picked up the pace considerably. I was puzzled by this late surge of effort until I glanced up and saw Rose standing at the edge of the pit, accompanied by Phil. For several minutes he said nothing, then he turned to Phil and said loudly enough for everyone to hear, "They're not working intelligently."

The picks and shovels fell silent.

Rob, working next to me, muttered under his breath. "How intelligent do you have to be to dig a ditch?"

Rose pointed towards a corner we thought we had completed. "You might already be too low over there."

"But Mister Rose," Phil protested. "we measured and its eight feet."

"Maybe it's eight feet somewhere, but unless you get a two-by-four and a level, there's no way of knowing where you're at." He glanced around at us. "By the way, I need eight of you down at the spring," he said, then turned and walked away.

In less than a minute he managed to make our job twice as difficult while cutting the work crew in half. The days of carefree digging were over. From now on, we would have to stop and measure every inch of the way.

A few days later when I showed up at the house at two o'clock for "The Numbers," I found a crowd gathered at the bulletin board. A notice in Rose's unmistakable hand proclaimed that from now on rapport meetings would be held daily at one o'clock. There was also a breakdown of who would be in the three separate groups that would be sitting together. I was disappointed to find I had been left out of what was generally considered to be the highest energy group. I felt slighted, even insulted, but tried to reminded myself that Rose made up the groupings based on potential energy compatibility among the members, not as rewards or punishments.

Strangely, no one seemed happy about the rapport meetings, even though Rose emphasized sitting in rapport as an important element in speeding up the development of insight and intuition. Instead, there was grumbling that since it was customary to refrain from eating before a rapport sitting, this new development in effect cut out the lunch hour.

A new state of mind settled in immediately. That afternoon there was no joking during "The Numbers." Afterwards no one sat on the porch and chatted, as had become our custom, or suggested a swim in the creek, as someone usually did. We just scattered to our private spots around the farm. That evening, too, there was none of the usual nervous chitchat before the meeting. We sat silently in the living room as we waited for Rose to finish up a phone call.

When he did, he sat down in what we had come to regard as his chair, even though it was no more comfortable than any of the others, and looked us over for a moment before he spoke. His voice was measured, and he seemed exceptionally calm.

"I've been thinking about you people, and why you're not moving spiritually," he said. The evenness of his words magnified their effect. We all thought we'd been suffering sufficiently to be making good spiritual progress.

"All of you are getting hung up on your egos. And because you're looking at it from the inside, you can't see it."

And with that, he started around the room, pointing out in each of us our primary personality trait—what Gurdjieff would have called our "chief feature." As he discussed each person in turn, Rose would identify his chief characteristic—with one it was selfishness, another, cowardice, a third, manipulation, and so on. He'd also give an example of it and explain how it permeated that person's whole personality. Then he'd talk about why it was psychologically or spiritually destructive to that individual. He proceeded counter-clockwise, and since I was two seats to his left, I had plenty of time to worry about what might be coming. Finally it was my turn.

"Now with Dave Gold, it's *vanity*. Somewhere along the line he got the mistaken idea that he's a tremendously important individual. The rest of us are just incidental characters to him. He's the star of the show and we're the extras. You take your life in your hands when you work with Dave Gold, because he doesn't pay attention to anybody but himself. And you can't tell him anything because he's convinced he already knows everything there is to know."

He didn't stop there, but continued to elaborate on my flaws in painful detail. Four or five minutes was all he gave anyone, and I had no reason to believe he spent any longer on me. It just *seemed* like hours, as each word stripped off another layer of skin. When he was through I felt as naked and vulnerable as I had after he laid into me at that first meeting.

From that point on, there was no relaxing around Rose. Every statement, every idiosyncrasy or habit was more ammunition for the relentless barrage of confrontation he directed at all of us. Sometimes his barbs were coated with humor, like when explained why he didn't bother confronting Craig very often.

"Nobody's going to give that guy any headaches," he said. "Craig's still tripping through the horse turds thinking they're marshmallows."

More often, though, his message was delivered straight up with an intensity bordering on anger. We speculated about this, as with everything Rose did or said, and wondered whether he was actually angry at these times, or if an enlightened man only allowed himself to manifest anger to get his point across.

That debate was settled a few days later when Rose discovered that someone had cut down an ancient walnut tree by the bunkhouse because it blocked the view of the sunset. We were struggling through The Numbers when he burst in, his face crimson with fury, veins bulging on either side of his neck. Rose never mentioned the transgressor by name, but for forty-five minutes he stormed and raged, recounting every item on the farm that had been lost, damaged, or destroyed that summer.

"This is my farm, damn it! These are my trees. These are my tools. I'm not tied up having to earn a living because my in whole life I've never discarded anything of value. Now a bunch of dopeheads are busting up everything I own."

Then he itemized the new farm rules. No trees were to be cut. No lumber could be used for any purpose without first clearing it with him. The shed would be padlocked and no one would get so much as a nail without signing out for it.

"And I'm tired of people taking a powder around here when things get too intense." He stared at Steve, who had gone to Cleveland the week before to be best man at his brother's wedding.

"Funerals are one thing," Rose said. "If someone in your family dies, then you've got to bury your dead. But you don't have to dance at their wedding and celebrate their folly."

Then his final pronouncement. "Once you leave the farm, for *any* reason, don't come back."

"The Great Walnut Tree Massacre," as the blow-up came to be known, marked yet another turning point in the Intensive. Before, you might run across Rose once or twice during the day, and usually he'd glance at what you were doing in silence. Now, he seemed to be everywhere with a comment about everything.

I turned out to be one of his prime targets. Once he assigned four of us to pull the rusty nails from a pile of scrap lumber and straighten them for re-use. It took several days and periodically Rose would come around to inspect the growing pile of nails. Every time he encountered a nail that hadn't been salvaged to his satisfaction, he called it a "Dave Gold Special."

At an evening meeting he jabbed at my vanity and got a good laugh to boot by referring to a conspicuous pimple in the center of my forehead as my "third eye." At the same meeting he later classified me as "semi-sincere," which to Rose is an oxymoron on par with "partial virgin," or "slightly dead." Two days later he demoted me to the "low energy" rapport group, and joked that it was because of the life-size blow-up Barbie doll I kept in my tent. But worst of all, and the most puzzling, was his steadfast refusal to accept anything from me, be it a cookie or an offer to mix his mortar.

Attempting to please him was like trying to hit a moving target. Just when we thought our farm labor might be living up to his expectations, Rose announced that we had turned ourselves into work machines. Our physical activity was just a distraction from the "real work" of facing ourselves, he said. From now on, he told us, there'd be no labor on Mondays—whether we wanted to work or not.

The following Monday passed tediously. A restlessness bordering on depression hung over the farm, and the evening meeting reflected our mood. Instead of the usual caginess or combativeness, people began confessing to hopeless inadequacies. Dale was particularly hard on himself, complaining that he wasn't getting anywhere, despite his summer-long stay at the farm.

Just then Rose walked in from the dining room where he had been reading the evening paper and listening to our meeting. He looked towards Larry and said, "You've been staying in the bus with Dale all summer. Have you noticed any change since he's been here?"

"It's kind of hard to tell," Larry said cautiously, "but he does seem more confident than he did at the beginning?" Rose had been riding Dale pretty hard and Larry was probably reluctant to say anything too positive.

Rose said nothing and turned to Mark. "What about you? Do you see anything different about Dale?"

Mark thought for a second. "He works harder than when he started. He's a lot more energetic."

Rose continued around the room, asking about Dale. Someone said he was easier to talk to, another mentioned that he had more poise. Rose waited until everyone had spoken.

"It's only in hindsight that you'll know whether you made a jump," he said. "Don't waste your time feeling sorry for yourselves. Keep working, keep pushing. Be relentless."

He moved from the doorway as if to leave, then turned back to us again. "There's a door open for you people—all of you," he said. "But you're going to have to fight your way up to it."

The next day in the pit, we debated what Rose meant by his last comment. A door open to what? Some thought Rose was referring to a door that was open into his head, his Enlightenment experience. Transmission. How long would the door remain open? How did a person become a worthy candidate for transmission? Was it an opportunity that always awaited us? Or was the Intensive a special chance?

We argued the point all morning. After work we went into the farmhouse with the intention of asking Rose what he meant, but there was a new face at the dining room table and the afternoon took on a different tone. Rose had mentioned that someone was flying in from Los Angeles and we assumed this was him, although there was certainly nothing about him that said "California."

His name was John. He was tall and lean, with an angular face and sharp Semitic features that made him appear older than he probably was. His face was perpetually serious—"dolorous," as Rob later described it—and I subsequently learned that both his parents were survivors of Auschwitz.

John had read some of Rose's books and had become interested enough to start corresponding with him. Now, having flown three thousand miles to meet him personally, he was apparently prepared to do *dharma* combat. He took a small spiral notebook from his shirt pocket and began to ask Rose questions from a long list. His inquiries were heavy and ponderous, concerning the void, oblivion, ego death, and darkness.

Rose was in high spirits, as he almost always was when meeting an interested potential student for the first time, and he answered the questions with appropriate, but light-hearted responses. John never smiled. He just kept reading depressing questions from his notebook.

"Doesn't it ever get tiring being a spiritual teacher, trying to bridge the gap between the mundane and the Absolute?" John asked.

"Do I get tired of people walking on my back? No, that I don't mind. It's the perpetual leaning against the bridge that makes me weary." Rose laughed good-naturedly.

"What I mean is," John went on, "it's almost like you're the tie that all these people have to God."

"No, no. Don't expect me to put in a good word for anybody with the man upstairs. Believe me, I have no standing."

Everyone laughed but John. He didn't blink.

"But doesn't a spiritual master have an eternal responsibility to his students, to make sure they all attain perfect Enlightenment?"

"Ugh," Rose said, as if there were something distasteful in his mouth. "When I die I'm leaving this place permanently. You guys won't get any more help from me. Don't pray to me for any advice, like I'm still floating around watching you."

John was still earnest. "But how can we find the road to the Absolute if we don't have a teacher to guide us?"

"Hey," Rose said, his voice now serious but his eyes still smiling. "There *is* no road. There are no teachers, no students. Nobody's here. Nobody's doing anything. You have to realize that. There's only a roomful of dummies sitting in the dark asking each other, 'Are we dummies?'"

Rose broke into deep laughter, all the lines in his face coming together in total, uninhibited glee. Even John joined in this time. When the laughter died down he said to Rose, "You looked like the laughing Buddha just then."

Suddenly we were aware that the phone was ringing. Phil went to answer it in the other room. When he came back he looked at me.

"Dave Gold," he said. "Your mother's on the phone."

The room fell silent. Embarrassed and a bit nervous, I shrugged my shoulders and walked to the telephone.

"Hi. What's up?"

"I'm sorry to call. You know I wouldn't interrupt unless it was important..."

"Is everyone okay?"

"Sure, sure. Everything's fine. It's your boss. He made a special call. He says something came up at work and he needs to talk to you. He seems like such a nice man. I promised you'd call him."

I took down the number she gave me, and promised I'd take care of it. After I hung up I sat on the ottoman, staring at the phone. Another burst of laughter came from the dining room. I folded the number and put it my pocket, then went back in.

Rose was in the middle of a story about his brother Joe. As soon as he finished he turned to me. "What's going on in Pittsburgh?"

The unexpected spotlight caught me off guard. I spoke before I had time to rehearse. "My boss called about something. My mother told him I'd call back."

"Call him," Rose said forcefully. It was more of an order than a suggestion. "He might be in some kind of jam."

"I know what he wants. He needs somebody to work and I'm the last resort."

"Well, if he needs you, you better go."

My thoughts were still of the "no return" policy Rose had recently instated.

"I don't want to leave," I said.

"That's not the point. This guy's been equitable with you, and you don't turn your back on a friend."

It was almost as if Rose was trying to get rid of me, to encourage me to leave then not let me come back. Dejected, I went back into the living room, and called my boss. As I suspected, he was in a tight spot and I was the last warm body available.

I walked back into the dining room and told Rose I had to leave right away.

"Good," was his only reply.

Minutes later I stood in front of my tent, too bewildered to know what to do next. Was I leaving for good? The thought of walking away and not returning was more than I could handle. I left everything as it was and packed only for a few days then went back to the farmhouse, determined to clarify my status before leaving the farm. But when I was face to face with Rose all I could say was good-bye, which was all he said to me.

My unexpected return to the world was neither as traumatic as I'd feared or as exhilarating as I'd secretly hoped. I was pleasantly surprised at how detached I felt from the play of life around me as I went about the business of fulfilling my commitments at work. It took only three days to do what needed to be done and before I knew it I was headed back to the Intensive.

As I drove the winding roads back to the farm that evening I speculated about what awaited me. Separation had sharpened my sense of what I had been a part of at the farm—the energy, community, shared sense of purpose—and I wondered if I would be able, or even allowed, to fit back in.

It was close to eleven o'clock when I arrived. Rose and a few stragglers were still in the dining room talking after the meeting. I watched carefully for smiles or frowns when I walked through the door, but there were only blank stares, first at me, then at Rose.

"We had a little accident while you were away," Rose said. He waited, as if watching for my reaction.

"There was a storm out here last night," he went on. "Lightning hit that big cherry tree north of your tent and took it down. Your tent's crushed."

I didn't know what to say or feel.

"We salvaged what we could of your stuff," Rose said. "Dale put it in the blue bus. You can stay there the rest of the summer."

Feeling somewhat dazed and not knowing how to respond, I thanked everyone. Then I borrowed a flashlight and hurried down to my campsite. The giant cherry tree that had shaded my tent was split in two about twenty feet from the ground, and the top half—at least two feet in diameter—lay flat on the ground, a torn piece of brown canvass peeking out from underneath it.

I shuddered involuntarily. No one in that tent would have survived. I was suddenly overwhelmed with a maze of conflicting emotions—sadness at the destruction of my tent, an almost giddy relief that I wasn't in it, confusion as to why I had to suffer this calamity, and most of all, bewilderment at the unlikely course of events that had quite possibly prevented my death. Feeling drained and tired I headed for the blue bus.

It was miserable. The bus was hot and musty. Breathing was difficult, sleeping impossible. Mosquitoes buzzed my ears, mice scurried about the floors and walls, and just before dawn the bats rattled the tin behind my cot as they returned from their nightly rounds. I was up and out at daybreak, taking deep breaths of fresh morning air and wondering how I was going to survive my last week on the farm.

"'Morning."

I turned around, surprised to hear a voice so early in the day. It was Rob, walking down the hill with a large backpack.

A few days before I left for Pittsburgh, Rob had set out for the back edge of the farm, where he had pitched a tent and apparently remained until now. He told me about his week in the woods as he loaded his car, and I joined him on the walk back to the campsite to retrieve the rest of his gear.

We proceeded to the hilltop at the west end of the farm, then down an embankment so steep that a few times we had to scramble on all fours to keep from falling. About half-way down I could see small sections of a meandering creek, and at the bottom of the hill we came upon a grassy plateau with a small tent sitting about ten feet from the water.

We followed the creek upstream a few hundred yards, and Rob showed me the waterfall where he showered each morning. As we sat silently on a large flat rock in the middle of the creek, staring at the steep shale walls that kept the sounds of civilization from penetrating the ravine, I knew what I wanted to do.

Rob grinned when I asked him if I could move into his tent for the remainder of my stay. "I was hoping I wouldn't have to lug it back up the mountain," he said.

He helped me think through the details as we made our way back to the farmhouse. He had fasted during his week-long stay and the prospect of dragging food and cooking gear all the way to the campsite convinced me to do the same. A sleeping bag, water jug, flashlight, and maybe a book or two was all I would need. I was able to haul it all out in one trip, and by nightfall, I was settled into my new home, listening to the rippling water and the sounds of the woods.

I thought I would miss the pit, The Numbers, rapport. But the time passed quickly, even pleasantly. Fasting relaxed my body and quieted my mind, and after a couple of days I forgot all about food. The weather was good, and the bugs weren't bad. Each morning I stood under the waterfall and whooped and hollered in the cold water. Meditation came more easily than ever before, and in the evenings I followed the stream to a clear blue lake and watched the sun set over the water.

On the sixth evening as I lay in my tent, wondering what I should to commemorate my final night on the farm, the wind, which had been blowing steadily all day, suddenly picked up, and I could hear rumblings in the distance. As I lay there the reverberations grew louder and closer and I knew that the peaceful weather was about to end.

I grabbed my flashlight and went outside to examine the tent. Only four of the eight anchor loops had stakes in them, and those were small plastic things that didn't penetrate very deeply into the rocky soil. I began hurriedly to fashion wooden stakes out of branches as the rain began to fall, and within minutes I was grappling with the tent in a torrential storm, trying to drive my makeshift tent stakes into the ground with the heel of my work boot. The lightning drew closer, until there was no longer any delay between the streaks of light and the bellowing thunder. As I struggled to keep the tent from blowing away, I found myself observing the process, impassively watching myself work with an uncharacteristic calm and thoroughness. It was such a pleasant sensation I even slowed my efforts slightly so as to prolong the feeling.

When I was done I stripped off my wet clothes and laid on my sleeping bag, listening with delight to the relentless thunder and the roar of the swelling creek, marveling at each flash of lightning that lit up my tent like daylight.

The following morning I awoke twice. First from sleep to waking consciousness, as usual. Then abruptly and without warning from waking consciousness to a level of awareness I'd never experienced before. As I lay there I was startlingly aware of being only a nameless entity lying in a tiny nylon cubicle, staring at a metal pole. I had no sense of my persona and all the negative baggage that came with it. I felt clean.

This, I thought, must be the observer Rose talks about. The one who objectively watches life through your eyes. The observer who can lead you to your True Self. In those moments it was glaringly apparent to me that this was the path to Reality, that regardless of what I might accomplish or acquire, or who I might surround myself with in life, that this entity, this being-ness, was the essential substance of my life, and was the vehicle of my destiny if I was to have one.

It was not a particularly joyous revelation. More like a childhood memory, long lost in the cluttered attic of my mind, that had suddenly surfaced. "Oh, yeah," it felt like. "I remember now."

I crawled out of the tent and waded up the creek, allowing the cool waters to rush past my ankles, shins, knees. I paused in the swift current, staring at the steep rock wall that bordered the stream, listening to the roar of the rain-swollen waterfall. Gradually my physical perceptions blended together, until I could no longer separate sight from sound from feeling. The surroundings became less and less real, until the outside world faded and my inner feelings created a new one in its place. For the first and only time in my life I was completely happy, and the world reflected it back to me in every way imaginable. I felt wrapped in a blissful light.

"So this is happiness," I thought, overwhelmed and awed by the sense of rapture and joy that surrounded me. Immediately, the feeling left, preferring, I suppose, not to be named, not to be captured in thought. I felt no sadness at it's leaving, however, only a clear knowledge that now was when the work began in earnest. Within an hour I had packed and cleared the campsite, careful to remove all traces of my visit, and started up the steep hillside that led to the farm.

I had packed all of my belongings before I moved into Rob's tent, so once I placed what I had carried back with me into the car, I was ready to leave. I had planned to take a final walk to my original campsite to organize my thoughts before saying good-bye to Rose, but when I closed the car door and turned around he was standing there, just a few feet away.

"Heading out, are you?" he said.

"Yeah, not much choice, really. Classes start Monday." I looked into his pale blue eyes—laughing, piercing, yet eternally neutral.

"I want to thank you for everything you've done for me," I said, suddenly aware of a catch in my throat.

Rose narrowed his eyes as if scrutinizing me for a moment, but said nothing.

"Is there anything I can do to repay you?" I asked.

He smiled warmly. "Just pass it on," he said. "That's all I ask of anyone. Just pass it on."

Chapter 10

Between-ness

Two years later, depressed about what felt like a lack of spiritual progress, I found myself thinking back to a conversation I'd had with Rose at that first summer Intensive. I'd asked him what I should focus on when I left the farm, what the next step was for me to make spiritual work a part of my regular life.

"Get control of yourself," he'd said. "Get control of your appetites and habits. Once you get control you'll feel powerful, feel as if you can take on some of the bigger challenges you'll have to face. Without control over yourself you'll always feel inadequate, inferior. You'll always be..." he searched for the right word, "remonstrating."

His word choice surprised me. In fact, I didn't know what it meant. Rose's natural speech was an odd combination of erudite and hillbilly. His basic pattern was very much a product of the mountains from which he came, and occasionally included the poor grammar and arcane usage one would associate with a backwoodsman or uneducated farmer. Yet the overall impression he left was that of an extremely well-educated man, but one perhaps whose education came from another era, or more accurately, of a man one might imagine had been self-taught from books found in the basement of an abandoned Victorian prep school, or maybe even a medieval monastery.

I nodded as if I understood. He could see that I didn't.

"You need to build your capacity for the work," he went on. "You need to be strong enough to withstand the forces of adversity that will rise up against you. The way to increase your capacity is to push beyond it. The measure of a man is his ability to endure tension."

Most of the tension in my life came from Rose and the group. Mainly through attrition, I gradually assumed more responsibilities in the Pittsburgh Pyramid Zen Society, first as treasurer, then as monitor. Sitting behind the table wasn't as easy as it looked — trying to stir everyone's thinking while keeping the peace, trying to lead people in beneficial confrontation without scaring them off, trying to talk intelligently about spirituality without being grounded in it myself. I thought back to when Ray was leading the group and wondered how many of the new people were judging me as harshly as I'd judged Ray.

Rose still showed up unannounced for meetings once or twice a month. Sometimes when I arrived he would already be holding forth, joking and talking with everyone. On those nights the meetings would pass with me as just another spectator. Other times he'd remain quiet and let me run the meeting while he sat sternly and silently a few feet away, as if mentally critiquing my competence for the job. On these occasions I tried to follow Augie's advice to just go on with the meeting as if Rose wasn't there, which sounded great in theory but in practice was like trying to make casual conversation with a time bomb ticking under your chair.

Every Friday evening the core members of the Pittsburgh group gathered to sit in rapport at the "ashram"—a rundown house in the Squirrel Hill section where several members lived together. Rose's teaching emphasized the importance of rapport sessions—sitting silently in a circle of fellow seekers—as a highly effective way to sharpen the intuition and to draw strength and insight from the energy of the group. I looked forward to these sessions as a time when the tensions of the week might fade and open the way for the calm clarity that so effectively eluded me in my daily affairs.

In other situations, I perceived and interacted with people as if they were two-dimensional supporting characters in the drama of my life. It was difficult, if not impossible, for me to see any characteristics in them that were not merely an extension of my own worrisome personality. But in rapport I would sometimes look around the room and see, as if for the first time, that other people were complex individuals with thought patterns totally different from mine. Occasionally I would get a strong sense of what it felt like to be one of the other people in the room—really "stand in his moccasins," as Rose would say—and it was an extraordinary revelation.

Usually Rose was not present for these sessions, but consistent with his unpredictability he would sometimes make the two-hour drive to sit with us. On these occasions—when I would walk into the ashram and see him drinking tea in the tattered overstuffed chair that had come to be his when he was there—my heart would instantly race, because with Rose present there was always the possibility of magic.

Unlike our normal sittings, which were preceded by a brief inspirational reading, there was no definite starting point for the actual session when Rose presided. Eventually he would just stop talking and remain quiet. Sometimes the energy level was similar to sessions without him. More often, however, it would take on an other-worldly intensity. Rose had the capacity to focus and direct this energy to a particular person in the room — sometimes in an unseen manner, sometimes by physically pointing at the person. When he did, that person's head would be *stopped* for a moment, and he would have an experience of some kind. Rose said that he himself did not know whether he was actually directing the energy, or whether his pointing was merely a recognition or pre-awareness of where the energy was headed anyway.

Rose never pointed to me, and the energy never headed in my direction on its own. The closest I got was at a session where Rose raised his finger to point — he told us later — at Edward, one of the regulars at our sittings. At that instant, however, Perry, a newcomer at his first rapport meeting, happened to lean forward into the line of fire and got hit instead. A startled look of shock came over his face and he began crying. As I watched this happen I realized I was crying, too. Not out of empathy for Perry, but at the stark recognition of the falseness of my life that overcame me at that moment. I carried that recognition for several weeks afterwards and it colored virtually everything I did. I don't know what happened to Perry. He never came around again.

Not long after that incident I was driving aimlessly one evening, depressed and confused about the uncertainties and conflicts in my life, when, without making any conscious decision about it, I suddenly found myself on I-79 headed towards West Virginia. I laughed at myself but didn't think I was actually going to go see Rose, only that I-79 was as good a road as any to do your thinking on. Even when I got out of my car in the school parking lot across from his house, I wasn't sure I'd actually knock on his door. It was after eleven o'clock by then, and it had been so long since I really talked with Rose that he seemed like a stranger in my thoughts. I walked up the steep steps to his house and noticed that the kitchen light was still on. I stood for several minutes on the back porch, then knocked.

The door opened slowly and Rose peered out at me. "Hello," he said, as if expecting me. "The wandering Jew returns."

Then he left me to come in and close the door myself while he turned his attention back to a local news story he'd apparently been watching on the old black and white TV perched atop one of the refrigerators. Though seven or eight group members lived in the house, Rose was alone in the kitchen. He, too, would probably have gone to bed in a few minutes had I not dropped by. I closed the door and sat down at the table. Rose stood in front of the refrigerator and watched attentively as the local anchor told of a fugitive in Moundsville who had barricaded himself in a trailer with his estranged wife, refusing to surrender to the police who surrounded him.

"I knew this guy's dad," Rose remarked. "He wasn't intimidated by cops, either. They arrested him for dynamiting fish down by Stahl's Run once, and he..." Rose stopped talking as the newscaster read a bulletin he was handed. The suspect had just committed suicide after exchanging gunfire with police.

"These guys always commit suicide," Rose said with disgust, "right after the cops shoot 'em."

The weather report followed and Rose turned up the volume. "The garden needs rain bad," he said. We listened in silence as the forecaster predicted hot dry weather for the next five days. "Guess I'll have to get out to the farm tomorrow and do some watering," Rose commented, almost to himself.

When the sports came on my own interest picked up. The Pirates had started the day only a half-game behind and I wondered how they'd done. Rose walked over and turned off the television.

"Half the news these days is idiots hitting a ball and looking for an excuse to pat each other on the ass," he said. Catching my eye he added, "Hard to believe there's actually intelligent people out there who give a damn about who's in first place."

I nodded in hypocritical agreement. He filled the tea kettle at the sink and put it on the stove.

"When I came back east from Seattle I stopped off in Cleveland for awhile," he said. "I was still too shaky from my Experience to come straight home. I checked into a room at a fleabag hotel in the Parma section and decided to head downtown, to see if the place had changed much since I was there in my twenties. Ever been to Cleveland?"

"No, I haven't."

"Well, I'm walking down by Lake Erie there, and all of a sudden I see this mass of humanity coming towards me. They're marching four or five abreast, with tremendous intensity in their faces, and nobody's saying a word.

"I was still very out-of-touch from my Experience and I thought to myself, there must have been a catastrophe of some kind. An earthquake. Maybe an atom bomb. So I stop somebody and ask him what happened. He looks at me like I'm nuts and keeps on walking. Same thing happened with the next couple of guys I stop. No answer. They just keep moving. Finally I stop a fellow who sees I'm sincere and he says, 'What do you mean, what happened? Nothing's happened.'

"'Where's everyone going, then?' I ask him. He just looks at me like I'm crazy and points to this big stadium a couple blocks away. 'To the ball game,' he says. 'The Indians are in town.'" Rose took two cups from the drain board at the sink and put a tea bag in each without asking me whether I wanted any or not.

"I couldn't believe it. I just stood there watching these stone-faced people flood past me, looking like they'd just seen death. And the only thing they've got on their minds is a ball game? All I could think was, 'My God! This is what I came back to?'"

The teapot whistled. Rose filled our cups then sat down across from me.

"So what's new in Pittsburgh?" he asked.

It was my opening to tell him what was on my mind. But even then, sitting across from him in his kitchen, I didn't really know what had brought me.

"Same old stuff, really. The meetings are going okay. I finished the bar exam. It'll be a few months before I get the results, but in the meantime my work at the law office is keeping me pretty busy. I'm just trying to figure out what comes next, I guess."

He nodded his head. "Sometimes a person's mind is so cluttered up with details they don't take the time to think about the future. That's when you get into trouble. You've always got to be looking ahead for the next step."

"That's just it, Mister Rose. I don't know what's up ahead. I'm not sure I even know what I *want* to be up ahead. It's hard to move forward when you don't know where you want to end up."

"You have no choice. None of us has any choice. In spiritual matters or in ordinary life, you either grow or you die. There's no such thing as standing still. As soon as you quit moving, you start slipping into death.

"I'm facing the same situation with the group," he went on. "Everybody's comfortable with things the way they are. Nobody wants to rock the boat. But I keep telling everybody the *zeitgeist* is changing. The group has to change with it.

"You can't just put up a few posters and get a hundred people at a lecture anymore. The government's putting the squeeze on people, and these kids in college are thinking about how to earn a living when they get out, not about the meaning of life. Spirituality is going to be a luxury no one will think he can afford."

"What about the people in the group now?"

"Most of you will give up and return to the drama of life, but a few will stick with it. They'll be the spiritual giants of tomorrow. And whoever these survivors are, they're going to have to join together in a common direction, and to keep looking for their fellows.

"They're still out there—people looking for Truth. You just have to change your words to suit the times. Talk their language. The physical dimension is the only common reference we have. Any philosophy that can't be explained in the current language and paradigm of Earth won't be believed or understood."

"What are you going to do, Mister Rose?"

He smiled like a man without a care in the world. "Relax," he said, folding his hands behind his head, as if demonstrating the concept. "Relax, then work like hell when the light turns green."

It was an unexpected philosophy from a man who maintained that bull-headed determination was the key to spiritual growth.

"You can't force things if they're not meant to be," he continued. "When you try to make things happen, all you're doing is feeding the forces working against you. Everything that's ever happened in the group has been a miracle. The group itself is a miracle. For years I tried to get something going and nothing happened. I was beating my head against walls that wouldn't move. Then, suddenly, a door opened and I just walked through it."

"But you had something to do with that door opening, didn't you?"

"Yes and no. The years of fruitless struggle were necessary to build up a sufficient head of steam. But I didn't *do* anything. You quit and things happen. You *let* the door open. You stop the obstruction, you eliminate the ego. This is *between-ness*."

"I've never really understood between-ness," I said.

"You can't learn between-ness," he said. "But if you *live the life* it will come naturally to you."

"Come to you how?"

"When you finally realize that you're not doing anything in this life—that you're *incapable* of doing anything—then you stumble into a state of mindlessness that proves to be creative, that's all."

He laughed at my puzzled expression. "Don't try to figure this out. You'll break something."

We stayed silent for a minute or so, then he unexpectedly continued to explain, as if he thought there really might be a way for me to understand through words.

"The ego is the single biggest obstruction to the achievement of anything," he said. "Between-ness is the act of acting without ego. You act, but you are not the actor. You do things, but you are not the doer—and *you know* you are not the doer. It's the ability to hold the head at a dead standstill in order to effect certain changes. You desire the change, *but you do not care if it comes to pass*.

"Between-ness does not change the eternal fact. It's a way of *discovering* the eternal fact. It occurs when you want what is right, independent of your own desires. There's a mechanism for holding your head in this half-way state, in between caring and not caring. You *will* it, then forget it—without fear of failure or hope of gain. Between-ness is the product of a lifetime of egoless-ness.

"Children know about this," he said. "I stayed at an orphanage for awhile when I was a boy to be near the Catholic school I was going to. I remember seeing this kid with his nose pressed against the window one day, saying, 'Snow, snow go away. Come again some other day.' The rest of us *wanted* it to snow, so I asked him why he didn't. He said, 'I want it to snow, too, but if you want something too much, it knows, and you won't get it.'"

He looked at me intently. "Did you pick up on that? He said '*It knows.*' That kid knew something."

I nodded and took a sip of tea.

"Between-ness isn't necessarily a spiritual thing," Rose went on. "It's a law, like gravity. It works on all kinds of mundane stuff. There was a period while I was married when I was pretty sick. I don't know what it was. One doctor said I had a mild stroke. I think I was just deflated from fighting with my wife all the time."

I laughed but Rose did not.

"Whatever it was, it made me constantly tired. I'd come home from painting and sit down in a chair and would hardly be able to get up. So I started going down to a beer joint in the evenings, just to get myself moving and out of the house. I didn't drink, but I'd have a soda and shoot the bull with my neighbors, just to pass the time and get my mind off my troubles.

"Anyway, there was always a poker game going on in the back room, and eventually I started sitting in. They loved it because I didn't know how to play and they took all my money. Just penny ante stuff, though, so I didn't mind. I figured it was as good a way to pass the time as any. Then they raised the stakes to a quarter. *That's* when I started practicing between-ness." We both laughed.

"I didn't care if I won or lost. In fact, if I had a cinch hand I'd tell everyone to fold. But I was winning every night just by calling people and never folding unless they had me beat showing. When I needed a card I'd think of it and the dealer would give it to me. I was amazed. It got to where I started calling for the cards I needed out loud. Crazy stuff like filling an inside straight. I'd say, 'Steinie, give me a nine and a jack.' And that's what he'd give me. It drove the other guys nuts.

"I didn't know exactly what I was doing, but I knew the reason it worked was because I didn't care and I never got greedy. After the game I'd take everybody to an all-night restaurant across the river in Bellaire and buy 'em a steak dinner with my winnings. If I'd started to care about the money, I'd have lost that point of grace and balance. See what I mean?

I nodded. I was beginning to understand the concept, at least intellectually.

"There's a tremendous power in between-ness," he went on. "When circumstances are right, things happen. When it's used in spiritual work I call it *ultimate* between-ness. Every true spiritual system expresses the same thing in one way or another—try like hell while at the same time surrendering to God."

We sat in silence for a few minutes. Once again he had answered questions I didn't know enough to ask. For the moment, at least, I stopped worrying about my future.

"I wonder what time it is," he said, turning to a small travel clock on the shelf behind him. "Wow, it's after two. Do you want to bunk here tonight?"

I quickly stammered the beginnings of an excuse, but the fear I suddenly felt must have showed on my face. Rose laughed uproariously.

"Hell, this place isn't so bad. Nobody's died here in weeks."

"It's not that," I protested weakly. "It's just that I'm supposed to meet with my bosses in the morning about my legal plans. I've got a ton of loose ends to tie up now that the bar exam is over."

"Well, drop down again when you get a chance. I'll be out of town this weekend. Maybe next weekend you can get free."

I promised to come down the following weekend and headed for the door, but for some reason he kept on talking. For several minutes he stood with me at the door telling me about an invitation he'd received to speak at an outdoor symposium in northwestern

Pennsylvania the following Saturday. It was late and I was tired. I was mystified as to why he was bothering to tell me about it on my way out, or at all, for that matter.

"Well, I guess you better hit the road," he said finally, turning the porch light on for me. "Get those loose ends tied up and come on back down."

I carefully walked down the uneven stone steps then crossed the quiet street to my car. True, I would have made up an excuse if necessary to keep from staying in Rose's stark, crowded Benwood house. But I really did have a meeting the next morning with Don, the senior partner at the law firm where I worked, to discuss my future now that I had taken the bar. I enjoyed working there, and it provided a secure source of income, but I had decided it was time to move on and start my own practice. On my drive home from Benwood that night my head was alternately filled with thoughts of between-ness and with what I would say to Don in a few hours.

The next morning my meeting was over quickly. What's to discuss when somebody makes you an offer you can't refuse? Don proposed that I start my practice within their office. They would provide a secretary, take care of all my overhead, steer me some clients, even pay me a salary. In return I would work twenty hours a week for their firm. The rest of the time would be my own, to build my practice, or, as Don said with a wink, to stand on my head and meditate on my navel if I wanted to. We agreed that I would continue to work as an hourly employee through the summer, and begin this new arrangement on the first of September.

It was an arrangement so perfect I could not have imagined it in advance. Not only would it provide me both freedom and security, but evidently my bosses had somehow caught wind of my interest in esoteric matters and did not openly disapprove. In one swift stroke a nameless tension I'd been enduring but unable to identify was simultaneously unmasked and eradicated. I was intoxicated with a giddy rush of relief.

I couldn't wait to talk with Rose and tell him what had happened, to ask him if this was the kind of thing he was talking about the night before in the kitchen, if this was the result of some kind of accidental between-ness on my part—or his.

At the Thursday meeting I overheard Augie tell someone that Rose had summoned him to Benwood for the weekend, so I called Augie and we arranged to drive down together.

Maybe because I was doing the driving I did almost all the talking. I recounted for Augie in detail the conversation Rose and I had about between-ness, and the unbelievable job offer I got the very next day.

"It's just like you told me on our first ride down," I said, excitedly, "there's some kind of magic about the man."

Augie wasn't even pretending to be interested. I studied his face and saw something I had never seen in him before.

"You look exhausted," I said.

"I am." He continued staring straight ahead. "Two years setting up groups in Pittsburgh and Ohio. New groups last year in New England. This year, the traveling Intensives with Rose. I feel like a soldier who's marched across Europe. Then just as he's about to take his boots off, he gets called to headquarters for another mission."

"Another mission? Are you sure? When Rose and I were talking in the kitchen, he didn't know where to take the group. In fact, that's what started the whole conversation about between-ness."

"Well something at that symposium last weekend got him all fired up again, I guess. We'll hear all about it soon enough, whatever it is."

I had a hard time believing that anything at that symposium could have solved Rose's dilemma about the future direction of the group. That night at the door before I left Rose told me he wasn't even sure why he was going. He said it would be full of "piddlers," which is what he called people who dabbled in spirituality the way others watched birds or collected stamps. He'd showed me a copy of the program: massage therapy, crystals, spirit guides, spiral staircases ascending into heaven—exactly the kind of spiritual pabulum Rose was always ridiculing. What's more, at sixty years of age, he would be one of the youngest people there, and he was always warning us to steer clear of people who'd lived too long to change. People whose lives were too complex or heads too hardened to undergo the radical and traumatic adjustments necessary to *become*.

But as Rose wrote in *The Albigen Papers*, even a sick chicken can lay a healthy egg. He was in high spirits as he recounted his experience at the symposium. True, the program was insipid, the crowd ancient, and the facilities primitive, but Rose was sure he had caught a glimpse of how the group could survive, maybe even prosper, during the coming spiritual recession.

"Hell, we could put on a much better program," Rose said excitedly. " You could pull ten speakers out of a beer joint and hear more wisdom than what they put out. And the farm has it all over where they put this show on—they were meeting under a circus tent. Sure, we're not going to get serious people at first, but we'll keep expanding our contacts, and eventually find a few people who are material for the esoteric core."

Whether truly inspired, or simply too worn out to resist Rose's enthusiasm, Augie began lacing up his marching boots again.

"Maybe we could put one on in a city first," he said. "Get the bugs out of the operation before we bring the show to the farm."

Rose nodded encouragingly, and Augie pressed ahead. "I know some people who would probably speak for nothing in Pittsburgh. Jim belongs to that Unitarian Church in Mount Lebanon. We could probably hold the first one at his church. And Dave here has some time on his hands now that he doesn't have the bar exam as an excuse to keep from doing group work."

Later, after six hours of uninterrupted caffeine and brainstorming, I felt I'd witnessed the birth of an empire. The only thing that worried me was how often my name came up in the conversation. After all, it was more or less a coincidence that I was there for the conversation at all. On the ride back home I explained to Augie that I had just over a month to make extensive preparations for my life's work, and that I had little or no time to give to this enterprise.

"No sweat, Attorney. All I need from you is a place to work. Just let me in to use your office at night, and I promise not to interfere with your spiritual corruption."

The first few evenings Augie was true to his word. About seven o'clock, I'd let him into the office, then do my legal work while he used the equipment and made phone calls from Don's thick leather chair. Then one night he asked me to look over a press release he'd written, and even though I knew better, I agreed. Within a few days I was typing letters, helping him work the phones, and lining up interviews for our speakers on local talk shows.

Each day the "Chautauquas," as Rose had named our symposia, took over more of my life. Augie and I moved into a small apartment his grandfather owned in Lawrenceville, so I was never far away when Augie wanted help. He thought nothing of working at the law office until two or three in the morning because he could sleep until noon, while I had to report back to the office by eight the next morning for a full day's work.

After a month of this I was stretched pretty thin, but my spirits were high because I kept thinking about September, when I would begin my new arrangement with the law partners. I wasn't sure what, if anything, would be different from when I was just an hourly employee, but in my mind the new arrangement was of great importance because to me it marked the beginning of my legal career.

When that morning finally came I rejected my polyester ties and borrowed a silk one from Augie. I rode the bus to work instead of hitchhiking. In the building lobby I studied the office directory and wondered if I should have my name included on it. I whistled as I rode the elevator up to "our" law offices, and imagined the good-natured welcoming handshakes that might formally mark my transition from lackey to equal.

When I stepped into the reception area, however, the office manager gave me an icy stare that froze me in my tracks.

"Mr. Hartwell wants to see you," she said.

Don was waiting for me in the hall. "Let's go where we can talk," he said, and I followed him into his spacious corner office.

He motioned for me to take a seat on the couch, while he slid into the high backed leather chair behind his massive mahogany desk.

"I've always regarded this office as sort of a family," he said. "I've tried to treat everyone that way, and I think for the most part I've succeeded."

He paused as if waiting for me to agree. I felt as if I were being set up for something, and said nothing.

"And like a family, each member's actions reflects on everybody else. If somebody in the family does well, everyone profits. If somebody embarrasses themselves, everybody looks bad."

He reached into a desk drawer and pulled out a yellow pamphlet, which I immediately recognized as a flyer for the Pittsburgh Chautauqua. He pushed it across his desk towards me as if presenting evidence to a witness.

"I knew you'd been coming in here in the evenings working on something, and quite honestly I didn't care what you were doing. But I absolutely cannot allow this law office to be associated with whacko stuff like this!"

He stared at me, waiting for an apology, a confession, an obsequious explanation, perhaps. My face burned but I could think of nothing to say. He leaned back in his chair and waited a full minute before speaking again. When he did his tone was softer.

"I'm sorry Dave," he said, tapping the tips of his long narrow fingers together, "but you'll have to find another place to work."

I left the office building in a daze and stepped into the jostling pedestrian traffic of attorneys hustling down Grant Street on their way to the courthouse. Never before had I felt so much like an outsider in their world. They had jobs, lives, careers, futures — vectors of success that shot by me as I wandered aimlessly through the crowded city streets. I caught the first bus back to Lawrenceville and found a seat among the old men and women whose business in town could be completed by ten o'clock. Some held bags from pharmacies, others, government envelopes from the Social Security office.

I walked into the empty apartment and laid down on my bed, trying to come to grips with the reality of my situation. I had nothing to fall back on. I didn't have the legal contacts to land another job, or the money and know-how to open my own office on short notice. Immersed in self-pity, I ignored the ringing of the telephone, until I realized that it might be someone returning one of Augie's innumerable Chautauqua-related phone calls. I was surprised that the caller was still on the line after all of those rings, and even more surprised by the voice on the other end. It was Rose.

"Christ, I thought maybe the police had raided the place and you were both in jail," he said. Over the phone it was difficult to gauge his level of seriousness.

"No, nothing quite that dramatic," I said, though at that moment I'm not sure I could have felt much worse even if I *were* in jail.

"Augie's not here," I said. "He had an early meeting with a philosophy professor at Carnegie Mellon. He's trying to get him to bring his whole class to the Chautauqua."

"I wasn't looking for Augie, anyway," he said. "I was looking for you."

My legs felt like rubber. I sat down on the floor. Rose regarded long distance telephone calls as an unnecessary evil, an expensive indulgence to be used only in emergencies. For him to call me, and in the middle of the day no less, was almost unthinkable. I wondered just how bad a day this was going to be.

"You know," he began, in a reflective West Virginia drawl, "I just had an idea. And you don't have to give me an answer right away."

Now my heart was really pounding.

"I don't know how flexible your work situation is up there, but I think these Chautauquas have real potential. There's no limit to what we could do with them."

He proceeded to elaborate on his plans. It was clear as he talked that the blueprint for the Chautauquas had already been laid out in his mind, taking into account every detail, and its relationship to every other detail. Pittsburgh was just the beginning. From there we'd move on to Columbus, then Cleveland, Akron. After each Chautauqua we'd leave behind a study group that would hopefully attract those few serious people Rose was really after. Rose would get the guys on the farm to start building a pavilion—he already had the spot picked out—and by next summer we'd have a place to meet and contacts from the surrounding cities for the Chautauquas at the farm, which, as I recalled, was the original reason for the entire operation.

"Augie's a great idea man," Rose said. "But sometimes he's a little weak on the details. He needs someone to come along behind him and pick up the broken glass, and you two seem to get along okay.

"Now you know I'm reluctant to interfere in people's lives, but I was wondering if you thought it might be a good idea to take a year off before you start lawyering and help Augie out with this operation. That way you'd see a little of the country before you settle down to get fat and rich. Maybe we could season you up a bit."

I could no longer hold my excitement. "Mister Rose, it's perfect. I'll do it."

"Well, maybe you should think it over. Sleep on it and call me back."

"No, I'm sure this is what I want to do. You're not going to believe this but I just got fired about an hour ago. Today was supposed to be my first day of work, and when I walked into the office they—"

"Okay, well, I don't want to give any more money to these thieves at the phone company than I have to," he said. "Maybe you and Augie can come on down this weekend and we'll talk about it."

Chapter Eleven

The Chautauquas

The first Chautauqua was a qualified success. It was held in the Mount Lebanon Unitarian Church outside of Pittsburgh, and as the first day neared an end I was feeling pretty good about what we'd accomplished. The small church was packed, and the mood all day had been friendly and harmonious. People kept walking up to the information table and thanking us for bringing all these different people and ideas together. A few even bought memberships in the Truth and Transmission (TAT) Society, which was the official name for the organization that had formed around Rose. Even Rose, who had forced us to plan for every conceivable negative contingency, had remarked earlier in the day that things seemed to be going well.

Near the end of the day, however, Augie looked distraught as he paced nervously up and down the hallway outside the sanctuary where Rose was currently appearing as the last speaker. Periodically Augie would crack open the door and observe the proceedings for a moment, then resume pacing.

"What's wrong?" I asked him.

"Just what I was afraid of," he said. "These crowds are wrong for Rose. Take a look."

I quietly opened the side door to the sanctuary and stepped inside. Rose stood behind a podium on the small stage, speaking to an audience of about seventy-five people who were staring at him with confused, skeptical, even angry faces.

"Maybe it's for the best," Rose was saying to a heavy-set man standing at the end of a row of chairs, as if ready to walk out at any moment. "If people really thought about what they're promised in church, they'd realize how absurd it all is. I mean, who wants to spend eternity sitting around with a bunch of cherubs playing harps? After awhile people would want to go to Hell just for the change of scenery."

"Well, I don't agree with everything organized religions may espouse," the man said, in a tone that indicated their disagreement had been going on for some time. "But they do give people a reason to strive for goodness and for a better world." Many in the audience nodded their heads or voiced their agreement.

"No they don't," Rose said firmly. "What they do is give people an excuse to keep from working to improve their personal state of being, and perhaps their after-death state as well. Religion tells you we're all going to the same place. People think God has to operate under the human concept of justice, and it wouldn't be fair if we all didn't go to the same place. So they figure they can just sit back and ride the tide of humanity into Self-Realization.

"The worst of it is that these kinds of beliefs keep people from looking for real answers," Rose went on. "Every sentient being needs to know his cause, needs to know if he was created or merely the product of accident. What he doesn't need is to be placated or silenced by some political social group that hands out fairy tales and calls them the word of God."

The questioner had been moving toward the door and now stood right next to me as he turned back to Rose.

"These 'political social groups,' as you so disparagingly call them, provide great solace for a great many people," he said. The crowd nodded its approval again.

"Maybe," Rose shot back, "but for how long? If a man has even a shred of curiosity or self-honestly, he'll wake up one day and realize he's been deluding himself for thirty years. Society and religion brainwash a man into thinking he has to believe a certain way. So he tries to assume a posture he thinks will mesh with what's expected of him. First he puts one over on society—convincing them he fits in, that he's a nice fellow, that sort of thing. Then he puts one over on himself by believing his own act. By this time he's hopelessly caught in the web of lies that has become his life.

"But the thing is," Rose said, his voice rising, "there will come a time in everyone's life when you come to doubt everything you ever thought. Unfortunately, for most people it doesn't occur until it's too late to do anything about it. In the meantime, the majority of people just slide along, reasoning that because the public doesn't complain about their social behavior, they must be on the right track on all levels. They pay their taxes, get along with the fellow next door, do a decent job at work. To them, these are the signs of a sufficient theology."

"What your alternative, then?" the man persisted.

"You mean something I can explain to your satisfaction in twenty-five words or less? Forget it. It would take twenty-five hundred just to get you confused, then a lot more to try and explain away the confusion."

"Well, then I'd say the problem lies with your inability to communicate," the man said. Then, as if suddenly realizing he'd just spoken a perfect exit line, he hurriedly opened the door and left. Rose watched impassively, then turned to the rest of the audience.

"Maybe he's got a point. There's times I find it difficult to even know how to begin delivering a lecture. I have trouble communicating because when you find out that this whole existence is a projection, you lose enthusiasm for feeding people what they want to hear about the significance or appeal of the illusion.

"You see, I don't want to bring you peace of mind. I want to bring you trouble. I want to stir you, to shake you. Because protoplasm tends to inertia. You have to keep irritating it to keep it alive, so to speak. It has to be continually stimulated. Complacency is a very negative trait for a person who wants to progress in his mental capacities.

"In fact, if you're interested in finding your self-definition, you need to abandon any philosophy or system that quiets you down. You need to continually awaken yourself, to arouse yourself mentally, to attack your systems of thinking. Because you don't want peace, you want an answer."

Rose talked for awhile longer and when he finished the audience silently filed out. I had seen Rose irritate people before. It comes with the territory for a man who places Truth above all else. But whether due to Rose's bluntness or to natural attrition, the Sunday sessions only had about half as many attendees as Saturday's, and all day long I'd hear snatches of conversation about that "negative man from West Virginia." Overall, though, the Chautauqua feedback was positive. We broke even financially, and with one semi-successful program behind us I was ready to take the show on the road.

Augie was not as optimistic. On the drive down to Benwood the next day to post-mortem the week-end, he was obviously very worried. The next Chautauqua was planned for Cleveland, and in light of Rose's reception in Pittsburgh, Augie saw trouble ahead. I talked up the positive points of the weekend and tried to transfer some of my optimism to him. I couldn't understand how Augie, whose near-childlike faith in Rose had carried him through so many successful projects, could now be so worried.

"These Chautauquas just aren't going to attract the kind of people who can listen to Rose being Rose," he said with finality. We rode the last few miles in silence.

When we arrived, Rose was in high spirits. He had always made me feel welcome, but now that we were working together I felt like a special door had been opened for me in his home. We sat around the kitchen laughing and drinking tea, Rose poking fun at Augie's frightened look after he had introduced him as a speaker, and at my inability to sit still behind the table where I belonged while he was talking. I felt like the three of us were sharing a special joke, one that we might even be playing on the rest of the world.

And then, almost offhandedly, Rose announced, "One thing for sure, though. I'm not talking at any more Chautauquas."

I figured Augie would be relieved by this unexpected and almost unbelievable news. But his arguments were from the heart.

"Mister Rose, I'm not interested in putting a year of my life into bringing together a bunch of astrologers and crystal gazers. The whole reason for these programs is to find people who can understand your message."

"Yeah, but my message is sour music. You can't sugarcoat the truth, and I'd rather say nothing than be dishonest with people. These Chautauquas have real potential, and the group is larger than any one individual. I'm hoping the group will survive long after I kick the bucket.

"Besides," he added with a smile, "someone has to make sure the toilets are clean."

The next day Augie and I left for Cleveland with Rose's blessing and not much else. We had little more than pocket change between us, no income, and of course, no TAT expense account.

We moved into the local "ashram," a tiny rundown apartment in the Little Italy section of East Cleveland. Four members of the local TAT group were already living there in a space designed for two, but Augie and I squeezed in anyway.

Each morning we'd walk to Lopresti's Bakery for two loaves of Italian bread hot out of the oven, then over to the Mayfield Emporium for a stick of butter and a package of figs. After eating we'd head out to the appointments Augie had set up the day before—dream analysts, astrologers, numerologists, psychic healers, theosophists, Jungians, palm readers, mediums. I never knew what to expect.

Augie was fearless, self-assured and overwhelmingly optimistic about The Grand Work of the TAT Society. He exuded success and confidence, and nearly everyone regarded him as some sort of New Age boy wonder. Strangers invited him into their homes, agreed to speak at the program for nothing, introduced him at their group meetings, placed announcements for the Chautauquas in their newsletters, and provided names and references for our next day's work. It was magic and momentum—the Albigen System in action— and I was thrilled to be a part of it.

We met sincere people who knew a little, and charlatans who professed to know a lot more than they did. I was intrigued by the occultists who had so fully explored their chosen paradigms that they somehow managed to derive some insight, if not wisdom, from a relatively narrow field of study. I met a psychic who informed me that late in life I would marry my high school girlfriend, a Virgo by the name of "Jan" or "Jane." A tarot reader examined her cards and advised me I would be practicing law in West Virginia within a year. An iridologist looked into my eyes and correctly told me which bones in my body had been broken. All of them saw the Chautauquas as a chance to reach people who otherwise wouldn't know they existed.

When I was the monitor of the Pittsburgh group, promoting the Pyramid Zen Society was a pretty straightforward affair. We were looking for Truth, plain and simple, and for people who were desperate enough or fed up enough to look with us in earnest. Pitching the Chautauquas was a different matter. We were dealing with a much more diverse set of people, many of whom had mixed motives. But Augie adapted quickly, and became very adept at convincing the greedy there was money to be made, the vain there was glory to be had, and the fringe groups that we were all taking different paths to the same end.

Every couple of days Augie would call Rose and report in careful generalities the highlights of what was going on. If Augie did most of the talking he'd come away from the call upbeat and revived. If the call was long and Augie did the listening, he'd come away deflated and depressed. Within a hour or two, though, he would have worked himself back up to his normal level of self-confidence—which sometimes bordered on a conviction of infallibility. As we set about our next tasks after a call like that, I sometimes wondered whether we were operating under the advice Augie had heard from "headquarters," or from the personal instincts he felt were his prerogative as field commander.

Whatever his method, in less than three weeks he had set a date, secured a hall, and lined up twelve speakers for the program. We left Cleveland for the farm feeling proud of what we'd accomplished in such a short time, but the closer we came to West Virginia the more nervous Augie became.

"I know that dream analyst from the bookstore is money-hungry but I had to put her on the program to get her mailing list. Besides, how bad can she be. Right?"

"Right, Aug."

"And that guy with the speech impediment from the psychic research group. You can still understand what he's saying, can't you?"

"If you concentrate hard enough, eventually you get his drift," I assured him.

"I mean, how many quality speakers can you find in a place like Cleveland, especially who'll talk for nothing?"

"Relax. Mister Rose doesn't expect the twelve apostles."

"Don't be too sure."

It was easy for me to be upbeat. I wasn't the guy on the hot seat who had to live up to Rose's standards. I was just along for the ride, enjoying the feel of the path beneath my feet. I had no reason to believe that our motives were anything but pure, our efforts diligent, and our results commendable.

We drove straight to the farm, where Rose was supervising the building of the summer Chautauqua pavilion. The first thing I noticed as we pulled into the parking area was that a new road had been cut through the deep woods behind the farmhouse and a lot of noise was coming from that direction. Augie and I got out of the car and headed that way. As we approached, the sounds of shouting, trucks, hammers, and chain saws got louder and more distinct. At the end of the new road was a scene of high activity—maybe fifteen or more men engaged in various construction tasks.

The tangle of trees and underbrush where my original tent had been pitched—and destroyed—was now part of a large clearing, in the center of which sat the crude framework of an enormous building. Twenty oak logs at least two feet thick and two stories high had been sunk deep in the ground, while logs about half the width and twice as long crisscrossed the huge posts.

Larry was dragging more trees out of the woods with an old truck, while Al and a guy I didn't recognize chain-sawed the logs to size. At the peak of the framework, twenty feet off the ground, Rose sat astride a log, supervising the hoisting and placement of the next cross-beam.

I wanted to jump right in and help, but instead took my cue from Augie, who did not like physical work. He stood well back from the action and surveyed the activity agreeably, like a general watching his well-disciplined troops on the battlefield.

Rose, who was aware of our presence, continued to oversee the setting of the posts and beams, standing on the cross-members, rearranging ropes, shouting directions and occasionally pulling on the lines himself until his face was red from the strain. Though nearly sixty years old, when he worked strenuously alongside youths he became youthful, and looked the equal or better of any twenty-year old on the crew. After setting the last of the posts, Rose climbed down the ladder and greeted us. It was lunch time and we walked with him down the road towards the farmhouse, along with Chuck, who acted as foreman for the building project.

"It's amazing no one's been killed down there," Rose said, smiling but serious. Despite the coolness of the overcast autumn day, he was still perspiring from his efforts. "I lost my grip on a sledgehammer and it zigzagged through ten men like somebody was steering it. It's a miracle it didn't hit anybody."

"We were all convinced he did it on purpose as some kind of magical feat," Chuck said.

"Magic, hell," Rose said. "I lost my grip. And yesterday one of the ropes broke carrying a two-ton log..."

"Five seconds after Mister Rose warned us not to get underneath the ropes because they might break," interrupted Chuck, shaking his head in amazement. "Two guys moved out from under the beam after he warned them, and boom, the rope snaps."

"They were old ropes," was all Rose would offer on the subject.

We followed him into the farmhouse, which was overheated by a roaring fire in the wood stove. Rose got a coke out of the refrigerator and took a seat in the meeting room. "So how's the circus going in Cleveland?" he asked, snapping the pop-top then taking a long drink from the can."

"Circus is right," Augie said, jumping at the opening Rose had given him. "You've never seen such a bunch of fruits and freaks. We've been from one end of that city to the other and we're lucky if we've met a half-dozen sincere people."

"Well, that leaves you six people short. You said there'd be twelve speakers, right?"

Augie looked uneasily, even a bit irritably, at the guys who were drifting into the room to listen in. Whatever he was hoping to accomplish with this visit wasn't going to be any easier with an audience.

"Oh, we've got twelve," he said. "And they aren't too bad. Some of them are pretty good, actually. None of them are devil worshippers or anything. But it's hard finding heavyweight speakers on lightweight subjects."

"I don't care how much they weigh, Augie. We're not running a sale barn where we get paid by the pound." The guys who now ringed the room laughed. "I don't want you snapping up the first twelve people you meet just so you can fill up the program."

"I didn't take the first twelve people I met," Augie replied, the restrained evenness in his voice revealing both hurt and anger. I could understand Augie's reaction. There were a lot of times he had to reject potential speakers without hurting their feelings. I also saw Rose's point, because occasionally, swept along by humor or flattery, Augie would extend an offer to someone we'd previously agreed wasn't up to the task.

"This is the real world we're dealing with, Mister Rose. Everybody's got an agenda out there. I just don't think we're going to find perfect people with what we've got to offer."

"I know what's out there, Augie. I don't expect you to find speakers who are enlightened." The way the guys nodded, it was obvious Rose had been talking about this while we were gone.

"A lot of those people are interested in money," Rose went on, "and in a way I don't blame them. Money's not the most important thing, but it's more important than most things. If it weren't for money, I wouldn't be able to do what I'm doing. But if money's their primary game, we don't want anything to do with them. They'll twist everything they say to get that almighty buck. I just don't believe in eating at the alter.

"I know you're doing a helluva lot of work up there, Augie. I don't want to see it wasted. But the easiest person to sell is another salesman. And I don't think you see how easily you get snowed into thinking that you're getting something from somebody, when you're the one who's really being enlisted into the other guy's power trip."

Augie slumped in his chair and kept silent. Probably because it was not directed at me, I could see the wisdom in Rose's warning. All the while Augie was pitching people to help out in our venture, I could see they were sizing him up, trying to figure out what they could get out of him. Although we never discussed it, I figured Augie knew what they were thinking, and even led them on a bit to believe that if they really came through, maybe he could be talked into working for them.

"To some people it might look like all we're doing is putting out some half-baked speakers to talk about piddling topics," Rose went on, "but the overall aim of this venture is the highest work of man, and consequently, it attracts the most insidious forms of adversity. No matter how clever you think you are you've got to constantly be on guard against your own vanity. Otherwise, the fox gets caught."

Augie looked hurt and confused as Rose continued.

"That goes from the top on down. Nobody is immune. In order to keep this group from becoming a personality cult, I try to have no personality. Maybe I try too hard," he chuckled.

The telephone rang, and Rose got up to answer it. He listened, voiced a few words of concern, wrote down some directions, then hung up.

"The stake-body truck broke down with a load of lumber from the saw mill." His words were like a call to arms. Everyone left the room and moved outside, where Rose gave orders about tools, a tow bar, and who would drive which vehicle to where.

Augie and I stood in the yard watching everyone scurry about us, the "highest work of man" completely forgotten.

"Looks like we came a long way for nothing," Augie muttered. I disagreed but said nothing. Not yet in the line of Rose's fire, I still had the luxury of believing that we must have gotten what we came for.

We started over to the van. Rose, carrying a length of thick rope, joined us.

"Damn junkers. We just put a new transmission in that truck and already it's shot. It'll probably take the rest of the day to haul it back here." Then, as if remembering something, Rose stopped and leaned against Augie's van, his face transformed by a look of calm serenity and understanding.

"Maybe you think I'm being unreasonable," he said softly, "expecting you to fill the programs with saints and virgins. Believe me, I know what's out there. I've spent the last thirty years looking for one person who would pick up this work and really go with it. One person who would say, 'Yes, this is it, this is what I want more than anything else. What do I have to do to find out who I really am?'"

He took the rope off his shoulder and placed it on the hood of the van. "Well, I haven't found that person and I'm not getting any younger. Eventually, my life's work will come down to what I leave behind. And I'd rather leave nothing than have my work twisted by some phony or pervert, especially somebody I let lecture under the group banner."

The roar of engines called him back to another role. He picked up his rope and climbed into the passenger seat of an old blue flatbed truck, and with a wave he was gone.

Back in Cleveland the next day I reassured myself that good results on the Chautauqua trail would iron out these minor differences of opinion between Rose and Augie. Instead, success seemed to highlight what I came to recognize was an essential philosophic difference between them.

A hundred and twenty-five people attended the Cleveland Chautauqua in December. Over two hundred people came to the February event in Columbus. To Augie, bigger crowds were proof that we'd hit upon a successful format that we could package and take to the next city. Rose warned that we were getting lazy and complacent and merely looking for an excuse to put on "more of the same." To

Augie, more revenue meant more opportunity and bigger budgets. Rose still sweated every nickel and chided us about the "extravagances" and "flourishes" of long distance calls and newspaper advertising. Augie complained about being second-guessed over every move and started making more decisions on his own. Rose intervened less and less, which relieved Augie and worried me. I knew Rose wasn't the type to ignore problems for long, especially those that might interfere with The Work. We still had city programs to put on in Akron and Washington, D.C. before we broke for the summer Chautauquas, and I hoped we could get through them without any major blow-ups.

Akron was our biggest success yet, with more attendees than seats to put them in. Augie moderated the program while I handled operations. I rushed around giving orders, making decisions, and feeling important—until I bumped into Rose in the church kitchen, supervising a half-dozen women who were frantically trying to prepare two hundred and twenty-five meals before noon. I felt a sudden wave of guilt for the ego-high I had been riding, and had the urge to confess, explain, apologize—anything to let him know I hadn't forgotten who he was and why we were here. But it was Rose who spoke first.

"Who's minding the gate?" he asked irritably. I immediately hustled out of his kitchen and back to my post.

The tension eased in the afternoon, with the program running smoothly and Rose's meals out of the way. I wandered over to the book table where Rose was joking with Tim, our remarkable book salesman. Each Chautauqua, Tim had managed to sell forty or fifty copies of *The Albigen Papers* to people who probably never made it past the first chapter, assuming they opened the book at all. That day he had already sold a book to everyone who had stood still long enough to listen to him, and with nothing left for either of them to do, he and Rose were relaxing in the foyer.

"You know, Mister Rose, you're always selling yourself too short," Tim said loudly, still in his ebullient salesman mode.

"That's because I *am* short," Rose replied with a chuckle.

"You know what I mean," Tim said. "You've had an Absolute spiritual experience, but you're wrapping hoagies in the kitchen while some nut's in there preaching about flying saucers."

For several minutes Tim continued to press Rose to take his rightful place in the spotlight while Rose did his best to humor him. The presence of an older lady standing within earshot of Tim's flattery clearly made Rose uncomfortable. Unable to curb Tim's enthusiasm

Rose finally turned to her and explained, "I've got his wife locked up in the trunk of my car. He has to say these things."

The old woman smiled politely, and Rose started to walk away. But Tim was not finished. "Mister Rose, do you know who you are?" he said, his voice rising and filling with emotion. "You're God. That's who you are. You're *God*."

Rose smiled and pointed towards the woman. "If I'm God, then she's the Virgin Mary." Everyone laughed except the woman. She turned noticeably pale and quickly disappeared down the stairs.

"You better go check on that lady," Rose said to me. "We may have offended her."

I went downstairs and found her sitting on a couch, sipping her coffee with trembling hands. I sat next to her and made small talk.

"Oh, you don't have to worry about me, young man, I'm all right. It's just that, well, that person upstairs..." She took another sip of coffee then continued.

"You know how that tall boy was going on and on about how the other man was so wonderful and smart and holy?" I nodded, but I don't think she noticed.

"Well, it was really getting on my nerves. I was thinking, 'What kind of cult is this?' And finally, when he said to the older man, 'You're God,' I thought to myself, 'Yeah, right. If that guy's God then I'm the Virgin Mary.' And the thought had no more popped into my head than he said it out loud, in words, just the way I thought it!"

She put her hand on my elbow. "Does he do that sort of thing all the time?"

"Not all the time, no. But often enough to keep us on our toes."

She shook her head and stood up. "Well what's he doing in the kitchen, then?" With that she hurried up the stairs to the exit.

After the Akron Chautauqua, Rose suggested Augie and I split up. He sent Augie on to Washington, D.C. to arrange the next event, and me back to West Virginia to help prepare for the summer Chautauquas. Being around Rose at the farm each day, I was there for the aftermath of Augie's phone calls reporting how it was going in D.C. It became clear that Rose was becoming exasperated with their disagreements and lack of communication. He began to say that the whole operation was "slipping," the ominous term Rose used to describe an irreversible descent into mediocrity and eventual failure. Although his criticism was directed at Augie, it was obvious my name was somewhere on the indictment, too.

"Augie keeps saying he wants to shine a light on me," he said once. "But what he really wants to do is shine a light on himself by bouncing it off of my bald head."

I knew he was right. Seeing Rose in the kitchen during the Akron Chautauqua had crystallized what I knew in my heart was true. Augie and I had been on a giant ego trip, with the Chautauquas as our vehicle. I vowed to myself to bring the programs back in line with Rose's vision, but when I tried to come up with ways and means, I drew a blank.

While Rose's criticism was direct, his solutions, especially in regard to particulars, were vague—maybe purposefully so. Despite the fact that he foresaw Augie's personal ambitions eventually getting the group into trouble, the complaint he voiced most often was that the rest of us were leaning on him, and never did any thinking on our own.

Nothing we did seemed to please him, but doing nothing displeased him more. How we were to find quality speakers, or get the word out with less expense, or recognize the sincere seeker among the crowd, was never made clear. Evidently Rose saw his role as pointing out the problem, and our challenge, to find the solution. By the end of a few weeks of this Rose felt certain that the Washington Chautauqua was going to be a bust. As a last resort he suggested I leave for D.C. to see if I could help out.

I arrived in Washington with a new perspective on the Chautauquas and my role in them. Since the first day I met him, Rose was always pressing people towards action, inspiring them to *do*, to put effort into the search and to transform themselves into a *vector*. The Chautauquas were the first chance I'd had to do what he was always prodding us to, which was to put every spare minute into The Work. Naturally, I assumed there'd be some automatic "spiritual benefit" to the process, and in my hurry to collect my reward I confused the hot ego rush of self-importance with spiritual progress.

The forces of adversity, which Rose said were always working in opposition to genuine spiritual effort, had found easy prey in Augie and me. We'd been fed just enough success to fatten up our heads to the point where we could no longer hear the man who set us on the path.

Through a combination of graceless bludgeoning and subtle surgery, Rose had finally gotten the message through to me and I hoped I could pass it on to Augie before it was too late. But within a day or two of arriving in D.C. I realized that Augie was operating in a different world, with a different state of mind, and nothing I might do or say was going to change it. Augie lost no time educating me to the fact that the Washington area was too vast and cosmopolitan for the homespun approach that had served us so well in Pennsylvania and Ohio. This was the big leagues, he said.

I tagged along with him as he made the rounds and it became clear that — whether due merely to a swelled head or to an accurate assessment of the situation — Augie had definitely changed his style. Instead of the eager, sincere, and somewhat naive seeker from West Virginia, Augie was now a spiritual power broker with a string of successes under his belt.

The group leaders we met were more polished, cynical, and worldly-wise, and I was surprised at how confidently and effortlessly Augie talked their language. His phone calls to Rose grew less frequent and more contentious, and often ended without the friendly note that Rose normally tossed in to let us know that, whatever our differences, we were all in this together.

In the end, only about eighty people attended our Chautauqua at the Kay Spiritual Life Center at American University, including one resigned, irritated man from West Virginia who had come to work the kitchen and witness what he predicted would be a "fiasco."

The people who attended the earlier Chautauquas were most often friendly dabblers in the occult who were grateful for the chance to get out of the house and meet some kindred souls. The Washington, D.C. audience, however, was sophisticated and generally unimpressed with the "more of the same" fare we presented.

Augie kept up a good game face and tried to put a positive spin on the situation, but by the end of the first day his facade was cracking, even though he still clung to one last hope of claiming victory. Our prize speaker, a physicist from Kent State, was scheduled for the next day. His main claim to fame was that he had tested Uri Geller's psycho-kinetic powers while a professor at Stanford.

"I really think these people will respond to him," Augie said. "He's got credentials."

Unbeknownst to us, however, our headliner had agreed to allow an eccentric hypnotist, Ander P. Jobe, to share the stage with him. Physically, Ander P. Jobe looked like a wild man, with a scraggly beard and long gray hair flying out in all directions. In later years, retelling the story, Rose would describe him as looking like an "anarchist," after those nineteenth-century political cartoons of unkempt men in waistcoats holding bombs with lit fuses.

During the physicist's talk, Ander P. Jobe proceeded to perform a clumsy demonstration of his hypnotic powers, which were pedestrian at best. Then he worked himself up into a wild frenzy and, incredibly, pulled a gun. As the audience gasped he shot three times at a young man on stage, who screamed loudly then slumped to the floor. Rose, standing at the back of the room shaking his head, was one of the few people present who recognized it as part of the act. The rest of the audience went into a panic. Terrorized men and women screamed, threw themselves onto the floor, or fled on hands and knees towards the exits. It was indeed a fiasco.

Augie was so depressed afterwards he literally climbed into bed and stayed there for several days, refusing to see anyone or take any calls. When he finally emerged and accepted a call from Rose, it quickly escalated into a heated argument that resulted in Augie either resigning or being kicked out of the group—depending on whether it's Augie or Rose telling the story.

Chapter Twelve

Transmission

A week or so after the Washington Chautauqua I found myself sitting in Rose's kitchen in Benwood listening to the litany of offenses that led to Augie's departure. Some of Rose's criticisms seemed trivial—like Augie allowing the people from the farm to sleep on the floor in D.C. while he occupied a bed—but others were more substantial, and by now, indisputable. As Rose painted on and on with his very wide brush, I wondered how much of the stain was meant for me as well. It was not uncommon for Rose to confront someone by using a third party as an example of the faults in question.

"Well, what do we do now?" I asked, eager to change the subject.

"We keep moving, that's what we do," he said angrily. "Nobody's indispensable in this group. That was part of Augie's problem—he thought we couldn't live without him."

That kicked off another ten minutes of painful Augie anecdotes, after which I tried again to divert him. "Where do we go from here, Mister Rose?"

"I don't know where the Chautauquas are going," he replied, putting the kettle on, "but you're going to start your law practice."

I was stunned. If there was anything I was sure of after my year on the road with Augie, it was that the feel of this path beneath my feet was now more important to me than anything the mundane world, including a law career, might offer.

"I want to stick with this project, Mister Rose. I think I can—"

His eyes flashed. "I'm not going to sacrifice the future of this group just so you can continue to build up your ego. You've had your fun, now it's time to get to work."

I was so surprised by the harshness of his words that it took a moment for them to sink in. By then he had changed his tone.

"Look," he said, softly, "I don't like to interfere in people's destinies. You've put years in so that you could be a lawyer. I'm not going to get in the way of what you're supposed to do. Maybe you'll still have time to help out on the Chautauquas, maybe not. But what's important is that you don't use the group as an excuse to keep from taking the next step."

"I haven't given any thought to law for months. How to start, where to—"

"Start right here. Wheeling's got plenty of crooks to go around. Bunk upstairs if you want. Gary's moving out tomorrow, so there's a bed available."

My mind was still reeling from the sudden turn of the conversation. "Mister Rose, I..."

"Think it over," he said, laughing at my stunned expression. "Everybody's got to grow up sometime."

A week later, full of second thoughts and reservations, I moved into Rose's house in Benwood. The population there was fluid, ever-changing. People moved in excited and inspired, then grew weary or perplexed or angry, and left. Sometimes only a few people were living there, but when I moved in the house was full.

I shared a bedroom with Al, Dan, Frank, and occasionally Rose's son, James. Linda and Jean, Dan and Frank's wives, stayed in the middle upstairs room, while Carrie and Brenda, two single women, occupied the bedroom farthest from the men. Downstairs, Mister Rose was crammed into the smallest room, while his daughter Kathy had recently moved into the other with her two-year old daughter.

The atmosphere in the house was a reflection of its owner, an eclectic blend of the miraculous and mundane, where mind-readings were as common as reprimands for putting a tin can in the burnable trash bag, or leaving the lights on when you were the last to bed.

Some of his rules, like strict morning bathroom schedules and rigid division of shelf space, would have been necessary in any house where so many strangers lived so close together. Others were a function of our peculiar circumstance, where men and women were welcome to live and work together for a higher purpose, as long as no other purpose got in the way.

Rose was extremely sensitive to the subtleties of the human sexual mechanism and maintained strict protocols, even in areas others might not consider suggestive. For instance, his rules for the disposal of sanitary napkins read, as Al once remarked, like federal regulations for the dumping of nuclear waste.

Discipline for rule infractions could range anywhere from a wisecrack, to days or even weeks of relentless confrontation. This was not pleasant, but it was expected. Supposedly we had all chosen to live with Rose in order to accelerate our progress on the spiritual path—to "Know Thyself." Rose's preferred method for helping us get to know ourselves was to constantly confront us about as many of our frailties as we could take, and then some.

My behavior, and everyone else's, became somewhat schizophrenic under this kind of pressure. My spiritual self *wanted* him to know me better so he could tell me what blocked my progress on the path to enlightenment. But my ego self shrank from criticism of any kind and tried to cover up my flaws with smoke and mirrors. Ironically, it was no use anyway. No matter how many masks you wore or subterfuges you tried you always felt transparent around Rose. He seemed to see through everything with laughable ease.

The kitchen was the center of the house. In the winter it was the only heated room, and at all times of year Rose used it as a combination living room, dining room, office and study—as well as kitchen. For those of us who lived there it was a magical place of community, solace, embarrassment, pain. A remarkable place to visit or ponder in the abstract, but tough to endure when you had no where else to go.

Mornings were especially unpredictable. For the first hour or so of the day Rose's mind seemed suspended between the world of his dreams, which he took quite seriously, and the world of waking reality. The kitchen vibrated with a tense otherworldliness. The women seemed especially sensitive to it, and I noticed that they usually tried to get out of the house and off to work as quickly as possible. When one lingered too long in conversation with Rose, she invariably left unsettled, angry, or on the verge of tears.

Evenings had a slightly different feel. People would drift in from work stealthily, or with forced cheerfulness, buying time until they could remember where they left the spiritual face they tried to wear around Rose. After a day spent being themselves they knew their egos were closer to the surface and more exposed. With harder and bigger heads to work with, Rose adjusted his tactics, and more often it was the men who got hit at night.

Dan was the biggest target. He never let down the tough guy act, whether it was bullying three crews of drunken hillbilly carpet installers during the day at work, or trying to ramrod his way into a little spiritual wisdom in the evening. Like Rose, he could be harsh, demanding, stubborn. Unlike Rose, he seemed to have no other facets.

Dan worked the hardest, made the most money, and was usually the last one to come home. We were sitting at the table one evening watching the news when Dan came in, grunted a hello and immediately went to the telephone in the hallway. Rose kept one ear on the television set and one ear on Dan, who was on the phone for the next half hour, first haggling with the owner of a carpet store about some money he thought he had coming, then arranging to pick up his wife after work and take her to a movie.

The news was over by the time Dan returned to the kitchen. He took a sirloin steak out of the refrigerator and threw it into an iron skillet. When the steak was done he sat down at the table, sliced off a big chunk of meat, then looked up at Rose.

"Mister Rose," he said, putting the meat in his mouth, "I've got a question about enlightenment."

Rose, who was washing his hands at the sink, didn't look up. "Which enlightenment are you talking about? The cheap brand, or the high priced spread?"

"You know what I mean. I was reading something yesterday about the void."

"The void? You've been reading that pornography again." Rose smiled but his voice had an edge.

Dan cocked his head at Rose as he chewed. "You're not taking me seriously."

"That's because you're not taking *me* seriously." Rose's smile was gone. He left the sink without drying his hands and walked over to where Dan sat at the table. "You march in here like a big shot. You've got plans to make. You argue about your money, line up a date with your wife, fry up a big steak. You're an important man. And now the big shot wants a little enlightenment talk to go with his meat, like onion rings. Forget it! If you want to be entertained while you eat, go to a fancy restaurant and hire a singing waiter. If you want to talk with me about enlightenment, prove it by changing your life. Show me you're serious about something besides money, sex, and food. *Then* we'll talk!"

I suppose living with him was very "Zen." He kept us all "attension." You never knew which ego or attitude you had betrayed until he pointed it out in front of everyone. Most often they were trivial offenses that Rose saw as indicators of larger issues. One woman was crowding everyone out of the cupboard because she "thinks she's the chief hen in the chicken house." Another, he said, was leaving the door to her bedroom open with her underwear draped over a chair in full view, "hoping one of the billy goats in the far room might get downwind." Al never washed his silverware because "he thinks he's on a first name basis with God, and God would never let one of his best friends get food poisoning." I left the house unlocked several times because I was "still a kid thinking his mother's gonna come along behind him and take care of everything."

But just when you caught yourself wondering why you were there, you'd get a glimpse of that mysterious *something* that lay behind the man and his personality. Something that made the rest of your life seemed like a foolish dream.

One Saturday a dozen of us gathered at an enormous dilapidated building the TAT Society had recently purchased to house various group enterprises. One of the supporting walls was ready to collapse, and we had put out the call to the Pittsburgh and Ohio groups for manpower to help repair it. The response was overwhelming. Twenty guys showed up, but it was pouring rain and we sat around all morning waiting for it to let up. At noon we tuned in the news and the weatherman announced that it would continue to rain steadily all weekend.

"Well, I guess I'll just have to stop the rain, then," Rose said. Everyone laughed, but Rose just raised his eyebrows like a man who knew a secret. Within minutes the skies cleared. Working frantically, we got the wall rebuilt in record time. Then, as we loaded our tools in the truck the rain resumed and didn't let up for two days.

Several days later when we were alone in the kitchen I asked Rose about the incident. He reflected a moment before answering, as if deciding how much I should be told.

"It is permissible for man to implement magic," he said, "as long as he doesn't *willfully* implement magic."

I must have looked very confused by his explanation because he burst out laughing.

"Don't try to think about it," he said. "You'll blow a gasket. You either *know* this yourself—intuitively, in a single grasp!—or you haven't a clue. There is no room for thought or partial understanding. It can be *known*, but never understood."

Even though I was living in the same house with him, it was rare that I had a chance to talk to Rose alone there. For this reason the times I treasured most were when we were traveling together. Out on the highway, away from the crowded, contentious kitchen, I invariably felt as if I were discovering Rose for the first time.

It was generally Chautauqua duty that provided those opportunities. I had taken over the title of "Program Coordinator," but it was a title without substance. After his experience with Augie, Rose handled all but the most mundane tasks himself. He said I should be concentrating on my career anyway, so I spent the summer months of 1977 preparing for the West Virginia Bar exam, looking for a place to set up my law practice, and tagging along with Rose on Chautauqua business whenever he'd let me.

Towards the end of August we took a ride to Steubenville, Ohio, a depressing mill town thirty miles up river from the depressing mill town of Benwood where we lived. Rose had set up an appointment to meet a man who supposedly knew a lot of healers, which was the theme of our next Chautauqua.

I had a long list of things I wanted to talk with Rose about during the ride. I had no idea how or where to start a law practice, the Chautauquas were going downhill on my watch, and I felt like I was making very little progress on the long hard task of overcoming my unwieldy ego. But after a few miles those things seemed to fade in importance. Gliding down the open road with Rose, the evening sun turning the Ohio River into a glistening gold, my worries melted. We rode in silence for awhile. Rose was the first to speak.

"You know," he said, staring out the window at the water, "healing used to be more common in the old days because it served a pragmatic purpose. Back in Christ's time, they didn't have any newspapers. All your advertising had to be done by word of mouth. That's why you needed miracles. If you heal a guy of leprosy, word gets around."

"Do you think Christ really performed all those miracles?"

"If he really was a son of God—in other words, if he really had transcended the illusion—then yes, anything is possible. Once you visit Reality, you know that miracles are nothing more than tinkering with the fiction we think is real life."

"Does a person have to be enlightened to do what Christ is supposed to have done?"

"Not necessarily. Some people have a way of maintaining that state of mindlessness that proves to be creative. Somehow they stumble on a condition of high indifference, and from there you dream it—you *will* it—then you forget it."

"But there must be limits," I said. "You never read about anything really incredible."

Rose paused a moment as if thinking how to phrase his words so that even I might understand. "Once a person has the formula," he said finally, "anything can be changed, *even the future*. Through determination, a man can discover how to completely change his destiny. There's thoughts—which are not yours, but come from elsewhere—and there gaps between thoughts. When you get into that gap between thoughts, you have the opportunity to completely reshuffle you life. This may sound impossible to you now, but try not to let your ignorance get in the way of understanding. I have just told you something of priceless value."

"I think I understand what you mean," I said weakly.

"No, you haven't a clue," he smiled. "But that's to be expected. If you understood there would be no need for talking."

He stayed silent for awhile as if to let me experience how little I did know. Strangely, my mind was almost totally blank. I could barely remember what we were talking about. When he spoke again his voice startled me.

"The formula for this is *between-ness*. A person doesn't have to be enlightened to practice it. Between-ness is the ability to anticipate what is going to happen in the dimension of the Manifesting Mind. You can do almost anything, as long as your will accords with the will of the Manifesting Mind. Actually, you could say that when you are in a *between state* your will *becomes* the will of the Manifesting Mind. This is how destinies are changed.

"But in a practical sense, you're right. For all but the most powerful beings there are limitations. You notice that none of these healers puts a leg back on, for instance. That's because they're operating on a 'faith' quantum, and there's too many people without that faith, too many people believing it can't be done. Moving mountains requires agreeable, movable mountains.

"It's like in the Bible where it says that Christ did not do many great works in his hometown. That's because he was tapping into people's belief and faith. People meeting Christ for the first time were more open to the possibilities and Christ could use their energy and belief to perform miracles. But in his hometown they remembered him as just a kid, a common carpenter, and he did not have enough personal power to overcome their disbelief.

"Even when conditions are right for you to do something, like take away a sickness, you might decide against it. Sometimes you're not doing a person a favor by healing them. Generally something's got their teeth into them, or it's their lifestyle that's gotten them into trouble and that's what has to change. I don't believe in patching tires. I believe in removing the nails from the highway."

I drove with uncharacteristic slowness, partly because Rose insisted on allowing two hours for a forty-minute trip, but mostly to prolong each untroubled moment. After all, this was the same guy who had given me hell that morning for leaving the kitchen spigot dripping.

Our directions led us to a modest, well-kept brick home in a quiet neighborhood. As we got out of the car I realized we hadn't discussed strategy.

"Do you have any particular approach in mind for this guy?" I asked, mindful of Rose's criticism that I was always "working off the top of my head."

"Just be a friend," he replied.

I followed Rose to the rear of the house and stood behind him as he knocked on the door. A tall man about Rose's age answered.

"Slim. Just call me Slim," he said, as we all shook hands. He motioned for us to follow him down to the basement. Inside the spacious cellar, we walked past various work stations of spotless machinery and eventually took seats in a small cubicle which served as office for the machine shop he ran out of his home.

Slim was an easy man to like. Within minutes he and Rose were laughing and joking like old friends. It was a stark contrast to the year before, when Augie and I viewed every contact as a challenge and every signed-up speaker as a conquest.

An hour passed while the two veterans of the occult swapped stories about healers and healing. Rose said there were two methods of healing, one drawing on the combined energy quantum of those present, while the other involved a "way of holding your head" which drained neither the healer nor the audience.

Slim nodded thoughtfully. "Yes, that makes sense," he replied, "how else could Ambrose Worrels have healed people well into his eighties?"

I began to wonder when Rose would get into the business of our visit, which was to tap into Slim's extensive healing contacts for our next Chautauqua. Rose seemed totally unconcerned with business or time and launched into yet another story, this one about a famous faith healer whose assistants slyly kicked the crutches out from under those about to be "struck by the Lord."

Slim interrupted. "You know," he said to Rose in his pleasant drawl, "you're healing *me*."

Rose barely reacted. "Yeah?"

"Yes, that's a fact," Slim said, grinning broadly. "I've got a bad case of emphysema—had it for years. But while you and I have been talking my chest has cleared, and I tell you I feel like a damned kid again."

"Well, if I did it was an accident," Rose said, then he finished telling his story.

An hour later we were driving home in the dark, the bright colored lights of the power plants dancing on the blackened Ohio River as we followed it to Benwood. Rose seemed tired or preoccupied, or both, and we rode mostly in silence. I wanted him to talk about the incident at Slim's, but his mind was elsewhere. Finally I brought it up myself.

"Mister Rose, did you try to heal Slim down there in the basement?"

"Hell no. I didn't even *know* I was healing him."

"What happened, then?"

"Hard to say, really. His office was so crowded with stuff there wasn't much room to sit. You were off to one side of us, but me and Slim were right in front of each other, our knees almost touching. I didn't want to stare right at him at such close quarters, so I picked a button on his shirt to focus on. He said something happened in his chest, that's all I know."

That night in the kitchen I related the story of Slim to the others. There were only a few of us there—Mister Rose, Frank, and Jeff, a visitor from the Cleveland group who had come down for the night. When I finished talking the others looked to Rose.

"I didn't know I was healing him," Rose said. "But there's a tremendous power in between-ness. When circumstances are right, things happen."

"Like with Jane that time, Mister Rose?" Frank asked.

"Well, yes, in a way. Although her experience that day was on a much different level. In that case I was actually inside her head."

Jeff looked puzzled. "Inside her head?"

Rose started to explain, then apparently decided to begin at the beginning.

"Jane was a woman who came down to my place a few years ago with her husband, although for the life of me I don't know why. Not only wasn't she interested in what we were doing, she was downright antagonistic. Her only concern was to get her husband out of the group as quickly as possible."

"Her husband was a friend of mine from the Pittsburgh group," Frank explained to Jeff. "We decided to bring our wives down to meet Mister Rose that weekend."

"Yeah, well, I gave 'em the usual tour," Rose said. "Took 'em out to the farm for a look around. Jane was very cold towards me and not even civil in her conversation. A funny thing happened, though, on the way out there. We were riding in their pickup truck with her sitting in the middle and me sitting next to her in the passenger seat. It was a small truck and we were pretty close. The whole ride I kept feeling this sensation like an electric current passing between us. It was hitting me in the stomach, just below the navel, and was uncomfortable. I didn't think much about it. Just figured it was tension of some kind from the awkward situation, I guess. Later I found out different."

Frank picked up the narrative. "We all came back to Benwood and that evening Mister Rose decided to hold a rapport sitting in the middle room. There were about six or seven of us, I guess, sitting quietly in a circle..."

"But Jane didn't sit with us," Rose interrupted. "She didn't want no parts of us. She stayed out in the kitchen, here, and while we were sitting I heard her make a cup of coffee and use the sugar bowl."

"The energy in the room got real strong," Frank said. "Real strong and—"

"I can see it when it's strong enough," Rose said. "It was visible to me that night."

"See it?" Jeff said.

"Oh, yes. Usually it looks like a hazy humanoid form floating horizontally over the heads of the people in the room. I can see where it's going, or direct it. I don't know which."

"It went to me," Frank said.

Rose nodded. "It hit Frank and—"

"I never felt anything like it. I felt like I was taking off somewhere. It scared me, but I was also—"

"His eyes was like this," Rose chuckled, making big circles with his fingers around his own eyes.

"Mister Rose nods at me—"

"Just to let him know everything was going to be all right."

"Then Jane walked in and stole it." Frank shook his head slowly.

Rose laughed. "Happens every time. A woman will steal a man's energy one way or the other. Probably Frank's one shot at an Experience and she—"

"I don't understand," Jeff said.

"Women are more sensitive," Rose explained. "That's why I usually separate men and women for rapport sittings. If there's energy around, most of the time it will go to a woman."

"But, I mean, what happened?"

Rose went on. "Jane came to the door of the living room just as Frank's on the verge of going into something. I looked over at her and said, 'I see you've been in the sugar bowl.' I didn't mean anything by it. It was just something to say. But as soon as I said it the energy left Frank and went to her. Boom. Down she goes. Hits the floor like she's been clubbed, and immediately she starts weeping. She went into an experience right there. I knew what was happening to her because our heads were locked. I pulled up a chair next to her and said, 'You know what's happening don't you? I'm in your head.'

"She says, 'I know. You've been there all day.'" Rose leaned forward. "That electricity I felt in the truck. She'd felt it too. Something was starting then."

"What was happening to her, Mister Rose?" Jeff asked.

"She had what I call the 'Mountain Experience.' This is where you see the world as an illusion. You attain an awareness that's superior to this dimension and the reality of this world evaporates. She kept looking at her husband and reaching out towards him, saying 'You're not there. I know I can see you, but you're not there.' She was on the floor weeping for two hours straight." Rose made a large circle with his hands. "Left a puddle of snot on the rug this big. I ain't kidding 'ya. We used up a whole roll of paper towels on it."

"You were experiencing all this with her, in her head?" Jeff asked.

"It was my Experience she was having," Rose said simply. "Our minds were one. My thoughts were her thoughts, her thoughts were my thoughts. Because mine is the more deeply rooted mind, it's dominant. This is how *transmission* occurs. While our heads were locked I entered the mood of my Experience and she came with me as far as she could. I tried to take her farther but she couldn't go. She saw the world as a shadow but she never saw what *is* real. After two hours I could see she was wasn't going any farther, so I just turned my head away—my internal head, I mean, of course—and she came out of it."

"What was she like afterwards?"

"Ecstatic, literally beaming. Radiant. She kept following me around, thanking me over and over, asking what she could possibly do to repay me. I told her, 'You pay for this by working with someone else.' She says, 'Oh I will, I will.'"

"Did she?"

"I never heard from her again until a year later—a year to the day, as it turns out. Late one night in the rain there's a knock on my door and it's her. We had a long talk. She was in bad shape. Said she couldn't hold a job. Separated from her husband. She told me she'd been spending most of her energy trying to push the experience out of her life so she could be a normal person again. The last I heard she was in Texas somewhere."

Frank held his head in his hands. "Pushing it away. I just don't get it."

Rose shrugged. "She wasn't prepared for it, that's all," he said. "She hadn't done any of the necessary work beforehand. It's a strange paradox. On the one hand it's true that spiritual work and disciplines are useless because we're all just robots responding to our programming—we can't really *do* anything on our own. And besides, there's nothing that needs to be done anyway—except wake up to the fact that we're robots.

But it's also true that a person must make monumental spiritual efforts to have any hope of becoming something more, of discovering one's True Self. Because the experience of Reality, of Truth, is a tremendous shock. In order to make use of it, or even survive it, you need to prepare yourself. You need to be vaccinated for that dimension."

Chapter Thirteen

Citizen Rose

A few months after moving in with Rose I received a letter welcoming me to the West Virginia Bar Association. I had decided to open my office in Moundsville, the county seat of Marshall County, where Rose lived, rather than the bigger town of Wheeling, a little further up river. I rented a small storefront a few doors down from the courthouse and started making the rounds, trying to get my name around town.

My first formal contact with the local bar was an ethical interview required of all new members. The lawyers I had met while taking the bar exam told me this was mere formality, and that their own interviews had consisted of nothing more than a handshake and a warm welcome. My interview was of a different sort. I was ushered into the office of an ambitious, fair-haired Moundsville attorney whose first question dealt with a name that appeared on my bar application.

"I see you've used Richard Rose as a reference," he said, thumbing through my paperwork like it was a criminal's rap sheet.

"Yes. Do you know him?" I smiled, glad to see we had something in common.

"Everyone knows Richard Rose," he said with a withering glance over his half-frame reading glasses. "Make yourself comfortable, Mr. Gold. I have a few questions about your application."

That evening I related to Rose how I'd been grilled for over an hour after my interviewer had seen Rose's name as a reference. Rose asked who the attorney was.

"Oh, *that* guy," Rose said. "He's still mad at me over the golf course deal."

Rose explained that several years before, the County Commissioners had voted to condemn a thousand acres of rural property, including Rose's farm, to develop into a golf course. Rose immediately organized the neighboring farmers to fight the condemnation, and they successfully defeated it. The lawyer who interviewed me had represented the County Commission in the case.

"I remember I was speaking at a public hearing," Rose grinned, "and I'd gotten people pretty stirred up. Things weren't going the way the Commission wanted. The farmers started shouting that they'd get lawyers and fight this thing to the top. Then that fathead you talked to today yells back at 'em, 'You don't need lawyers. You've already got Richard Rose doing your talking for you!' He looks at me like I was a bug that should be squashed."

It wasn't the best way to kick off a career, but I couldn't expect everyone to like me. Rod, the attorney I was renting my office from, had promised to introduce me around town the next day, and I assured myself that tomorrow would be better.

On the walk over to the courthouse the next morning, Rod explained that Marshall County had two judges who disliked each other so much that each refused to mention the other's name, referring to each other instead as "Part One" and "Part Two."

"Part One and I don't get along very well," Rod confessed, "but the one you're meeting first, Part Two, we're really close." Rod gave me a reassuring wink then disappeared behind a door marked, "Judges Chambers - Part II."

Through the door I could hear Rod's muffled voice, then the judge's loud response. "Gold! What the hell'd you rent to somebody like that for? I heard about him already. He's a disciple of that loose cannon from Benwood, Richard Rose."

I heard Rod say something else I couldn't catch, then a few seconds later he emerged from the judge's office.

"It's all set," he said with a big smile, holding the door open for me.

With some misgivings I walked into the unkempt office where a portly man with a flushed face stared without expression at me from behind a large ornate desk. I started to offer my hand but it seemed clear he would not have reciprocated so I thought better of it.

"Welcome to the Marshall County Bar," was all he said. Then he spun in his chair to look out the window behind him. The introduction was over.

Out in the hallway again, Rod pointed towards a door at the opposite end of the hall. "That's Part One's office," he said, heading for the elevator. "I'm not as tight with him so things may not go as well. You're on your own."

I stood there for a moment staring at Part One's door, then decided one judge a day was enough. I granted myself a continuance and returned to Benwood for lunch.

As I walked up the steps to the house I heard a rustling in the apple tree that shaded the narrow walkway on the south side of the house. There in the uppermost branches stood Rose, picking apples and carefully placing them in an old black bucket he'd wedged between some branches.

"Did they run you out of town early today?" he said, tossing an apple down to me.

"I met another one of your admirer's," I said. I told him the judge's name then took a bite of the apple.

"Oh, *that* guy," Rose said with a chuckle.

I wondered how many "that guys" I was going to have to deal with in Marshall County.

"He's probably still upset over the State Road deal."

I found a spot to sit on the porch where I could see Rose through the branches.

"You see that garage back there?" he said, pointing towards the back yard. I'd often wondered about that building. It was a solidly built block garage, but the vehicle entrance faced the cliff-like incline that rose abruptly to the four-lane highway bordering Rose's back yard at about rooftop level. There was no way a car could get into it.

"Yeah," I said. "The 'garage-to-nowhere.' I figured it was some kind of Zen *koan*."

"It was a *koan* for me, that's for sure," he said. "And I hope for some of the courthouse gang, too." I could hear the rustling of branches and the steady plunk of apples falling into the bucket as he spoke.

"There used to be a house that went with that garage, up there where the road is now. Built it myself, right after I got married. My parents still lived here and I wanted a decent place to put the family, so I decided to build on the lot back of here—what used to be a lot. I cut the timber myself off the farm and sawed it into lumber with a rusty old sawmill rig I bought off a guy for eighty bucks. I was alone so it took me most of a winter to do it. Then I hauled it all into town in the spring and started building the house.

"I mixed the concrete and poured the footers myself by hand—the stuff you get in the trucks is watered down. When I framed it I only used seasoned oak and locust—wood so hard that every nail I hammered into that house had to be held with vice grips. I used cement instead of mortar when I laid the bricks. It's hard to work with, but lasts twice as long.

"Must have been one helluva house."

"'Build for a thousand years and live as if you're going to die tomorrow,'" Rose quoted softly, more to himself than to me.

"What happened to the house?"

"It was in the way of where they wanted to put their highway," he said, changing positions in the tree. "A guy down the road — who was the mayor's cousin — got five thousand dollars for an empty lot. Me, I got six thousand for my lot and house both."

"And they got away with it?" I walked over to the tree.

"Not without a fight. First I took them to court. That's where I met your new friend the judge. He was just a lawyer for the State Road Commission at the time, and I made a lot of trouble for him. Of course, fighting these thieves in court is a battle you can't win. I paid some other lawyer five hundred bucks to tell me the fix was in and there was nothing he could do."

He stared down at me from under his wide-brim hat. "Naturally, my lawyer didn't tell me this until he had my money in his pocket." As if to emphasize my guilt by professional association he shook the branch above me and I was showered with apples, several bouncing off my head and shoulders. Rose let out a high-pitched, childlike laugh, then continued.

"I saw that I wasn't going to get anywhere by myself, so I got all the neighbors together who weren't in with the politicians and we formed a property owners association. We went to the newspapers and held rallies and drove to Charleston. I think we really had 'em worried for awhile.

"But then that State Road lawyer — your judge — went to them, one by one, and raised the offers on their houses. Naturally, they all caved in.

"So then it was just me. I made a picket sign and marched in front of the construction trucks, telling the TV cameras and anybody who'd listen that this country was no better than Russia if they could steal the roof over your family's heads whenever they got the notion, and pay you what they damn well wanted to!

"But eventually they took my house, of course. The bulldozers were brought in and they just ran along that little ridge up there, flattening every house they came to. When they hit my house, though, it wouldn't budge. They kept taking longer and longer runs at it, trying to take it down. Finally they got it leaning and on the next run they knocked it off the foundation.

"But you know what? That house came off in one solid piece. Doors, windows, porch, roof — nothing so much as creaked. There was just a solid perfectly good house laying there on its side. The demolition guys said they never seen anything like it."

Rose chuckled at the memory and started down the ladder. I reached up to take the bucket from him but he seemed to either ignore me or not notice. It made me think again of that first Intensive when he refused to accept anything from my hand.

On the ground he began examining apples that had fallen and putting the good ones into the bucket. I bent down to help him and he seemed not to mind my adding some apples to his bucket.

"Funny thing is," he said, "everything worked out for the best. Those bastards at State Road actually did me a favor. I was going nuts trying to manage the two farms and the three or four pieces of property I had in town. After the house was gone, I realized that all they did was take away one of my headaches."

He stood up and made circular motions with his right shoulder, trying to work out the stiffness. "Not to mention the fact that every one of those politicians, from Governor Barron on down, ended up going to the penitentiary."

In the weeks to come I gradually learned that it wasn't just former legal adversaries who had memories of Rose. The next day I had lunch at a little diner a few blocks from my office. As I paid my bill at the register the waitress studied me curiously.

"Mind if I ask you a question?" she said.

"No, go ahead."

"You're the new lawyer, right? The one who's living with Richard Rose?"

"Yeah," I said cautiously, "I'm the new lawyer."

"So how's he doing? He must be, what, sixty by now?"

"Yeah, close to it."

She counted out my change carefully, the way people do who aren't too sure of their addition.

"My husband and I used to run a little bar there in Benwood near his house. Rose would stop in some evenings. He wasn't a drinker, but he'd order a soda and shoot the bull with some of the guys from the mill. Played a little poker in the back, sometimes.

"I remember when he first started coming here I thought he looked like he was different from everybody else. Like he didn't fit in, or something, and I asked my husband who he was. My husband says, 'The meanest, toughest son-of-a-bitch in the valley, that's who.' She laughed at the memory.

"I was a little wild in those days," she said, giving me a knowing look, "and that aroused my curiosity. I remember I went right over to Rose, gave him a soda he didn't order and said, 'You don't look so tough to me.'"

"'Is that a fact,' he says.

"'My husband tells me you're the meanest, toughest son-of-a-bitch in the valley,' I say to him, standing kinda close to his chair.

"Rose looks me over a second then says, 'That's what I want 'em to think. That way people leave me alone.'" She laughed again, then told me who she was, even spelled out her last name. "Make sure you tell Rosie you saw me, okay?"

The news of my arrival in town spread quickly among the locals. Everywhere I went people recognized me as the new lawyer who was somehow connected with Richard Rose, a man whom, I quickly discovered, was liked by some, despised by others, and understood by no one. People knew him variously as a friendly farmer, loyal friend, political loose cannon, belligerent fighter, that 'poet fella,' or 'that mystic guy who runs the hippie farm out on the ridge.' The only common thread that ran through all the ways people thought of Rose, was that in one way or another everyone respected him, even if it was, for many, a grudging respect. After awhile I was no longer bothered by people's reaction to my association with Rose, except in one very big area.

Regardless of their other memories and impressions of Rose, everyone knew him as the man who gave the Hare Krishnas a foothold in the Ohio Valley. A foothold they used to establish a sprawling empire by buying up all the land for miles around — except for the Rose farm, which was not for sale at any price.

No one knew that Rose had been "duped" into the deal, as he later laughingly admitted. All anyone knew or cared about was that the "Hairy Critters," as the locals called them, were now dancing and chanting and parading around on McCreary's Ridge, and that Richard Rose was to blame for it. Few knew the story of how it came to happen.

As Rose told his wife on the day he married her, his real purpose in life was to teach, and if that chance ever came along he would take it. For twenty years that chance never came. In post-World War II America people were interested in jobs and families and suburban tract homes, not in the musings of a man who spoke about *becoming the Absolute*.

But Rose was not idle. He carefully planned in his head and on paper the organization and structure of an esoteric spiritual group to be centered on his farm, should the opportunity ever come. By the mid-sixties he'd about given up hope, and with his health failing at the time, he began writing down his discoveries to leave behind — a "note in a bottle," as he called it. These writings would later be compiled into *The Albigen Papers*.

As Rose was finishing these writings, and preparing for what seemed like his impending death, young people from the fledgling counter-culture in Wheeling inexplicably started drifting out to his farm. Some were the children of his friends, others the friends of his children. They'd heard whisperings and stories and came to check him out. They found that Rose was, well, Rose, and they kept coming back. It was fun to get high then hang out with the Zen farmer with the quick wit who seemed as intrigued with them as they were with him.

Rose had never seen kids on drugs and they had never met a man who could read minds. Although none of the visitors were serious enough to settle down and do any real work, Rose interpreted their interest in his philosophy as a sign that the "door had opened." It was time to make a move.

He placed a small ad in underground newspapers in New York and San Francisco, inviting "serious seekers" to join in the establishment of a "non-dogmatic philosophic ashram" in the hills of West Virginia. Instead of serious seekers, however, Rose got serious dopers, but he opened up his farm to them anyway, believing then, as he still does, that he should work with whoever comes through the door until someone more serious shows up.

Among the wave of West Coast hippies who made the pilgrimage to West Virginia were Keith Ham and Howard Wheeler, the first people Rose met who seemed to want more than a place to relax in the country. They told Rose they were former Hare Krishnas, but that they'd left because of philosophic differences with Prabhupada, the founder of the Krishna movement in the United States. They expressed interest in leasing Rose's "back" farm for the purpose of starting a non-denominational spiritual community. Rose, pleased to find people who seemed serious, gave them a ninety-nine year lease on the place, a 160 acre farm he had purchased when he was twenty and used as a meditation retreat.

As soon as the papers were signed, however, his new tenants, as Rose says, "put on bed sheets and started chanting gibberish." Using their newly leased farm as a base, the two men eventually established the largest Krishna commune in the country, and built the "Palace of Gold," an extravagantly garish edifice featuring two hundred tons of imported marble and a rotunda covered with twenty-four karat gold leaf. As more and more neighbors sold out to the Krishnas at inflated prices, Rose found himself inhabiting an island farm on what was now becoming known as "Hare Krishna Ridge."

The Krishna shadow followed Rose's shadow which followed me. None of this helped get my practice off the ground. I continued to make the rounds, meeting everyone I could, hoping one of the contacts would pay off. But after two weeks of being open for business, I had yet to speak to a single client.

The storefront office I'd rented was subdivided into two units. On the other side of a thin plywood wall was the Moundsville chapter of the American Automobile Association, one of the busiest places in town. The previous tenants had occupied both offices so there was a large opening between the two rooms, and no door.

My landlord had been promising for weeks to correct this, but so far nothing separated me from the crowded waiting room of the Triple-A. Each day I sat in my rocking chair behind my table—the only two pieces of furniture on my side of the wall—trying to look like whatever I thought a lawyer should look like, while a steady stream of West Virginians passed by the door like visitors in a zoo, staring through the opening at the Semitic-looking oddity in the polyester suit.

Every day I waited for the phone to ring, an important piece of mail to arrive, or a stray client to walk through the door. Nothing. Each evening, as a matter of principle, I waited for the Triple-A office to close before I turned off my lights and returned to Benwood.

One night when I arrived Carrie was the only one home. Everyone else was still at work, and Rose, she said, had gone out to the farm. Then she left to meet a friend for a movie and I was alone. I switched on the TV and tried unsuccessfully to interest myself in the one channel it got. I switched it off and left for the farm.

When I walked into the farmhouse I found Rose, Phil and Mark sitting at the dining room table. In the middle was a small glass ashtray with three pennies in it. Rose was reading from a hardback copy of the *I Ching* and Phil, sitting next to him, was leaning over to get a better look at the text in Rose's hands.

Earlier in the week Rose had mentioned that Phil was leaving the farm after a four-year stay as farm manager. It appeared that Rose and Phil were consulting this ancient Chinese book of prophesy to get a hint about Phil's future. I judged from the mood that the oracle's judgment was not favorable.

"Yeah, but should a person place any stock in fortune telling like this, Mister Rose?" Mark asked, perhaps trying to cheer Phil up.

Rose looked up from the book. "I don't know the mechanics of it, but there is validity to some of these things. Anytime people endow something with belief status over a long period of time—

whether it's the rosary or the tarot or crystals or whatever—it gives that object a power it might not otherwise have."

Rose closed the book and turned to me. "So how's the law business going?"

"Not too encouraging," I replied, joining them at the table.

"Well, let's see what the *I Ching* has to say about our fledgling thief," he chuckled, handing me the ash tray and the coins. I had always been skeptical, even fearful, of occult practices, so I had never played with the *I Ching* before. I shook the three pennies and dropped them into the ash tray. Mark recorded the combinations of heads and tails that came up. After my sixth and last toss, Rose located the corresponding hexagram in the *I Ching*. He stroked his goatee as he slowly perused the text, then handed the book to me.

> *Success through modesty. You are in the*
> *the company of inferiors, but will succeed*
> *because of a strong and good friend.*

I looked over to Rose, but he had turned his attention back to Phil. "Just because you're leaving the farm doesn't mean you can't do spiritual work," he said. "Hell, I was married, working, raising kids, and I still went up to Steubenville every week for meetings. It wasn't even much of a group. Just a bunch of old women. Piddlers, really. But they were good people, and at least it was movement in the right direction."

I only half listened to his story as I read through the *I Ching*'s commentary on the prediction I'd drawn.

"I went up for a meeting one Friday night, and I was a couple of hours early. I had junkers back then, too. So just to kill time I dropped by John's Miller's hardware store. His wife was in the group. He thought it was nonsense, but he was a friendly sort and I liked being around him.

"While we were talking a customer came in and asked John how much his air compressors cost. John gave him the price, and the customer said, 'I can get that same compressor at Sears for a hundred bucks less.'

"John said, 'Yep. You can get it even cheaper. A lot of this stuff you can get cheaper other places.' He goes on to tell the guy where he can get the best prices on the same things he's trying to sell in his store. Then he said, 'The only difference is I take personal responsibility for everything I sell. If you ever have a problem, I make it my problem. And I won't rest until it's taken care of.'

"So John tells him to think it over, and the customer starts walking out the door. But he stops and comes back in. 'Ah, what the hell,' he says, 'I'll just take that one.'

"After the customer leaves I told him, 'John, you're the one who should be in the group, not your wife. You already know the formula!'

"John just laughed. 'I used to be a real selfish guy,' he said, 'until my father-in-law set me straight. He told me that if I ever wanted to be a success, all I had to do was make myself of service.'"

I looked up from the book. Rose was staring right at me.

"That's all any of you have to do if you want to succeed," he said, holding my eyes with his. "Just make yourself of service. The rest will take care of itself."

As the weeks went by I took his advice to heart. When clients finally started appearing I did my best to help whoever walked through my door. Invariably, these were cases that no one else wanted. My professional colleagues delighted in sending the poorest people with the toughest cases and the worst hygiene down the street to my office. I took hopeless cases to trial, fought city hall, represented undesirables, and, in almost all instances, I lost. I worked for little or no compensation, and my clients ended up thinking I was worth even less. Rather than thank me for my efforts in defeat, they were often abusive, wondering out loud what the outcome might have been had they scraped together enough money for a "real lawyer."

In the evenings I came home to a chaotic kitchen ritual that did little to bolster my spirits. As everyone drifted in after the workday, they would fix themselves dinner, and for an hour or more the kitchen was a noisy blur of people in motion. Stove use was at a premium and the four burners worked continually. As soon as a pot or frying pan was removed another took its place. Everything was either boiled or fried because Rose discouraged oven use, saying it used too much gas.

In the midst of the turmoil Rose sat impassively watching the evening news on the old black and white TV perched atop one of the refrigerators, the sound turned up as loud as it would go so that he could hear it above the talk and noises of cooking and eating and dish washing. The news was the only thing Rose ever watched on TV, and he invariably used it to illustrate and support his observations about the planet.

"You see this guy here?" he would say to whoever was sitting closest to him, pointing to someone on the set. "That's a fish head.

See how his face comes out to a point, like a fish? People with heads like that are always cowardly and sneaky. I was in C.C. camp with a guy by the name of Green who had a head like that. He was one of the most...." And with that he would launch into what was usually a very humorous story illustrating that psychological type.

Rose was a student of human nature and he gathered his information from all available sources. At one end of the spectrum, he could read minds, and had an incredible intuition about people and events. But he did not limit himself to these rather esoteric inputs. He observed and studied the behavior of animals, particularly farm animals, saying that human behavior was not much different. He believed that family and social backgrounds predisposed people to certain behaviors and destinies, and that a person's racial and ethnic heritage was of great importance in coming to an understanding of the person.

He judged you by what you said, how you said it, and what you could have said but didn't. He watched the way you moved, the things you did, the things you avoided. And, contrary to the "can't judge a book by its cover" homily, Rose also drew a variety of conclusions about people from their physical appearance. This often came out most dramatically during the evening news, when appearance was all he had to go on.

Rose's catalog of psycho-physiological types included, among others, such classifications as blockheads, muttonheads, pinheads, and stovepipe heads. For each one Rose had a prototype, (some famous actor or politician), a distinguishing characteristic, (invariably a weakness or compulsion), and a story involving one of his friends or neighbors who had that appearance.

Then, as the news ended Rose would say, "Turn off that idiot box, will you?" and we'd all sit in an uncomfortable silence as we tried to readjust ourselves to the fact that there was an enlightened man in the kitchen.

It was impossible to assume a "spiritual" state of mind at will, and even if we could, Rose wouldn't have bought it. The best we could do was take turns offering up incidents from the day and hope that he would seize upon one or more of our stories and dovetail it into a discussion of philosophy. In this way we hoped to avoid direct personal confrontations.

"You should've seen this guy who walked in today," Al began one night. Al worked as a counselor at the penitentiary in Moundsville, and he seemed to view every inmate-client as a potential case study for the evening's discussion.

"This guy's doing habitual life. All real stupid crimes. Skinny, wild eyes, hears voices coming up from the drainpipe in his sink."

"Does he have deep black circles under his eyes?" Rose asked.

"Yeah," Al said with exaggerated surprise. "Looks like hasn't slept in months."

"Kidney trouble. Wrong kind of sex." Rose's diagnosis was purposefully inexplicit in deference to the women in the room. "Probably went to reform school as a kid."

"Yep. He was sent off to Prunytown when he was ten years old," Al confirmed.

"Same thing happened to a kid down the street," Rose said. He got sent up and the older kids raped him. Then when he gets bigger, he's the one gets to be on top. And that's the sexual association he'll carry with him the rest of his life. He's never comfortable outside of prison, and eventually the voices will goad him into doing something that'll land him back in jail where he can get all of that kind of sex he wants.

"That's why a man has to protect himself," Rose went on. "When my dad was in the pen, he said that if someone whistled at you, you'd better grab something sharp and stick it in him. Otherwise, the next day somebody'd be putting his hands on you, and before you know it, you're no longer a man. And when your self-respect is destroyed, you've lost all spiritual hope as well."

Dan was next. "I put carpet in a house in Glendale, today. The woman was a real bolt cutter." He paused to chew the last bit of his steak from the bone.

"The husband comes out to talk. A little guy, you know, Wally Cox type, always apologizing. It turns out he used to lay carpet, so we're talking. Then the woman comes in and sees him.

"'You, get back into the kitchen!' she yells at him." Dan mimicked her with a threatening shake of his steak bone, and we all laughed. "He slinks away. Never saw him again."

"Was there a dog in the house?" Rose inquired.

Dan nodded. "German Shepherd. Stared at me the whole time like he wanted to tear my throat out."

"There's your explanation," Rose said. "The dog is the husband in that house."

It was my turn. "This old farmer and his wife came to my office today..."

Rose gave me an inquisitive look. "I don't think you'd know them," I said. "They just moved here from out of town and bought a dairy farm up on Robert's Ridge."

I explained that they'd come to me for the usual reason—no one else would touch their case. In this instance it was because of who they were up against.

"Their daughter was on her way home from town with some feed, when she has to stop while some cattle cross the road. While she's waiting for the cattle to pass, the cattleman who owns 'em—who I found out later has tons of money he inherited from his parents—walked up to her car and started touching her and making obscene suggestions.

"Well, he knew right away from her reaction that he'd made a big mistake, and when he found out how mad her parents were over what he did, he ran down to the magistrate's office and swore out a warrant against the girl. That way, he figured, they'd be too intimidated to file charges against him."

"How can he do that?" the others wanted to know.

"Magistrates will give just about anybody a warrant for just about anything. All you have to do is fill out the paperwork."

"So what'd you do?" Rose asked.

"I got angry," I said, watching Rose carefully for his reaction. "These are good, simple people. They have more than a dozen foster children at their farm besides their own. I called the magistrate's office and told them I was going to represent them in the case. Then, right after they left, I got a call from one of the women that works in the magistrate's office. Nice lady. I think she feels sorry for me because I get so many losers.

"Anyway, she told me the fix was in. Turns out this cattleman's been bothering young girls all his life. One of them even brought rape charges against him. But somehow he always manages to buy his way out of it. He's never spent a day in jail. Never even paid a fine."

My story was a big hit. Rose launched into one case history after another about corruption in the local judiciary, and for a half-hour none of us had to think about the questions we really should have been asking him.

"That's why these attorneys are so miserable," Rose said, finally winding down. "They drink with the judge, conspire with him about how to fleece the public, bribe him if they really get in a jam, then go to court and call him 'Your Honor.'

He turned to look at me. "Even your so-called 'honest' lawyers don't raise a peep when one of their clients gets sent to the penitentiary for stealing food to feed his family—just because the judge wants to look tough just before an election. The lawyers figure that's the way the game is played, and they just roll over. So they all end up like the punks in the pen—no self-respect, and no chance to rise out of the illusion."

No matter how many times I heard a variation of this speech it still bothered me. I felt like he was not only holding me accountable for the whole legal system, but that he somehow expected me to change it.

"Isn't it unrealistic to think one person can clean up the whole system?" I said.

Without a word Rose stood up and walked out of the kitchen. A few minutes later he returned with a bulging manila folder.

"The outcome of wars isn't determined by atom bombs," he said, handing me the folder. "It's determined by desperate men with satchel charges."

Everyone crowded around the folder. Inside were numerous newspaper clippings of "Citizen Rose" in action. A younger, thinner Rose holding a microphone at a public meeting. An angry Rose carrying a picket sign reading "The State Road Commission uses Communist tactics." An article describing Rose's campaign against certain practices of the local school board. On and on. Clipped to many of the articles about Rose were related articles, such as accounts of the governor and some top aides going to jail for accepting kickbacks on the State Road Commission deal. And there were dozens of Letters to the Editor submitted by "R. Rose, Benwood." The one on top began, "Why does Wheeling rhyme with stealing?"

When we'd finished looking at the last of the articles he gathered them up and replaced them in the folder. "I refuse to be intimidated by anybody or anything," he said. What he left unsaid, but what we all knew, was that he expected each of us to live the same way.

"Cops, judges, the government," he said, "these bastards all think they can intimidate people by virtue of their superior position. I won't stand for it. A few years ago the IRS called me out of the blue and asked me where I got the money to keep two daughters in college on a painter's earnings.

"I said, 'Go to Hell! I found it, I stole it, I cheated little old ladies. If you think I'm doing something wrong, get a warrant and arrest me. But don't call my home and try to intimidate me, or somebody's going to get hurt.'"

Knowing I had to face him each evening kept me in a perpetual state of alert all day. Rose saw challenges to integrity and threats to spiritual potential in events that seemed commonplace to me. Inconsequential incidents that I figured came with the territory — a judge making an example of one of my clients, or another attorney stealing one of my cases — were regarded by Rose as that first wolf whistle in the penitentiary, sounding the beginning of a chain of accommodations and compromises that could destroy my chance to become a man, or to break out of the illusion.

"You might as well face it," he said. "We're living in a physical and psychic jungle. If you let yourself get pushed around in the earthly plane, then you become a coward who'll cave in when things get rough in the invisible dimensions. You've got to face adversity in this realm, and conquer it. Then you'll have character at least, and possibly the chance to achieve something much greater."

Chapter Fourteen

Success

Living with Rose constantly exposed us to an unflinching example of a person living his life without compromise. Trivial events that most people would let slide set Rose off on prolonged campaigns of protest. He boycotted Pepsi because they got a monopoly in the county schools through what Rose believed was a bribe. He withdrew all his business from a local bank because a teller tried to charge him a dollar to cash a check. When a book order he'd shipped was returned because of an improper zip code, he created such a stir it eventually took a personal apology from the Postmaster General in Washington to appease him.

Not all his protests were boycotts or letter campaigns. If someone insulted Rose or gave him any guff to his face, there was trouble. "You don't go looking for a fight," he once said, "but if someone is trying to make you into a horse's ass, you let 'em know where the line is by whatever means necessary."

One evening after dinner I began a story about a client who had come in that day. When I mentioned the man's name Rose raised his eyebrows in recognition.

"Brakeman for the B & O?" he asked.

"Yeah. Do you know him?"

"In a way. I tried to stuff him into a roaring wood stove once."

Needless to say my story was forgotten as all eyes turned to Rose for the details.

"This guy is one of these people who's overwhelmed by sex. They think that's their whole purpose in life, and every minute they're not knocking off a piece is a waste of time. You can hardly stand being around them. They think everyone's got nothing better to do than listen to the sordid details of their pitiful lives.

"Well, one day I was getting gas at the station that used to be down there where the four-lane crosses Marshall Street. There were a bunch of guys hanging out inside the service station and this brakeman from the B & O is in there going on and on about sex—all the different women he'd had and all the ways he'd had 'em.

"There were a lot of young guys there from the high school, and he was getting them worked up, so I said to the kids, 'Hey, relax.

You don't need to be obsessed with chasing women. The number of sexual contacts you'll have is already decided before you're born.'

"Well, this degenerate doesn't like me taking his audience, I guess. He says, 'What's the matter, Rose, you a faggot or something?'

"I didn't bother saying anything, I just charged the guy and jerked him head over heels. Literally. Both his feet scraped the ceiling."

We all laughed, but Rose continued very matter-of-factly.

"It was wintertime, and there was a wood stove going in the corner. I had a bear hug on this guy, and I was trying to get his head into the stove, but I couldn't figure out how to do it without burning my hands, so finally I let him go."

My life would have contained a lot less tension if I could have dismissed Rose as paranoid or overly confrontational. But the longer I lived with him, the more I realized that by never giving in to bullying in any form, Rose maintained complete control over himself and his life. And because he was always ready to fight, and die if necessary, to defend his principles, a lot of potential confrontations were averted simply because people preferred not to mess with him.

Rose's belligerent stance was in apparent contrast to his admonitions that egos were the single greatest block to spiritual progress. On the one hand he exhorted us to stand up and be men. On the other, to drop our rooster egos and get real. Don't take abuse from anyone, and be of humble service to all. It was a razor's edge I had great difficulty walking, or even understanding.

On weekends I often went out to the farm to help with the maintenance and chores. Usually I stayed in the main house, but sometimes I'd sleep in someone's cabin. Rose allowed group members to lease lots on his farm and to build their own meditation cabins if they wanted to. There were a dozen or so cabins scattered throughout the woods.

Not everyone who wanted to lease a lot was allowed to. To ensure harmonious living, unanimous concurrence of all the other lot owners was required. As long as you were not out of favor with Rose, however, approval was generally given. You also had to agree to the lot precepts. Non-group members were forbidden to visit or even know about your cabin. Farm taxes were pro-rated to reflect the value of what you had built. And if you turned out to be too big a pain to have around, you could be kicked off the farm whether you'd built a cabin or not.

Eventually, I felt sufficiently committed to request a cabin site of my own, and sufficiently confident that my request would be granted. The site I chose was about a half mile from the farm house—close enough for accessibility but far enough away for privacy. It was also close to an old logging road, so building supplies could be transported to the site without too much difficulty. And best of all the land sloped gracefully to a small creek that provided me with the sound of water almost year round. I was very pleased with my choice.

When the time came, Rose suggested I hire Chuck, one of the farm residents, to build my cabin. I readily agreed. Chuck was a meticulous craftsman who had taught shop in high school. It took awhile to complete, but when it was finished I had the nicest cabin on the place. I began spending more time at the farm. Occasionally I took a week off work to stay in isolation in my cabin. Later I would work my way up to longer isolations—two, then three, then four weeks alone.

Rose had always recommended short periods of isolation for anyone serious about spiritual work. As a young man he'd bought what he later called his "back" farm strictly as a meditation retreat for himself. The time he spent there—reading, meditating, fasting—he recalled as some of the happiest and most spiritually productive times of his life.

He warned against too much solitude, however. In his opinion one or two 30-day isolations a year was about right. He believed that maximum spiritual progress was achieved through a blend of silent introspection and worldly life.

In my worldly life—my law practice—it seemed somebody was always trying to push me and there was nothing to do really but push back and hope I was at least holding my ground. I had a few victories and many defeats. No matter how well or badly things were going for me Rose continually emphasized effort for the sake of effort.

"A person has to keep working without worrying about results," he said. "You work because futility is futile."

Rose's whole life was a testament to this philosophy. I tried to live the same way myself, but I was never sure of my motives, or my relative success. Being the kind of lawyer Rose would approve of made my dealings with the judges and other lawyers almost always confrontational.

As my practice grew I seemed to be continually involved in cases that were decided by friendship, political influence, or outright corruption, and unlike my colleagues I could not simply shrug it off as "the way of the world," and go blithely on my way. I spoke up, accused, sued and counter-sued. I began to actually believe I'd become some kind of white knight fighting for Truth and Justice. Of course, brandishing this self-image around the courtroom alienated me even more from the rest of the legal community. But in the midst of everything I still hungered for an occasional slap on the back and a little of the professional camaraderie the other attorneys shared. Rose would hear none of it.

"Those people are snakes," he reminded me one night after I'd related a rare incident of cooperation with another attorney.

"I'm only treating the man as a friend," I said. "You've often said, 'There's no religion greater than friendship.'"

He pointed his finger at me and used it to punctuate his words. "Genuine friendship requires true rapport," he said. "Otherwise it's only a pretense of friendship—a convenient alliance of people who agree to excuse each other's weaknesses. The only thing you have in common with the courthouse gang is that you're all trying to rob the same corpse."

The distance I tried to maintain from that "courthouse gang" was never enough for Rose. His criticism filtered back to me through the guys at the farm, who told me Rose was of the opinion that I was "selling out."

This bothered me immensely, and when it came up in my conversations with Rose I defended myself to him by itemizing how many cops I'd sued, how many lawyers and judges I'd angered, how many people I'd represented for nothing. But somehow my loyalty and integrity were always in question.

Verbal arguments or assurances were useless. With Rose, only action had substance, and somehow my actions did not impress him. He was convinced that I conducted myself as I did, not out of selflessness or commitment to Truth, but to satisfy my own egotistical ends, and that I was driven by a variety of unsavory motives and insincerities I had successfully hidden from myself. One night when I tried to press him for details about why I aroused his suspicions, he just waved me off.

"Circumstances provide each man with an opportunity to express his being," was all he would say.

At work the next day his words kept going through my head. I absently looked through the stack of files on my desk, each one, presumably, an opportunity for me to "express my being." As I evaluated each case in this light, I also struggled with the realization that I had already been expressing my being all along. The problem was that Rose and I saw that being in entirely different ways.

I had to admit that I had lofty ambitions and dreams of success. To think that these inner drives would not show themselves in my actions was a bit naive. I wanted to be a good lawyer—no, I wanted to be a *great* lawyer. I wanted to be a lawyer other lawyers would point to in admiration. I also believed that the best lawyers had the biggest egos. Their belief in their own infallibility drove them towards perfection in their cases, and juries allowed themselves to be led along by an attorney's confidence and flair.

I knew that when I became deflated after losing a case or receiving some particularly pointed confrontation from Rose, I had a hard time getting fired up for the next battle. Working with both dynamism and egoless-ness was a balancing act I was not very good at, and I wondered at times whether I truly wanted to learn it at all. Perhaps this is what Rose wondered about me, too.

As it happens, two of the files on my desk that morning ended up being cases that not only offered me opportunities to express my being, but were also major turning points in my career. One case concerned an inmate on a hunger strike who had gone to court to prevent the warden from force-feeding him. The other was a grisly Christmas-eve murder at a local fleabag hotel.

As these cases developed I discussed them with Rose, as I did with most of my cases. In addition to enjoying the attention, I'd come to rely on his opinion in legal matters, even though he never seemed concerned with the laws involved.

In the hunger strike case, for instance, he said I should only be interested in the man's motivation. The inmate said he was protesting prison conditions. It made no difference to Rose that he was in jail for a brutal murder committed during a bungled kidnapping. It was of no concern to Rose whether prison conditions really were bad or not. For him there was only one criteria. If he was truly ready to die for a selfless cause, Rose said, then this inmate was a man of character and deserved my support.

In the murder case Rose was less specific at first. After I'd described a long list of almost indisputable evidence against my client Rose simply said he had a "hunch" the man wasn't guilty.

The press picked up the story about the inmate at the penitentiary. "Hunger Strike to the Death" was the page-one headline. On the day the judge was scheduled to hand down his decision, the courtroom was packed with reporters. Microphones from TV and radio stations I'd never heard of were shoved in my face. A reporter from the Pittsburgh paper was there, and all thoughts of ego-control and Rose's philosophy went out the window as I basked in the fantasy of my hometown friends and law school classmates—who snickered when I moved to West Virginia—now reading about me over their morning coffee.

That evening as the dinnertime chaos swirled around me in Rose's kitchen, I excitedly awaited the evening news. When the time finally arrived, I shouted for everyone to quiet down. Rose looked at me and shook his head. The lead story was about the hunger strike at the prison.

As I'd hoped, a film clip came on, showing the starving penitentiary inmate weakly shuffling into court to demand his right to die, and at his side, his concerned and somber attorney—David Gold, Esq. I experienced a thrill seeing myself on TV again, but was not too pleased with the way I looked on camera. The angle accented my large nose. The lights glinted off my glasses and made my eyebrows appear bushy.

"Boy, that inmate must be hard up for an attorney," Rose said. "He's got Groucho Marx for his lawyer." It was too perfect. The kitchen crowd fell out of their seats laughing as I smiled and nodded my head. At the end of the film clip the station cut to a laxative commercial. Rose used the break to turn to me.

"You know, I've been seeing a lot of you on television, lately," he said. "You remind me of a trained seal. They live for an audience. As long as somebody's watching they just keep performing, until finally they drop dead from the strain."

Outside the confines of Rose's kitchen, however, I began to be treated by colleagues and media with newfound respect. The judge had ruled that the warden's duty to keep order in the penitentiary overrode my client's right to starve himself to death. But since my client was in no immediate danger of starvation, the judge delayed enforcement of his order for three days to give me a chance to appeal his decision to the West Virginia Supreme Court.

During that time I got phone calls from reporters, attorneys, and inmates' rights organizations from all over the country and even the world. It began to look like the case could well end up in the United States Supreme Court. It was heady stuff, and despite Rose's constant reminders about my hair-trigger ego, I reveled in it. That's where it ended, though. A few days later my ticket to the Big Time succumbed to a bacon and egg breakfast pushed into his cell. The "trained seal" was left without a spotlight—temporarily.

By this time I had a partner in my practice, Lou Khourey, an attorney I met in Columbus during the Chautauqua tour. Lou was the monitor of the Columbus chapter of the Pyramid Zen Society, and Augie and I stayed at his house while we prepared the Columbus Chautauqua. Now, in addition to being my partner, Lou had also moved into Rose's house. Though only two years older than me, Lou was a generation ahead in maturity and dependability, and provided a much needed balance to my impulsive, high-strung temperament. Our first big case together was what became known in the newspapers as the "Christmas Murder."

The victim was a seventy-three year-old woman who worked as the desk clerk in a cheap hotel. Her body was discovered in the early morning hours of Christmas eve laying in a pool of blood in the manual elevator she operated for the patrons. She had been stabbed over forty times and the cash register was empty. Our client was Charlie Gordon, a black, middle-aged ex-con who'd drifted into town a few weeks earlier and had been staying at the hotel.

When the police arrived they sealed off the hotel and began a room-to-room search. Charlie, an alcoholic, was sleeping off a vodka binge, but was finally roused by the officers' loud knocking. He opened the door, then sat back heavily on his bed and watched in a daze as police filled his room. Based on a pair of blood stained shoes they saw in a corner, the police obtained a search warrant. Charlie's belongings were seized and sent to the FBI for testing. The results added to a long list of evidence pointing to Charlie as the murderer.

The fresh blood on his shoes was positively that of the victim, as were the gray hairs found on Charlie's coat. Wool fibers found on Charlie's hat matched those of the victim's sweater. And fifty dollars — in the same combination of coins and bills as the fifty dollars that was placed in the hotel register at the beginning of each shift — was found on Charlie's nightstand.

The deeper we got into the case, the worse the evidence looked. The friends Charlie had been drinking with on the night of the murder were certain that they drank until their money ran out, and nobody could explain how Charlie might have gotten the fifty dollars found in his room. Our own blood expert not only confirmed that it was the victim's blood on Charlie's shoes, but added that the "splatter pattern" indicated that the blood fell from above, destroying our theory that Charlie may have drunkenly stumbled upon the body.

Charlie himself was no help. He said he'd been drunk for five days before it happened and that he recalled almost nothing about that night — although he was sure he didn't kill the hotel clerk. Rose, who inquired about the case every evening, offered to hypnotize Charlie to see if he could get him to remember more about the night of the murder. From the beginning, Rose was convinced of Charlie's innocence, and no amount of evidence swayed him.

"The guy could have been set up," Rose replied one evening, after I carefully explained again how Charlie's blood-soaked shoes unquestionably placed him at the murder scene. "That hotel is a nest of thieves and degenerates. I knew a guy who stayed there once and he said the whores kept him awake all night knocking on the door. Your client would be a perfect pigeon. He's probably prison-simple from all those years behind bars, and he's got no friends or family to go to bat for him. I saw his picture in the newspaper. He's the kind of drunk who might grab a purse if he got a chance, but he's not violent. He reminds me of a dog I once had at the farm."

No matter how damning the facts, a trial lawyer has to believe that his case can be won. First he envisions a scenario he can argue to the jury with a straight face. Then he works madly to develop evidence to support that position, until the momentum of his own effort convinces him that the case really isn't as bad as it looks. This self-hypnotism keeps the attorney moving and motivated for awhile, but inevitably there comes a point when the bubble bursts, the hard truth sinks in, and he knows he's stuck with a loser.

Lou and I bumped up against that point of truth, that realization of hopelessness, early in the Gordon case, but we could never quite surrender to it because of Rose's oft-stated opinion that Charlie was not the murderer. Eventually, we came around to the beginning again and Rose's conviction became our conviction.

In the face of overwhelming physical evidence that no lawyer in his right mind could ignore, we both nevertheless began to believe Charlie was innocent, and we were able to prepare our case with the energy and zeal of the righteous. As always, Rose constantly reminded us of the link between our efforts in the mundane world, and our spiritual destinies.

"You people have no idea how much power there is in spiritual effort," he said one night. "You've got too much ego as it is, but even so, you still don't appreciate what you could have going for you. When a person is willing to persevere for what's right — whether it's looking for Ultimate Truth, or keeping a man from getting railroaded — there's no limit to what he can do."

No matter how long and hard you've worked getting ready for a trial, invariably there are critical loose ends that can only be tied up at the last minute. I poured over police reports, Lou contacted forensic chemists, and our private investigator checked out every suspicious character who had been in the Rogers Hotel on the night of the murder. Most nights I stayed at the office, grabbing a couple of hours sleep on the couch. At dawn I would awake with a start, then get up and go for a run along the narrow ridges above Moundsville, trying to think of what we might have overlooked.

The night before the trial I went home to sleep in Benwood. I had barely seen Rose for a week and I looked forward to discussing the case with him one last time.

"So tomorrow's the big day, eh?" Rose said. "How does it look?"

"Not too good," I began, trying to prepare Rose for the worst. "They have all that physical evidence, and Charlie still can't explain where the money came from, or how the blood got on his shoes. The main thing we've got going for us is that the police quit working once they arrested Charlie, so there are still other suspects. We've also got a doctor who'll say that Charlie wasn't physically able to do all the things the police said he'd have had to do if he killed that old lady."

Rose leaned back in his chair. "Well, it sounds like you've done just about all you can do. It's time to relax and let what's supposed to happen, happen."

I studied him to see if he was serious.

"It's kind of hard to relax when you've got a man's life in your hands. That's why we've been kicking over every rock." I intentionally borrowed one of his phrases to be sure he understood that I took this case as seriously as he did. But Rose was in a different mood.

"You never know what a man's destiny might be. If this guy's meant to spend the rest of his life in jail, nothing you can do is going to change that."

"But you said—"

"You have to *act* as if you can change things. Act as if your actions make a difference. That's the only way you can be sure you've played your part out to the fullest. But once you've given it a hundred percent, relax and let the gods work their magic."

The next morning I arrived at the courthouse feeling more confident than I had in weeks. In criminal cases, as in Rose's spiritual philosophy, the key word is "doubt." A defense lawyer isn't required to prove that his client is innocent. He need only cast enough of a shadow on the state's case to create a "reasonable doubt" in the minds of the jury. By constantly pointing out factors we hadn't considered, Rose kept Lou and me in a state of perpetual doubt. Now it was our turn to pass it on.

We hammered on the weaknesses of the prosecutor's case. If Charlie Gordon was the murderer, where was the murder weapon? An exhaustive police search of the hotel turned up nothing. What about all the other suspects the police had questioned, then ignored after they arrested Charlie? Isn't that where the murder weapon disappeared, with the real murderer who fled the scene? How could Charlie, so crippled that he needs a walker to get around the courtroom, have committed this brutal and physically demanding murder? By the prosecution's own account, Charlie would have had to run down to the lobby from the third floor—where the bloody elevator ride had ended—hop over the counter, rob the cash register, then run back up six flights to his room. Our medical expert said he was not physically capable of this.

This last point was the strongest. Whenever the details of the murder came up, different members of the jury would glance at Charlie, and the walker he had been using since his arrest. After the entire case was presented and the jury was being led away to consider their verdict, Charlie, who was standing, slipped from his walker and fell to the floor. Several jurors looked at him sympathetically.

While the jury deliberated, the week-long drama of the trial was put on hold and the opposing courtroom actors mingled on the set. Lou and the prosecutor discussed their golf games, Charlie joked with the deputy who guarded him, and we all waited.

Jury rooms are equipped with buzzers that ring back to the courtroom. One ring means they want to ask the judge a question. Two rings means they've reached a verdict. At eight o'clock that evening the buzzer rang twice. Files were gathered together, pop cans were hidden, ties were straightened and faces were adjusted to reflect our respective roles. The jury filed in.

My heart pounded as the verdict form passed from foreman to bailiff to clerk to judge and then back again to the clerk for reading. Charlie stood quietly beside me leaning against his walker, showing no more emotion than if he were waiting for a bus.

"We, the jury, find the defendant not guilty as charged."

Lou and I put our hands on Charlie's stooped back as he slumped into his seat in relief. We were surrounded by handshakes and congratulations. The handcuffs were removed. Charlie was a free man.

A couple of hours later Lou and I were sitting in our office, calling people who had helped, thanking them, accepting their compliments and wondering what we should do to celebrate. Neither of us drank, and yet clearly something was called for.

The phone rang and Lou answered it. It was Mister Rose. Lou laughed and talked for awhile then handed me the phone.

"I just wanted to congratulate you guys," he said. "I saw on the news that you got that poor guy off. Good work."

As we drove to Pittsburgh that night to celebrate with a late dinner at an expensive restaurant, Lou and I replayed the trial with a sense of awe and disbelief. "I can't believe it!" we kept saying to each other. "I can't believe it!" It was exhilarating.

A few days later, I received a call from the deputy who guarded Charlie during the trial. "Next time you're down by the jail, stop by, I have something to show you," he said, refusing to provide more details. I was curious, but it was almost a month later before I had the opportunity to visit the jail, and by that time I'd forgotten the call. As I passed by the control booth, however, that same deputy was on duty. He called me over.

"Come on downstairs," he said with a grin. "I've got something I need you to take off my hands."

I followed him down to the jail storage room. There, sitting among the guns and marijuana stalks and other pieces of tagged evidence, was Charlie Gordon's walker.

"We brought him back to the jail after the trial to get his things and he left this behind. He told us he wouldn't be needing it any more."

The deputy was clearly enjoying the expression on my face. I mumbled something to him as I took the walker, then rushed back to the office.

"What do you make of this?" I said, setting the walker down in front of Lou's desk. I repeated what the deputy had told me.

"Maybe the verdict healed him," Lou said with a smile.

"I'm serious. We worked like hell to get him off because we really thought he wasn't guilty. We convinced ourselves..."

"You mean, *Rose* convinced us."

"Whatever. We used our belief to convince the jury."

We sat in silence for a while. I noticed that Lou looked thoughtful, but not depressed or even disappointed.

"So what do you think?" I asked.

Lou still didn't reply for a minute or so. He is a very private person and it takes a while for his thoughts to find their way to the surface. When he finally spoke it was in slow, deliberate tones.

"It's like Rose said, our job was to extend ourselves to the fullest and then let whatever was supposed to happen, happen. And we did that. We got caught up in the case, and for the first time pushed past what we thought our limits were. We went beyond them and now we have new limits to shoot for. I was prepared to accept the verdict if we won, or if we lost. Or even if we won when we should have lost."

"But we did it all so a guilty man could go free."

"We still don't know who killed that old lady. We played out our parts, and left the rest up to God."

The clarity and conviction with which Lou expressed his thoughts was reassuring, but I needed to talk to Rose. I cleared a few things off my desk then headed home.

Rose had been working on a new book the last few months, a compilation of his lectures eventually published as *The Direct-Mind Experience*, and when I got home that night he was listening to tapes of some of his talks. It was late in the evening before I got the chance to tell him about Charlie's walker.

"Yeah?" he said, almost absently, squinting at a small clock on a shelf at the other end of the room. "It doesn't really matter. I didn't like the way the cops were trying to railroad him anyway."

Then he got up, switched on the eleven o'clock news, and left me to my thoughts. That was the last we discussed it.

I didn't have much time to ponder the lessons, if any, of the Gordon case. "Success breeds success," Rose often said, and Charlie's acquittal had definitely taken our practice up a notch. More and better cases walked through the door. The local bar grudgingly accepted that we were in it for the long haul and began to leave us alone. And most surprisingly, the judges started appointing us to high profile cases, which kept us in the public eye.

I was, as usual, easily disposed to getting an inflated ego, to believing that "I" was responsible for our increasing success. Rose, as usual, did his best to control the swelling.

"I'm a firm believer in fattening up the head before you chop it off," he remarked one night as I stared overly-long at my picture in the evening paper, "but it's getting so we're not going to have an ax at the farm big enough to handle the job."

Lou and I moved into a new suite of offices with two secretaries, a well-stocked library, and separate bathrooms for men and women. We began to resemble successful lawyers, and the temptation was there to begin to act like them, too.

As for Rose, I doubted if anything could ever tempt him. His immunity to enticements wasn't so much a matter of will power as indifference. Watching him, I realized that his detachment was a major factor in his remarkable intuition, which was in turn the key to much of his power.

"Intuition won't develop as long as you're obsessed with something," he told me once.

Mister Rose desired nothing so he perceived what was really there, not what he wanted to see. And often, as in the Charlie Gordon case, he seemed to see beyond what was there, as well—beyond the "small-t" truths he so ardently urged us to value in our daily affairs, and into the great matrix of indifference from which all creation is formed.

Chapter Fifteen

Entities

Within a month of the Gordon verdict another sensational murder landed on my desk. A local man had stabbed his wife to death while visiting friends, then fled the scene. An hour later he confronted a policeman in the street, the bloody murder weapon in one hand, a severed animal head in the other, chanting, "I am God—six, six, six. I am God—six, six, six."

After taking the case I visited the accused in jail and found him to be a shy, gentle, bewildered young man. His name was Tommy, and he spoke so quietly I often had to ask him to repeat what he'd said. I saw fear, confusion, and what I thought was honesty in his eyes. The psychiatric evaluations would later conclude that Tommy was legally insane. The man I talked to that day, however, was not.

Our private investigator found nothing in Tommy's past to explain the brutal murder. He had no prior run-ins with the law, not even a speeding ticket. His bosses and co-workers at the Fostoria Glass factory spoke of a dependable worker who kept to himself and never gave anyone a hard time.

Recently, however, there had been a change in Tommy's life. Nate, a co-worker of Tommy's, was involved in a fundamental Christian sect so strict and severe that many in town considered it a cult. Several months before, Nate had started preaching to Tommy about God, Satan, and the battle being waged on Earth for the souls of men.

Mainly to appease Nate, Tommy started attending services in the small storefront that served as their church. Gradually, however, he came to believe in what he heard there. He had long felt himself surrounded by negative forces, he said, and now that he had a name for his oppressor, he felt Satan's presence everywhere. He even had the church pastor come to his home to perform an exorcism of the evil spirits that he said were denying him sleep and destroying his peace of mind.

Tommy grew more agitated by the day. People at work noticed he had become moody and irritable, and showed little interest in anything but his church. He moved his wife and six-year old son out of their bedrooms, where he perceived the Devil had gained his strongest foothold, and made everyone sleep in the living room. He phoned other church members constantly, especially Nate, at all hours of the night.

The night of the murder Tommy was unable to shake a feeling of suffocating evil. All night he paced and prayed while his wife and son tried to sleep on their mattresses in the living room. At four a.m. he called Nate. Nate tried to calm him, but Tommy became even more agitated, then announced he was coming over.

At Nate's house Tommy paced the floor, jabbering almost incoherently while his wife looked on with sleepy eyes. Tommy's son, still in pajamas, sat on the couch clutching a stuffed animal. Occasionally Nate's children peeked out of their bedrooms, only to be hurried back to bed by their father.

Finally, things settled down. Tommy's son fell asleep on the couch. Tommy laid on the floor with his head in his wife's lap, his wife gently stroking his hair and speaking soothingly, trying to lull him to sleep like he was a child. Nate said later that he was going to let a few more calm minutes pass, then try to convince Tommy to return home.

But Tommy opened his eyes and saw Nate's two cats—one white, one black—perched on either arm of the couch. Between them was his young son, breathing rhythmically in sleep. As Tommy later told the examining psychiatrist, the forces he had been wrestling with for so long were now right in front of him. The white cat was God, the black cat, Satan, and they were battling for the soul of his sleeping son that lay between them. At that moment, Tommy said, he knew without doubt that his mission on Earth was to rid the world of evil. He jumped to his feet and before Nate could react, pulled out his electrician's knife and beheaded the black cat. His wife screamed.

Tommy then turned to her, and with a dazed, determined look, started pushing his wife ahead of him into Nate's bedroom. Nate, who outweighed Tommy by almost a hundred pounds, jumped on him, but Tommy arched his back and, as Nate later said, "threw me off like I was an insect." Inside the bedroom, Tommy locked the door and stabbed his wife until his arm was tired, then took off through the streets of Moundsville, a bloody knife in one hand, the head of the black cat in the other.

The whole case was bewildering to me. That night in the kitchen I told Rose about it. "The crime just does not fit the man," I said.

"Entities," Rose said, "plain and simple. I keep telling you people there're tigers in the jungle. It's only vanity that allows man to believe there's nobody here but him."

"How come nobody ever sees them?" I asked.

"There's a lot of things scientists can't see, but they still accept their existence because of their effects. Force fields, electricity, viruses. It's the same way with entities. You rarely see 'em, but their effects are manifest."

"Effects?"

"Loss of energy, mainly. 'Matter is neither created nor destroyed.' In passion, whether it's sex or bloodlust, there's a tremendous amount of energy generated, then it disappears when the passions are surfeited. That energy has to go somewhere. Whatever it is that drives us to indulge in these things gets the payoff from the act—whether its lust or anger or murder—in the form of energy."

Al, who worked at the Moundsville penitentiary as a counselor, joined in with a number of case histories of cons who had murdered or raped at the urging of distinct voices. Rose nodded, and added a few accounts he had heard of.

"Are these entities evil?" I asked.

"Not necessarily," Rose replied. "When you walk through the woods you've got to watch out for ticks. Ticks aren't evil—they just want a meal. I, for one, don't want to give it to them."

I started to ask a question, but Rose kept talking.

"Man is incredibly fatheaded. He believes he's in control, but the truth is he's just a robot in a dream—a puppet whose strings are pulled by intelligences he can't see."

"Both good and bad intelligences?" Al asked.

"Good or bad to what? These forces are just trying to survive like everything else. A farmer keeps cows, feeds them, takes care of them, maybe even names 'em. Then he steals their milk and slaughters their children. Does that make the farmer good or bad? Or is he just a parasite like everything else?

"Still," he went on, "there are some forces that seem to be interested in our spiritual aspirations, forces that could be called 'good.' I know I had help. I never would have been able to create the conditions necessary for my Experience in a million years. I believe that a person who makes a sincere commitment to find God at any cost will attract protection. That protection may put you through hell, but if you keep your nose clean you'll land on your feet."

"But where do these entities come from?" I asked.

Rose spread his arms. "Where does any of this illusion come from?"

The official diagnosis of Tommy's mental state was psychobabble at its most ludicrous: "...an hysterical homosexual panic resulting in a severe episode of non-repeatable, temporary schizophrenia." Tommy was judged mentally incompetent to stand trial and my responsibilities towards him ended.

Even though I resisted the idea of unseen entities being the instigators of Tommy's actions, by this time in my relationship with Rose the mystical and occult did not frighten me as much as it once did. Living with Rose gave me a direct, experiential feel that *something* lay beyond our vision, that this dimension was not the only game in town. Still, it was difficult for me to believe that spooks and spirits could control our thoughts and run our lives. While the psychological professionals obviously had no sensible theory for what had overcome Tommy, Rose's explanation remained too far-fetched for my tastes.

Then came the Labor Day TAT meeting. Four times a year — on the weekends closest to April 15th, July 4th, Labor Day, and Thanksgiving — group members from around the country congregated at Rose's farm. These gatherings were the official meetings of the Truth and Transmission (TAT) Society, but only a couple of hours each weekend were devoted to anything resembling group business. The rest of the time was spent catching up with old friends and just generally letting the mood and atmosphere reorder your life and renew your commitment to the real work. For many it was their only chance to meet and talk with Rose, and even those of us who lived in the area still ended up with a new appreciation of him, watching him function as teacher to anyone and everyone who wanted to talk or listen.

On TAT weekends Rose slept very little. He stayed up as long as the night owls wanted to talk, then he'd awake again before dawn to be available for the early risers. One of the new people asked him about this.

"After my Experience I had to invent a reason to live," he said. "I chose teaching. Now it's my only excuse for sticking around this madhouse."

That particular TAT meeting was especially enjoyable for me, both as a break from the office and a chance to visit with old friends, many of whom I hadn't seen in years. I got so caught up in telling and hearing stories I was almost disappointed when Al stepped onto the porch and announced there was to be a rapport sitting.

Everyone chattered nervously as they filed into the newly built farmhouse wing. Rose was already seated and we all tried to appear nonchalant as we selected and moved chairs in an effort to be "well positioned." This consisted, roughly, of being across from people you felt affinity with, away from people who drained your energy, and close—but not too close—to Rose.

The new room was fairly large, but the thirty or so people that filed in made it difficult to be very choosy about your location. I was not particularly pleased with where I ended up. Rose was almost obscured from my view, and I was a lot closer to Luke than I would have liked.

Luke was a short, soft-spoken man with piercing black eyes. He came to the Pittsburgh group about the same time I did, then moved to Washington D.C. shortly before I took off on the Chautauqua circuit. We shared a certain superficial camaraderie from our early days in the group together, and I always enjoyed seeing him at TAT meetings. But for the last couple years I had become increasingly uncomfortable around him for some reason, and as the last of the chair shuffling faded into silence I experienced a distinct physical uneasiness being near him for the rapport sitting. I attributed this to my general disappointment with my position in the room, and tried to ignore it. As I looked over at him, however, I noticed that he seemed nervous and agitated to a degree far beyond the restless anticipation that most of us felt at the beginning of a sitting.

Gradually, the various side conversations faded until only Rose was talking. He continued for several minutes, wisecracking in a quiet, almost soothing voice. Then he cleared his throat and remained silent. A few minutes later the silence deepened. The sound current in my ears became louder and changed in pitch. The air thickened and was filled with transparent motion.

Rose sat with his eyes closed, his head turning slowly as he "looked" at each of us through his eyelids. He had told us many times that only with his eyes closed could he *see* during rapport, and that this helped him know the minds of those present. As I watched, his brow would occasionally furrow, or he would recoil as if surprised, but always his face returned to the same state of impersonal, effortless concentration.

Then, without warning, he got up from his chair and stood before the young woman seated to his right, lightly placing his muscular right hand directly on top of her head. The girl's closed eyelids fluttered for a moment, then tears began to flow. Rose said a few quiet words to her but remained for no more than a minute before moving on to the boy in the next chair and placing a hand on his head in the same manner.

"What are you doing," the boy said after a few moments. He had met Rose for the first time that morning.

"Feeling your thoughts," Rose said quietly.

Fear and expectation filled the room as Rose made his rounds. As he did I gradually became conscious of a new sound that was slowly increasing in volume. I looked to my left and caught sight of Luke. His head was shaking in small quick vibrations and he was making rumbling noises in his throat that sounded like the low growl of an angry animal.

Others had also become conscious of Luke, but were trying to ignore him. After a few more minutes, however, that became impossible, as his growls became louder and his tremors grew more noticeable. Rose never looked in his direction, but continued to calmly and purposefully make his way from head to head as if each person he stopped in front of was the only person in the room. By the time Rose finally stood only a chair away from him, Luke's body moved and sounded like a snarling dog.

Cold chills shot through me, and probably everyone else. Only the complete calm on Rose's face kept the growing sense of panic from overtaking the room. Rose still did not look at Luke, nor did he hurry with the girl next to him, even though she was visibly frightened and had moved to the farthest edge of her seat. When he was done, Rose smiled at her then stepped in front of Luke.

Ignoring the growls and lunges Rose placed his hand directly on Luke's head in a manner no different than he had with the others. Unmoved by the snapping jaws a few inches below his hand, he stood impassively looking into Luke's eyes.

"A man's body is his castle!" Rose said in a sudden loud voice that caught me off guard and sent chills through me. "You have no right to be here! Leave this man!" he said sternly. Then he jerked his hand into a fist and ripped it from Luke's gyrating head. Luke let out a sharp howl of anguish, then his head dropped to his chest and he sat like that for a long time, sweating and exhausted.

I, too, was shaking. I closed my eyes and tried to replay what I saw—or thought I saw—when Rose jerked his hand away. Was it my heightened, anxious state feeding visions to my mind? Was it his quick motion leaving a trail of hand images in the air that gave the illusion of substance? Or did I see what my body was telling me I saw—a vaporous, terrifying being that emerged and vanished in the same instant.

Luke kept to himself the rest of the weekend, but before leaving he asked Mister Rose if he could speak to him alone. Rose said, "Sure, sure," as he always does, and the two of them took a long walk around the farm. No one saw much of Luke after that TAT meeting.

Back in Benwood, life went on as before. The exorcist was still our landlord, keeping order in his crowded house, raising hell when someone placed a pot too close to his papers or typewriter. Life with Rose was a truly inexplicable mixture of the magical and the mundane. Most of the time, especially in the rare moments when I was at peace with myself, I knew how lucky I was and gave thanks to whatever was responsible for bringing me to Benwood.

But other thoughts and urges were beginning to creep into my mind. As the law practice became a bigger part of my life, the pull of the outside world became stronger in other ways as well. I found myself first musing, then wondering, then finally dreaming about what I was missing by living in Rose's house. Sometimes the urge to leave became so strong I even began to wonder if "other voices" were speaking to me.

Autumn was a particularly difficult time of year. The approaching winter invariably brought on that same longing for warmth, security, and affection that had overtaken me so strongly on my first visit to Benwood, a longing for the very things that seemed in such short supply there.

As the days grew shorter I spent longer hours at the office in order to avoid returning to Benwood. I began to wonder if I could take another winter with Rose, stuck inside his stark house with no privacy or comfort, getting up in the middle of the night to feed the wood stove we'd moved into the kitchen, sleeping in a crowded room that rarely got above forty degrees from December to March.

The November TAT meeting that year proved especially depressing for me. People came to the farm, joked and talked, then returned to their comfortable lives and homes. For the first time since leaving Pittsburgh after law school, I wished that I could go with them.

I had gotten into the habit of working on Saturdays, mostly as an escape from the weekend tedium of Benwood, and on the Saturday before Christmas I sat alone in my office and stared out the window for a long time, lost again in a familiar mood. The air was full of thick, gently falling snowflakes. Christmas lights were on in the Courthouse across the street. Children with sleds and shoppers with packages passed by my window.

I thought of childhood snowball battles with my brothers. I remembered the snowy night at college when the telephone rang and my cousin told me my father was dead. I wondered what my mother would fix me for dinner if I was home. Fighting depression, I put away a few things in my desk, then locked up. Even Benwood was preferable to sitting alone in my sterile office.

The school parking lot was uncharacteristically empty. Only Rose's van was parked there, two inches of fresh snow on the roof and hood. I walked slowly up the snow covered steps and walkway, trying to gain control of my mood before facing Rose and my housemates. I kicked the snow off my shoes and went in. Rose was sitting alone at the kitchen table, glancing through a paperback book.

"Ho. What's it look like out there?" He sounded genuinely glad to see me.

"Coming down pretty good. Streets are getting bad. Where is everybody?"

"At a movie," he said with a mixture of humor and disgust. "It was Al's idea, so it's probably some war movie where the English charge the blockhouse and everybody gets gloriously killed." Rose was always chiding Al for his dramatic way of tackling every problem like he was a general going into battle.

I sat down at the table. Usually I went upstairs to change clothes when I first got home, but I suddenly realized it had been weeks since I'd been alone with Rose. Tonight he seemed especially warm and sociable.

"What are you reading?" I asked.

"Oh, some silly book that came to the Pyramid Press." Rose had adopted that press name to publish *The Albigen Papers*, and occasionally unsolicited books were sent in for review or possible publication.

"What's it about?"

"Heaven, and wonderful beings of light that help little old ladies across the street." Rose grimaced like he had a bad taste in his mouth and I erupted into laughter.

"There are such things, of course," he went on, "but whoever wrote this book doesn't have a clue about them."

"You mean like guardian angels?"

"Sure, you can call them that. I've always felt that something was watching out for me. When I think back on it, sometimes my whole life seems like a miracle."

"Do you think everyone has a guardian angel?" I was intrigued.

"Yes, I think so. I sure felt I was being watched over as a kid, and I'm nobody special. When you think of all the ways a kid can get ground up, there's no way so many could survive into adulthood without some unseen help."

"What about the ones that do get ground up?"

"That's necessary to keep the other parents on their toes."

We both chuckled then stayed silent for a moment. In the midst of my recent thoughts and speculations about what life away from Benwood would be like, I'd also been thinking about the other side of the coin, about the people I knew who had no spiritual interest and were already living a "normal" life. In the past year alone many of my friends and family members had been struggling through divorces or career setbacks, or were seeing therapists for a variety of modern miseries.

"I feel that overall I've been very lucky," I said. "Even blessed. I look at some of the events in my life and I sense some sort of guiding hand. But then I wonder if it isn't just vanity to think this. I mean, who am I to have some angel or spirit or whatever keep an eye on me, while so many other people seem so unlucky and miserable?"

Rose rocked thoughtfully in the swivel chair. "Not everybody has the same type of protection. I believe that each person has a guardian that's commensurate with their level of being."

"What do you mean?"

"Just that. For instance, there's only one thing I ever wanted in life—to find out who I was—and that's where I got my luck. But you take my brother Joe. There was a guy who lived purely on the instinctive level, and that's the level he had help on.

"He was absolutely fearless, so he was always getting himself into jams. It's literally a miracle he never got tore up. He had something looking out for him, too, even though he could be a real despicable character when he took a notion.

"Joe drove trucks for a living, and sometimes he'd ask me to go on a run with him if he thought things might get sticky. One time we pulled into a plant where some of the workers were on strike. There was a lot of grumbling because we were delivering supplies when these union guys wanted to shut the place down.

"Joe had me wait in the cab with a gun at the ready while he started unloading the trailer. There were a lot of angry men milling around and I was trying to keep my eye on all of them at the same time. All of a sudden I saw something out of the corner of my eye and when I turned I saw a brick flying right towards the back of Joe's head. Before I could even shout a warning, Joe ducked and the brick flew right on past him. If he hadn't ducked that brick would have caved his head in for sure.

"After we'd cleared out of there I asked him how he did it. There was no way he could have seen it coming. He told me he heard a voice inside his head say, 'Duck!,' so he did. That's what saved his life."

"Where do they come from, these guardians, or whatever."

"Hard to tell," he said, leaning back in his chair. "In the seminary they told us there were actually angels, you know, chubby little cherubs. One group I looked into out west believed they were relatives who had gotten attached to us when we were kids, and when they die they're still concerned about us and stick around to give us a hand."

The last possibility struck a responsive chord. "You know it's funny you should say that. I was just thinking about my father tonight. I was never interested in philosophy. But then after my father died I met you, and things started falling into place to put me here. Is it possible that he's..."

Rose shook his head. "I know you'd like to think that," he said quietly. "But, no, your father is not your guardian angel. He's aware of what you're doing, perhaps, but his concerns are elsewhere now. He's not the one looking after you."

Chapter Sixteen

The Krishnites

When I was first getting started in my practice Rose never asked me to do any legal work for the group. It was not until Lou joined me that Rose began to request our professional services. Either Rose waited until I had help in the office to ask, or it was actually Lou himself who inspired his confidence. At any rate, it was also about this time that Rose's feud with the Krishnas—or "Krishnites," as he called them—started heating up.

Rose never expressed outright regret over his decision to lease his "back" farm to Keith Ham and Howard Wheeler, even though they lied to him about their intentions and eventually turned it into a sprawling Hare Krishna empire that pressed against his farm from all sides. The New Vrindaban Community, as it was called, used their lease on Rose's farm as a base to buy up most of the other farms in the area, and build the "Palace of Gold," a huge structure featuring two hundred tons of white Italian and blue Canadian marble, and a dome covered with twenty-four-karat gold leaf.

"In some ways the Krishnites are better to have around than the hillbillies," Rose said once. "At least they don't get drunk and steal the radiators out of your trucks."

But over the years the tensions had been building. There were minor disputes over fences or livestock, and as the wealth and power of New Vrindaban increased, the leaders became more confident and arrogant.

Once, when Rose inquired about some missing goats, Ham—who by then had legally changed his name to Swami Kirtanananda Bhaktipada—said, "Even if we took them, there's nothing you can do about it. We've got you surrounded."

Gradually, Rose began asking me to intervene in these disagreements, and I made some calls. But the Krishna's attorneys shrugged off my threats to sue and almost dared me to take their clients to court. As the word got out that I was the opposing attorney in these disputes the Krishna devotees would scowl at me when they saw me, and began calling me a demon to my face. These border skirmishes turned out to be just the preliminaries.

As the incidents increased Rose turned more of his attention to the Krishnas. Almost every evening in the kitchen he talked about the problems he was having with them, or brought out some new piece of information he'd picked up about what was really going on inside the New Vrindaban organization. Rumors and stories of prostitution, drug smuggling, child molestation, and other crimes were commonplace. More than once I asked if he wanted Lou and me to do something about legally getting his farm back, but I never got a definitive answer. He'd say something like, "I know you guys are busy," or, "Well, if you get the time someday, maybe we can look into it."

Then one day as I was working at my desk in the office I heard a familiar voice out in the reception area.

"Are Lou and Dave here?" It was Rose. I was dumbstruck. He'd never been to the office before, and in fact made it a point to stay away, saying he didn't want his reputation as a loose cannon to rub off on our practice. I jumped up from my chair and was in the outer office before the receptionist had finished asking him if he had an appointment. Lou must have done the same thing. We arrived simultaneously.

Though it was a moderate fall day, Rose was wearing a long wool coat.

"I was out and about the town and thought I'd drop in on you guys," he said. "I took a bath today and didn't want to waste it."

Lou and I laughed nervously. Our receptionist looked puzzled at the whole scene.

"Come on in, sit down," Lou said.

We went into Lou's office, which was more spacious than mine, and sat down—Lou behind his desk, Mister Rose and I in the visitors' chairs. Rose glanced around Lou's office, taking in the few pieces of artwork Lou had put up to add interest to an otherwise dull and unremarkable room.

"Nice place you got here," Rose said, nodding approvingly.

"We're comfortable," Lou said, "but it's more or less a dump."

"Not compared to the places the lawyers in Marshall County used to have," Rose said. They really *were* dumps. Second story walk-ups that smelled like booze and cigarettes. Half the time you'd have to sober them up to talk to them. Then right away they'd put on their professional mask and look down on you like you were some kind of bug, like maybe they'd agree to save your miserable life if you proved to be worthy of their time—and if you took out a mortgage on your farm to pay them a huge fee..."

He paused and looked around the office again. "I tell everyone you guys are different."

We sat in silence for a few moments. It was time for him to tell us why he'd come.

"I was at the store yesterday and ran into Bob Burkey," he said. The Burkeys had a farm near Rose's. He and Bob Burkey had been friends for years. As we sat there, Rose proceeded to recount the long history of his friendship with Bob, even though we'd heard it several times before.

"Anyway, you already know all that. The thing is, though, I got to talking with Bob about the Krishnites and that back farm of mine. And he said, 'You ought to hire those new lawyers in town and see if you can get your farm back.' I told him I thought it was a good idea and I'd check into it."

He paused a moment and looked us over. "So what do you think? Should we take a shot at it?"

I experienced a moment of confusion and self-doubt. Surely he knew I would jump at the chance to help him and the group. Or did he? And why did he choose this time and this way to ask? Had he forgotten the occasions I'd volunteered to help get his farm back? Was it a lack of skill, determination, or trustworthiness on my part that had kept him from accepting my past offers? Was his past reticence somehow tied to his long-standing refusal to accept food—or anything else I offered—from me?

But these thoughts passed quickly. "Absolutely, Mister Rose," I said eagerly. "We can get to work on it right away."

"Good. Where do we start?"

Lou took out a legal pad and spoke in his usual methodical manner. "Just tell us the story from the beginning, Mister Rose, and we'll ask questions to fill in what we need."

We had heard the story before, but there was something about being in the office—lawyers and client—that brought a sense of order and chronology to it.

"It was about 1967, I guess when I placed an ad in the San Francisco Oracle. It had been probably twenty years or so since I'd had my Experience, and I'd almost given up hope of ever finding anyone to pass it on to. Outside of a few old ladies in the Steubenville group, and an occasional nut Bob Martin and I might meet, there was nobody to even talk to about spiritual matters.

"Then in the Sixties, the *zeitgeist* changed. I had always brought young kids from town out to the farm so that they could get the city out of their hair—the country is a beautiful place to a kid. But what started happening in the late Sixties is that young people—college-age kids, some maybe a little younger—started gravitating out to the farm on their own. I didn't put the word out or anything, but of course I didn't discourage them either. Before you know it we were having regular gatherings on the weekends. Nothing formal, just sitting around, shooting the bull about philosophy. If circumstances were right, maybe I'd read a mind or two.

"I became really curious about why these kids were suddenly so open and aware about esoteric matters. Eventually, I realized that it was dope—LSD in particular—that was opening up their heads. They saw other dimensions that seemed just as real as this one. And what's more, acid seemed to give them an artificial intuition—they understood me.

"Well, I figured, maybe the time has come. With the Experience comes an obligation. So I ended up putting an ad in a couple of underground newspapers in New York and San Francisco, letting people know I was looking for sincere seekers who wanted to take part in a philosophic ashram." Rose smiled. "I didn't know what I was getting into."

"I heard you had a lot of bums and drifters show up," Lou said.

"Yeah, when I was lucky," Rose chuckled. "Most of the people who came around turned out to be dope addicts just looking for a place to crash. Once a couple of gypsies came and stayed in a trailer on my place. Told me they'd been students in a Gurdjieff group, and I thought maybe I'd finally found some people with potential. I discovered later they were running a prostitution business outside of town. I kicked them out, but before they left they burned down my trailer."

He laughed at the memory and spoke without animosity or, apparently, regrets.

"Is this when Ham and Wheeler came," I asked.

"Yes, it was about this time. They told me they'd previously been in the Krishna movement, but had given it up. They said the Krishnites were too closed-minded, and that they were looking for some kind of non-dogmatic ashram, a place where people of different beliefs could come and meditate and exchange ideas. And of course, this appealed to me because this is what I was trying to do, too.

"So anyway, I had the back farm, and since I had the family in town and was raising cattle on the other farm, I couldn't keep an eye on the place. The hillbillies were breaking the windows out of the house, and it was growing up like a jungle, so when Howard Wheeler suggested I rent the farm to them, I thought, sure, why not. Maybe something good would come out of it."

He opened his old black satchel and handed me a three-page legal document. "This is the original lease between Howard and me," he said.

Rose continued talking as I read. "I went to Lawrence Evans," he said, referring to an older, impeccable lawyer whose office was just a few doors down from ours. "I knew him from the naval reserves. I told him, 'Lawrence, be fair to both sides.' That's why I went to him. I knew he'd be fair."

As I read through the lease I was impressed by its efforts at impartiality, and disheartened by the vagueness and lack of landlord rights that resulted. Rose had given Wheeler a ninety-nine year lease on the property for a very fair price, with an option to purchase for one dollar. And while Rose unquestionably knew what he was after when he specified that it be used as a "non-dogmatic, open-minded spiritual ashram," I wondered if a judge or jury would have the patience or desire to draw the distinction between what Rose envisioned and what Ham and Wheeler had created. It was true, of course, that his two tenants had, in Rose's words "put on bed sheets and began chanting gibberish" the day after the lease was signed, but it would be difficult to prove that such action legally constituted fraud.

We could not count on any sympathy from the courts, either. While it was true that the locals harbored no love for the Krishnas, their opinion of Richard Rose was not much better, especially since they blamed him for letting the Krishnas get a foothold on the ridge in the first place. And though my experience as a Marshall County lawyer had been relatively brief, I'd seen enough to know that the Krishna's vast wealth had produced a formidable influence in the court system.

The one ray of hope was a rather straight-forward provision that required the tenants to pay the taxes on time or forfeit the lease. Rose, who was meticulous with all his paperwork, had original receipts which irrefutably demonstrated that the Krishnas were often years late in the payment of the taxes.

"They intentionally pay the taxes late," Rose explained, "hoping the property will come up for Sheriff's sale so they can buy it."

"The lease is pretty clear on that point," I said, handing the papers to Lou. "We should win on that point alone if we get a fair shake."

Lou began reading the lease. "Around here, that's a pretty big 'if,'" he said slowly.

Two weeks later we filed a lawsuit seeking return of the property on four grounds: that Ham and Wheeler defrauded Rose when they said they were no longer Krishnas; that they did not pay the taxes on time as required by the lease; that they engaged in criminal activities on the property; and that Wheeler's assignment of the lease to New Vrindaban Community Inc., the Krishna's landholding corporation, violated the non-assignment provision of the lease. We had a good case, and by the time our court date arrived I was feeling almost confident, in spite of the powers arrayed against us.

But it was over in ten minutes. The Krishna's lawyers immediately moved for a pre-trial dismissal of the portion of our lawsuit dealing with the taxes. The judge not only quickly granted that motion but went ahead and threw out our entire suit as well. It would not be the last time we had reason to suspect that Krishna money and power had pre-empted justice in Marshall County.

Not long afterwards I received an unsolicited letter from an attorney for the Krishnas, offering to trade Rose's family farm for another tract of land a comfortable distance away from "Hare Krishna Ridge." The farm Rose would receive was almost twice as big, and, according to the letter, twice as valuable. I knew the offer would make for lively kitchen conversation and presented the letter to Rose that evening like I'd brought home a trophy fish.

After the usual search for his reading glasses, he sat down at the table and slowly read over the letter.

"They gotta be kidding," he muttered, slipping the offer back into the envelope and tossing it disdainfully in my direction. "They already offered me a million bucks for the place and I turned 'em down. Tell them to go to hell. Better yet, just ignore 'em."

There was also an interesting sidelight to this case that took on greater meaning many years later. In an early phase of the suit, we had a meeting with the Krishna's lawyers and they asked Rose a series of questions. At a certain point it appeared that the questioning was over. Then one of the lawyers asked Rose about his ex-wife, Phyllis. I thought it was a legitimate question since Phyllis' name also appears on the lease. But Rose took it as a direct threat to his family and came up out of his chair ready to do battle. Lou and I quickly worked to calm the situation, and although I played the part of Rose's loyal lawyer at the time, I secretly felt he had missed the mark and overstepped. I chalked it up to the "West Virginia mountain man" part of him and let it go at that.

But Rose might actually have sensed something deeper in the lawyers words that day. Years later, when the Krishna empire began to crack, I was told by one of the assistant U.S. attorneys that they had uncovered a Krishna plot to kill Rose in the aftermath of the suit we had filed to get his farm back. Though they had easily won the first round, the Krishnas apparently were fearful that Rose might persist and someday actually succeed in regaining the property that now had become the center of New Vrindaban.

As the enmity increased between Rose and the Krishnas, Rose became someone to whom local people would tell their stories about problems they were also having with the "Hairy Critters." And Lou and I, as the legal arm of Rose's feud, became the law office of choice if you had a beef with the Krishna's. Some of our cases were on behalf of Mister Rose, some were for other clients. One was somewhere in between.

"There's a woman out here to see you," my secretary said one day.

"Do I know her?"

"No, I don't think so. But she's with a friend of yours."

I walked into the waiting room. Mister Rose was there, sitting next to a gangly woman in her thirties, with short curly brown hair. Rose still tried to keep his distance from the office, and I wondered why he would bring this woman by unannounced.

When we got back to my office, he introduced her.

"This is Cheryl Wheeler. Howard Wheeler's wife."

"Soon-to-be *ex*-wife," she emphasized.

At Rose's urging, Cheryl began telling me her story. She had been initiated by Krishna founder Prabhupada in California during the Sixties. When Prabhupada decided that Howard Wheeler needed a wife, Cheryl had dutifully followed her guru's orders and moved to West Virginia where she and Wheeler were married. Years later they separated and Cheryl moved back to California where she filed for divorce. The divorce judge in California granted Cheryl temporary custody of her children, including an eight-year old son, Devin, who still resided at the New Vrindaban Community in West Virginia. She handed me a copy of the California court order, and continued to talk as I read.

"I came to Mister Rose," she said, "because I remembered him from when I first came here and the farm was just a broken down house. I don't know, it just seemed like he'd be a friend to somebody who needed help."

"From a purely legal standpoint, this is pretty straightforward," I said, looking up from the court order. "Based on this, a local judge should issue a Writ of Habeas Corpus, commanding the child to appear in Marshall County Circuit Court. Unless there's some compelling reason not to, the judge there would defer to the California order and your son can go home with you."

"This is not just any child at the commune," Rose said. "Ham will fight it with everything he's got."

"What do you mean?"

"My son is Keith Ham's protégé and constant companion," Cheryl said. "They eat together, travel together, and...sleep together." Her mouth tightened and she turned her head away for a moment.

I fought back feelings of anger and revulsion, but I wasn't shocked. I was aware of Keith Ham's long-standing homosexual relationship with Cheryl's husband, Howard Wheeler, and stories of child molestings at the commune were not uncommon. It came as no surprise that Ham's twisted mind would choose Wheeler's young son as the object of his perversion.

The next day Lou and I walked over to the judge's office and presented our Habeas Corpus Petition, which included a request for an immediate medical examination of the child to determine physical or sexual abuse. The judge impatiently scanned through our petition until he'd read enough to suddenly realize what it was about. Then he recoiled like we'd handed him a rattlesnake.

"Come back in fifteen minutes," he growled after regaining his composure. "I've got to think this one over."

We returned exactly fifteen minutes later, expecting the worst. The judge was gone, but surprisingly, his secretary calmly handed us the order we had presented, duly signed by the judge. Lou took the order to the Sheriff while I went back to the office to get Cheryl, who was to accompany the deputies when they picked up her son.

An hour passed, then two, with no word from either the officers or our client. Late in the afternoon Cheryl returned, alone.

"They knew we were coming!" she cried, slumping into a chair. "Someone tipped them off, and it had to be recent, because they didn't even have time to get their stories straight."

I called one of the deputies and he filled me in on the details.

"They had a bunch of stories, all of them bullshit," he said. "One teacher told us the boy was there a few minutes ago. Someone else said he hadn't lived there for years. Somebody else said he was out of town for the weekend. I'll tell you this," the deputy concluded, "that boy was there this morning, but you can be damn sure he's out of the state by now."

Over the next few days the Krishna community offered three different official explanations to the newspapers concerning the child's whereabouts at the time of the attempted pick-up. Everyone in Moundsville knew the Krishnas had hidden the boy, but nothing could be done. Without physical possession of the child, our Habeas Corpus petition was useless.

Matters did not improve when we began the process to have Marshall County recognize our client's right to custody of her son. Cheryl Wheeler, already distraught over the disappearance of her child, was dumbfounded at the treatment we received in court during the first scheduled hearing. The judge routinely granted every motion made by the Krishna's lawyers, and disdainfully overruled every request Lou and I made, repeatedly referring to us as "boys" in the process. It did not go well.

After the hearing, Cheryl vented her frustrations to a newspaper reporter. She expressed her belief that her child had been sexually molested, and said that the judge in the case was obviously partial to her son's kidnappers. Her interview appeared in the paper the following morning.

When Lou and I arrived at the office the next day, our secretary had already heard from the judge. He wanted to see us. Now.

Awaiting us in the court chambers were the Krishna's team of attorneys, a court reporter, and one seething judge.

"So your client thinks I'm a crook?" he said in carefully controlled tones, his lips tightening around each word.

Lou and I said nothing.

"You boys think you're going to try this case in the newspapers? Okay, we'll just put the newspapers into the trial."

He then read the entire newspaper article into the record, which he said would be sent to the State Bar Disciplinary Committee immediately after the hearing. Then he tossed the newspaper in our direction.

"Where's your client? I have a few words to say to her, too."

"She's in hiding because she fears for her life," Lou said, looking directly at the Krishna's lawyers.

"Well I can't answer to your client's fears, but I'm the judge here, and I'm running this court. I want to know the whereabouts of your client. Now."

"That's privileged information and we're not at liberty to disclose it," I said.

The judge picked up the phone and spoke to his secretary. She appeared a few moments later with a copy of the Attorney Cannon of Ethics. The judge opened it and read into the record the part that said an attorney must obey the mandates of the court.

"Now," he said, leaning forward in his chair until he was just a few feet from our faces, "I'm ordering you as attorneys practicing before the bar of this court to tell me where your client is."

"We can't do that," Lou said.

The judge slammed the book shut. "Make a transcript of these proceedings," he snapped to the court reporter. With that the hearing was adjourned.

I got in my car and drove straight to Benwood to tell Rose what had transpired. When I entered the kitchen I got the impression he'd been waiting for me.

"Well, what happened?" he said.

I didn't bother to ask how he knew that something had happened, I just launched straight into a blow-by-blow description of our inquisition, and its possible ramifications. The longer I talked the madder Rose seemed to get. Encouraged, I kept on talking. If there was to be a "round two" with the judge it appeared I would not only have God on my side, but a wrathful and vengeful God to boot. When I stopped talking, Rose spoke evenly, but with great force.

"You lost."

I was stunned. "Lost? What...?"

"You let that big bloat intimidate you, and then you just walked away with your tail between your legs, worried about what else he might do to you." He shook his head. "I would have expected more out of you."

I couldn't believe what I was hearing.

"What the hell else could we have done?" I cried out, forgetting myself in my emotions.

"If you're in the right, you don't just run away. Even if it's hopeless, you force yourself to fight. When you're in the right there are no minor battles, no occasions for retreat. You fight with everything you have, *every time*. That way the power of your conviction will deter opponents with weaker motivations than yours.

You fight, or you die in shame. Or worse—you live the rest of your life as a coward."

There were more words, lots of words, but I didn't really hear them. I felt as if my allies were attacking me. I didn't know how or where to make my stand.

"I don't understand, Mister Rose," I finally replied. "I just don't understand."

"Yes you do," he said. "You were right and he was wrong, but you're the one who ran away. You understand that don't you?"

"He's a *judge*, for godsake..."

"I don't give a damn and you shouldn't either! If you can't stand up to an earthly phantom in a black robe, what makes you think you're ready to *become the Absolute*?"

The next morning Lou and I asked for a private meeting with the judge—no court reporter—which he quickly granted, thinking, I'm sure, that we'd considered the possible consequences and were now willing to tell him what he wanted to know. Instead we told him what we should have told him the first time.

As he sat stunned behind his huge desk, his face becoming more flushed with each word, we told him that we not only agreed with and supported everything our client said in the newspaper, but that we strongly suspected him of being corrupt. We said we knew he was the one who tipped off the Krishna's in time to have Devin Wheeler kidnapped, and that we would do everything in our power to prove it. We told him several other things and when we were finished we stood up and left, solid on the outside, shaking to the core.

Cheryl Wheeler never regained custody of her son. We found out later that after Devin was whisked away from the commune that day, he was taken to a Krishna compound in Mexico where he remained until Cheryl Wheeler gave up her efforts to be awarded custody. Then he was brought back to New Vrindaban where he again became Keith Ham's—Swami Kirtanananda's—constant companion.

As a footnote to this case, twelve years later when Ham was indicted on federal racketeering charges the indictment also accused Ham of kidnapping Devin Wheeler to prevent the authorities from taking Wheeler into custody and thereby discovering Ham's sexual relations with the boy. During his testimony, Ham admitted receiving a phone call warning him that the authorities were coming to pick up the child, but the United States Attorney who was cross-examining Ham never asked him who had made the call or provided the information.

As time went on and word got out about the Cheryl Wheeler case, our office became a beacon for disaffected Krishnas from all over the country. Over the years we were phoned or visited by dozens of devotees with a cornucopia of complaints, from petty disputes over land or money, to desperate people like Cheryl Wheeler with tales of sordid sex, beatings, even murder.

These visits ceased to be novelties and eventually grew into burdens. The disaffected devotees who appeared in our waiting room — and scared our other clients — were always short of money and equally short of the resolve necessary to withstand the demands of legal process.

Eventually we grew tired of being used as weapons of revenge, but we never closed our doors to them, hoping that someday someone would come in who could crack the stranglehold that the Krishnas held on the legal and political community. One day that someone finally showed up. His name was Steve Bryant.

Chapter Seventeen

Murder

I had been out of the area for a couple weeks in late October and when I returned I went in to see Lou. He was uncharacteristically animated.

"Did you see this article?" he said. The Wheeling News Register was spread out on his desk, and I wondered what that particular paper could have to say that would excite anyone, let alone phlegmatic Lou.

I walked over to his desk, and was startled to see the headline at the top of the second section: "Former Krishna Devotee Claims Swami Bogus." The Wheeling paper, whether through inclination or intimidation, was extremely pro-Krishna, and rarely printed anything negative about them. Sometimes we would read of a Krishna murder or defection in the Pittsburgh, Columbus, or even Philadelphia paper, but there would be no coverage in the local news.

"It's Bryant," Lou said.

"Who's Bryant?"

Lou looked at me quizzically, then realized that I really didn't know.

"Steve Bryant. That's right, you weren't here when he first came to town."

Lou filled me in. Bryant, a disenchanted Krishna devotee had dropped by the office in early August while I was on vacation.

"He was off the deep end, of course," Lou said, "but in a coherent sort of way. While he was talking it occurred to me he could probably make it in the real world."

Lou went on to tell me that Bryant had kicked around a number of Krishna communities, then had settled in New Vrindaban a year or two before. Bryant imported and crafted Indian jewelry, and his Ford van served as a kind of mobile metal shop and crafts store. Most of his customers were in California, and earlier in the year he had traveled west on a business trip, leaving his wife, stepson, and two toddler children at New Vrindaban.

"Anyway, while Bryant was in California, Ham initiated his wife," Lou went on. "That really made him angry. Bryant spent an hour explaining to me why it was such a big deal to him. Apparently, in the Hindu culture a wife's primary master is her husband, and the guru is supposed to work through the husband if he wants to bring the wife into the fold. That's all he really wanted to talk about. He just kept quoting Prabhupada on the letter of the law and rambling on about Ham going too far this time."

"So where did you leave it with him?"

"Nowhere, really. He was pretty manic, and didn't have any real goal in mind, so I just tried to get him out of the office as soon as I could. But it looks like he's back." Lou held out a pink message slip. "You can talk to him if you want to."

I shrugged. "Doesn't sound like he's got much to go on."

I took the message anyway and read it. Bryant had called our office from the county jail and asked for me.

"What's he doing in jail?"

"Protective custody," Lou said with a slight smile. "Read the article. I think you'll find it interesting."

I returned to my office with the newspaper. I expected the News Register to paint Bryant as a fanatic, but the writing was surprisingly even-handed. It confirmed the reason for his disenchantment with the Swami, and reported that Bryant had returned to Moundsville to expose the Swami as a false guru.

Most of Bryant's accusations were doctrinal: the Swami was untrue to Vedic teachings and the directions of their beloved deceased guru, Prabhupada. But at the very end of the article, almost as a throw-away, there were additional allegations. Bryant claimed to have evidence of "drug dealing, child abuse, and murder." I put the article in my pocket and quickly headed for the Marshall County Jail.

I was led into the attorney visiting room and a few minutes later Bryant was brought in, wearing the standard blue jumpsuit all inmates were issued. The overall impression I got was one of incongruity. He looked like neither a Krishna devotee nor a convict. He was tall, blonde, and fairly good looking. What kept him from being truly handsome was a touch of goofiness in his face and smile, the same quality of expression that made him look out of place in jail.

I introduced myself and he seemed pleased and amused that I'd come. He placed the bulging manila envelope he'd brought onto the table, then offered me his long, slender hand. As a rule, I avoided shaking hands with inmates. I didn't like to extend a hand in friendship before I knew what kind of client I was dealing with. Besides, I was just squeamish enough to worry about where those hands might have been a few minutes before. But there was something about Bryant that made me let down my guard and shake his hand.

"You're becoming something of a celebrity in these parts," I said.

His smile broadened. "Yeah, I've been getting the word out. The TV crews were here this morning doing an interview. One of the guards promised he'd tape it for me tonight."

"What did you tell them?"

"Just the highlights. Whatever I could think of that would get Kirtanananda worked up if he saw it." His smile disappeared. "There's no way I could tell it all in a short interview. I know things you wouldn't believe."

"About the Swami?"

"Swami?" he spit the word out like a bitter seed. "What a laugh. He doesn't have a spiritual bone in his body. He's a phony, an impostor. He's gone directly against almost every one of Prabhupada's mandates. He's doing more harm to the Krishna movement than any outsider ever could."

Bryant then launched into a diatribe against Swami Kirtanananda that went on for fifteen minutes. As I listened I became aware that there was definitely something different about him. I had talked with a lot of disgruntled Krishna devotees over the years, all of whom had tossed out various insults and accusations about the Swami. But regardless of how angry or disillusioned they were, they still referred to Kirtanananda in tones of respect, even awe. In contrast, Bryant spoke without fear or reservation.

"Why are you doing this?" I asked him.

"Because he stole my wife."

"I didn't think Ham was interested in women."

"He isn't. He's a queer. He hates women and encourages all the men at New Vrindaban to beat their wives. He didn't want my wife for sex. He wanted her for money. And power. That's his game. That's all women are good for in his eyes—tools to get money and power. Sex he wants from men.

"He has other uses for women. If they're ugly he puts them to work in the fields, like mules. If they're pretty he sends them out on the "pick" to beg for money. If they're *really* pretty he'll use them as rewards for his cronies. That's what he did with my wife. He gave her to someone else—a gift from the guru." Bryant's tone, while bitter, remained composed.

"Kirtanananda quotes scripture about why its okay to abuse women, and why they're second-class citizens. But he violates scripture whenever it serves his ends. That's how he talked my wife into initiation."

Bryant proceeded to tell the story of being away on business in California and learning that Ham had initiated his wife into the Krishna faith. Evidently, "initiation" is a crucial and sacred step in the Krishna movement, and one that should never be made without the husband's knowledge and consent. When Bryant learned that Ham had initiated his wife, he called him in a rage.

"Ham told me the same thing he told my wife, that a woman's line to God is through the guru, which is not what Prabhupada said at all. Prabhupada made it clear that the woman's link is through her husband."

Bryant picked up the large envelope he'd brought as if it held the proof of what he was saying.

"If a guru initiates a wife without the husband's consent, the wife is now devoted to the guru instead of her husband. The chain of command flows directly from her spiritual teacher, and the husband is cut out of the loop. She becomes the guru's slave, and he can do what he wants to with her. That's how Ham got my wife to divorce me and marry Raganuntha.

"And he couldn't have chosen a worse mate for her." Bryant's voice rose and he began pacing. "Raganuntha is a pervert. That's why he couldn't get a woman on his own. But his parents have money, and Ham didn't want him to leave. So he gave him my wife! And you know what that son-of-a-bitch said when I called him about it? He said I should surrender myself to him."

Bryant sat back down in his chair. "Surrender," he repeated quietly. "Total, complete surrender." He fell silent, then contemplative, as if Ham's directive had a ring of Krishna truth that even Bryant could not deny. Surrender to the guru. Surrender to the guru—even though he steals your wife and gives her to a pervert. Bryant studied his hands in silence for a moment then stood up abruptly, the force of his sudden movement sending his chair flying backwards.

"Bullshit! There's no way I'll surrender to that faggot!" he shouted. "Maybe he can con a soft-headed woman, but he's not going to make a punk out of me."

I let him go on for a minute or so, then tried to steer the conversation into more concrete areas. "What's next,?" I asked him. "What's your plan?"

His eyes flashed. "I know the truth about Kirtanananda, and I'm going to bring him down."

"How?"

"Everyone believes Ham is a great Vedic scholar. He was with Prabhupada from the beginning, and claims to know all the sacred writings inside and out. I knew he was wrong when he initiated my wife, so I got my hands on everything Prabhupada ever wrote. I learned a lot about Vedic doctrine, but I also learned a lot about Kirtanananda.

"Everyone figured that Ham was Prabhupada's chosen successor. But right there in his writings were all kinds of warnings about Kirtanananda. Prabhupada said he was arrogant and ambitious, and that he didn't trust him. The people in the movement need to know this."

"But why did you call me? What do you need a lawyer for?"

"You've got to understand, Kirtanananda is considered to be like a God. Infallible. Above reproach. Nobody questions him. People are in awe of his power. But when I started showing this stuff to other devotees I found out everybody had their own story to tell. Everybody had some dirt on Kirtanananda. It's just that they were either too scared or worshipped him too much to talk about it before. Drugs, people getting killed, kids getting molested. And that case you had about Wheeler's son? Everybody knows the truth. Kirtanananda's been diddling that kid since he was out of diapers. When you and his mother tried to get him out of there, Ham had him taken to Mexico."

I tried to hold an objective, lawyerly pose but inside my heart was pounding. The Cheryl Wheeler case still ate at me, and the prospect of restoring some kind of justice or balance to the situation truly piqued my interest.

"I've dealt with disgruntled Krishna's before," I said. "They all have stories, but they won't follow through, or they want to remain anonymous."

Bryant picked up the bulging manila envelope he'd brought and emptied the contents onto the table. He separated the papers into two large piles.

"Here are some of Prabhupada's writings and commentaries," he said, placing his hand on one stack. "I've highlighted all the places where Kirtanananda has directly disobeyed the Vedic doctrines."

I was impressed with his research, and maybe it would help him break up the Krishna's from the inside, but to me that stack was legally useless.

"What's in the other pile?" I asked.

"Letters from my friends," he grinned, pushing the pile toward me. "I figured I could use some references for the battle."

I picked up the first letter and began reading. It testified to Bryant's good character, then it went on to say that the writer was aware of numerous women who had been beaten at the commune. The next letter contained similar testaments to Steve's sound mind and strong moral character, then the author, a woman, told how Kirtanananda had intentionally destroyed a number of families so that he could use the women for the street begging operation.

The next letter was from a man whose daughter was molested at the ashram school. Another man said Kirtanananda had encouraged him to beat his wife. Another writer, who remained anonymous, said he was ordered to smuggle heroin from Thailand and turn over the proceeds to Kirtanananda. Someone else reported that they knew who the killer was in an unsolved murder at New Vrindaban. I was elated.

"These are dynamite," I said. "We've heard rumors about stuff like this for years, but no one has ever been willing to step forward, let alone put anything in writing. Can you get any more of these?"

"Sure, all you want."

"If you can do that, you've got yourself a lawyer."

A week later, Bryant handed me twenty-four letters. All contained allegations and sometimes eyewitness accounts of physical abuse, dope smuggling, child molestings, even murder—and all were signed. I began to think we might have a chance.

But Kirtanananda must have thought we had a chance, too. Six months later Steve Bryant was murdered in California. Federal and state indictments in the case accused Kirtanananda of giving the orders.

Shortly after I had met him in jail Bryant was released from protective custody. For awhile he kept on the move, calling me every week or so from different hotels or different towns. Often he would call twice within a day or so, first to let me know where he was, then again the next day to say he thought he'd been discovered and had to move on. Once, when I thought he was in Missouri he dropped by the office wearing a false beard that was so cheap and phony looking I broke out laughing while he was telling me how much he feared for his life. During those few months, in a strange way, we became friends.

Bryant had produced a flyer entitled "Jonestown in Moundsville?" and printed a couple thousand copies. Part of his plan was to distribute this flyer to Marshall County citizens, and thereby, he hoped, incite an uprising that would bring down the Swami. But by the time he came back to Marshall County to expose the Swami once and for all, Kirtanananda had made a few moves of his own. Some of which Steve had anticipated, some which he had not.

One key miscalculation was that Bryant thought the Sheriff was on his side, and so he kept him informed of his moves to keep ahead of the Krishnas. In reality, Kirtanananda and the Sheriff were on the same side of the table.

Shortly after Bryant's return, Art Villa, the president of New Vrindaban, sought and received a warrant from a Marshall County magistrate charging Bryant with assault for threatening the Krishna community. The warrant was granted even though verbal threats are not a crime in West Virginia. And because Bryant had been telling the Sheriff of his moves, the arresting deputies knew just where to look for him—in a small boarding house just south of the Moundsville city limits.

When the deputies pulled into the boarding house parking lot, Bryant waved to them and stepped down off the porch. He had just seen the same deputies earlier in the evening, and filled them in on his plans. He thought they were merely stopping by for another chat. Instead, they placed him under arrest for assault. During the patdown search they found the loaded .45 he carried for protection, so they also charged him with carrying a concealed weapon.

The Sheriff got a search warrant and seized all of Bryant's papers. Then he invited the Krishnas to come down and look through them, and encouraged them to make copies of anything they thought might be of interest to the Swami. Included in these papers were correspondences between Bryant and me in which I had urged Steve to collect as much dirt as he could on the Swami. Any doubts Ham might have had about my intentions and methodology were now removed.

I went to see Bryant in jail. He was crushed, truly defeated. The Sheriff had betrayed him, and everything had gone terribly wrong. He thought he was on a holy crusade, but now he'd been arrested and painted as a killer, not a savior. He said he didn't want to live if this sort of thing could happen. He said he was going on a hunger strike, and for a few days he did.

At Bryant's hearing we got the bogus assault charge thrown out, but lost on the gun charge. We appealed and Bryant was freed on bond. His case was to be reset in Circuit Court sometime later that summer.

In the meantime, Bryant went back to California, followed by Thomas Drescher, Krishna devotee and hit man. Drescher had been trailing Bryant under orders from Kirtanananda for several months. His opportunity finally came in California when Drescher followed Bryant's van home one night. Bryant pulled up in front of his house and shut off the engine, but stayed in the van to do his chanting ritual before going into the house. Drescher came up quietly from behind the van and shot Bryant twice in the face through the side window.

Bryant's murder was the beginning of a long downhill slide for Swami Kirtanananda, mainly because it happened in California, beyond the reach of his millions. The two investigators assigned to it, Paul "The Stump" Tippin, and Leroy Orozco, were experienced Los Angeles detectives who had worked on several high-profile murders. There would be no cover-up.

The trail first led to Drescher, and finally back to Ham. The detectives even stirred up some dust about a 1981 murder in Marshall County, West Virginia, the murder of Chuck St. Denis, which undoubtedly would have stayed unsolved had it not involved the same suspects as Bryant's highly visible, out-of-state murder. The FBI even jumped into the St. Denis investigation, so a lot of rocks got turned over, and pressure was put on members of the New Vrindaban Community to come forward and talk.

Gradually the details of the murder of Chuck St. Denis came out. Dan Reid, a devotee, had gone to Kirtanananda with a story that St. Denis had raped his wife. Ham listened, then suggested Reid talk to Tom Drescher about it. Reid knew what that meant and was delighted. Reid went to Drescher and told him what Ham said. Drescher, too, knew what it meant when Kirtanananda sent someone to him with a problem, and he began making plans.

Then one night, when he was ready, Drescher told Reid to lure St. Denis to Reid's artist studio in the woods by offering him cocaine. It worked. When St. Denis arrived Drescher and Reid emerged from the darkness and leveled .22 pistols at him. They told him to get inside the house but St. Denis turned and ran. Both men fired at St. Denis repeatedly until he went down. He was hit twelve times.

The killers lowered their empty pistols and approached the prone figure of St. Denis. Suddenly, St. Denis stood up shakily and stumbled towards his car to escape. Drescher ran after him and tackled him, then yelled for Reid to get a knife. While Drescher and the wounded St. Denis struggled, Reid ran inside the house and returned with a knife. Drescher took the knife and held it poised high above St. Denis' chest.

"Chant!" he screamed at St. Denis, "Chant!"

In his mind Drescher was doing St. Denis a favor. In the *Bhagavad Gita* Krishna says, "Those who remember me at the time of death will come to me." St. Denis knew this too, and even as he continued to struggle he began to chant.

"Hare Krishna, Hare..."

Drescher plunged the knife deep into St. Denis' chest. St. Denis screamed but continued to chant as he coughed blood and tried to throw Drescher off. Drescher plunged the knife into him again and again until the blade hit a rib and broke.

"Krishna, Krishna..." St. Denis would not die and still tried to fight back. Reid, almost in a panic by now, ran into the house and came back with a screwdriver. Drescher took it and began stabbing St. Denis with it. St. Denis screamed in agony, but still he would not die. Reid looked around and found a hammer. He handed it to Drescher. Drescher hit St. Denis in the head with it as hard as he could, crushing his skull. St. Denis finally went limp.

Drescher, exhausted and arm weary, climbed off St. Denis. He and Reid stood for a moment looking down at the mutilated body, catching their breath. Suddenly from the bloody mouth of St. Denis came a high-pitched shriek of agony that froze the insides of the two killers. Then there was only silence.

"Help me carry him over there," Drescher said to Reid.

The day before the murder, Drescher had prepared a way to hide the body. He'd diverted a nearby stream with a makeshift dam, then dug a shallow grave in the stream bed. St. Denis was a big man and it was a struggle for the two killers to carry him to the grave site. When they finally arrived and dropped the body, Reid collapsed in exhaustion.

"Get up! Let's go!" Drescher hissed.

Reid pulled himself to his feet and they rolled the body onto a large sheet of plastic and began to wrap it up. As they were about to cover his bloody face St. Denis opened his eyes again.

"Don't do that," he said calmly, "you'll smother me."

Reid screamed in terror and fell backwards. Drescher kicked St. Denis then rolled him into the hole and shouted at Reid to help him. Panting and muttering they quickly shoveled in the dirt, stomped it down and covered it with rocks. Then they broke up the dam and the stream returned to it's natural course, covering the grave. Somewhere in the process, St. Denis finally died.

Chapter Eighteen

The Gun

One several occasions the guys who lived at the farm suggested I carry a gun when I was out working with them or staying in my cabin. But despite all the stories and evidence of violence the Krishnas had engaged in, I never actually feared them or felt physically threatened. My battles with them were relatively sanitary affairs, conducted through the medium of the law and their phalanx of attorneys. Occasionally when I was at the farm there would be a face to face confrontation over a missing goat or something, but these were brief and, while distasteful, never held a threat of violence. In general I felt comfortably insulated from the sordid realities of the cases I was involved with.

I did, however, have a psychic uneasiness that seemed to accompany each case I pursued against the Krishnas. The closest I can come to describing it is that it felt like I was opposing a powerful negative force, perhaps even pure evil. Whenever I was involved in a case against the Krishnas things began going wrong in my life. Once my sister became very sick. Another time so many things on my car broke at the same time I had to sell it for junk. On another occasion I had to be hospitalized for emergency surgery.

One night in the kitchen I told Rose that it felt like I was fighting an unseen intelligence when I had a case against the Krishnas, that my life invariably became more troublesome and complicated, while the Krishnas seemed to effortlessly maneuver around every legal trap I tried to set for them.

"There's two kinds of magic," Rose said. "White and black. White magic is what I call *between-ness*, and I recommend everyone learn how to use it. But there's black magic, too, and the Krishnites are dealing in it, whether they know it or not."

"How?"

"By attracting certain types of entities. Different kinds of entities are attracted to different kinds of human acts. Entities gain energy from our actions—our expenditures of energy. Sex is the primary release of energy the entities feed on, and some feed on particular kinds of perversions. Keith Ham and his outfit are feeding the pederastic entities. Naturally these entities want to protect the Krishnites so they can continue to get fed."

Rose also went on to say, however, that these entities would eventually turn on the Krishnas and bring about their downfall. This, he said, was the price one inevitably paid for dealing with the dark side. I took some solace in thinking that the Krishnas might someday be on the short end of things, but in the meantime I was not comforted by the thought that "pederastic entities" were interfering with my personal life.

So it was psychic protection I felt more in need of than physical protection, and consequently I never thought seriously about owning or carrying a gun. I came from a strictly pacifist household. My father never touched a gun in his life and he passed this aversion on to his children. I was thoroughly intimidated by guns, and firmly convinced that if I carried one there was a far better chance I'd accidentally shoot myself than come up against a situation where it might save my life.

Everyone who lived on Rose's farm, though, did carry a handgun, partly to shoot feral dogs who occasionally attacked the baby goats, but mostly as a symbol of readiness against the Krishnas. Somehow the farm residents managed to carry their weapons with a casual mindfulness that did not seem to conflict with the high spiritual purpose that supposedly brought them together. I found myself simultaneously disgusted and fascinated by their machismo. It was appropriate enough for the situation to make me look hard at my own aversion to weapons, and to face it as a possible fear and weakness, not as an expression of principle.

Several months after Bryant's murder I received a call from Tom White, the Marshall County prosecutor. He said he had something to tell me and he wanted to meet with me to talk about it. This was an odd request for several reasons, but it was obvious he didn't want to discuss it over the phone so I agreed to come by his office the next time I was in his building.

The call itself was unusual because Tom and I were not on good terms. We were about the same age and had gotten along fairly well while we were both Moundsville attorneys. Then in 1980, to my astonishment, Rose advised me to run for County Prosecutor to get my name in front of the public. Tom White also decided to run that year and we opposed each other in the election. He was a Baptist Democrat hometown boy. I was a Jewish Republican outsider.

Running for prosecutor turned out to be one of the best pieces of professional advice Rose ever gave me. I lost badly, of course, but got more votes than anyone thought I would, and after the election I noticed a change in attitude towards me in the legal community. If

I'd won I would not have fared nearly so well. The prosecutor's office in Marshall County was not a desirable job. Traditionally, candidates were attracted not by the position itself, but by one or more of it's three side benefits: it was a stepping stone to the judiciary, you got all the female divorce clients you wanted, and you could supplement your income with a little graft.

My relationship with Tom had deteriorated after the election, partly because we had been opponents, but mostly because Tom let the office go to his head. He tried to be a big shot and get tough on petty crime in a community where no one really cared because there was a thief in every extended family, and very few people got seriously hurt. Tom went overboard trying to throw the book at some of our minor offenders and we beat him soundly a few times before he backed off.

Adding to the friction between us was the fact that he had become somewhat jaded. After the election he quickly fell in step with the local power structure and the people who had backed him. It was also obvious that the Krishnas had nothing to fear from him. Whether he was in their pocket or merely sensitive to his own compromised position, the result was the same. Children continued to get molested at New Vrindaban, bodies kept turning up, and raw sewage was being dumped into streams running through Rose's and other non-Krishna farms.

Nothing was done. Several times I confronted Tom about his lack of action against the Krishnas and our conversations were not friendly. All in all, it was odd he would call and invite me over for a chat. So odd, in fact that I delayed several days before stopping by his office. I even talked to Lou and John about it, trying to figure what Tom's angle might be.

When I finally did call on Tom his secretary informed me he was out of town for the day. As I started to leave I heard someone call my name. I turned to see Fred Gardener, an assistant prosecuting attorney with whom I'd had several friendly dealings, standing behind the counter that separated the prosecutor's staff from the public. We greeted each other warmly, then he motioned for me to follow him to Tom's office.

"I know why Tom called you," he said.

When he closed the door behind us I looked around and was amazed at what I saw. Tom's normally tidy office had been turned into a war room of Krishna research. Stacks of overstuffed manila file folders were piled on the desk and floor. A sea of telephone message slips were laid out on a credenza. One wall was covered with aerial photographs, most of them of Krishna properties.

"Wow," I said. "I had no idea. I thought Tom was..."

"On their side? Yeah, I know."

"That's not what I meant, exactly. He just never seemed interested."

Fred sat down in Tom's high-back, red leather chair and leaned back.

"That may have been true at one time, but not anymore. Too much has happened."

I sat down. Fred gestured broadly to the stacks of files around the office. "We've been interviewing everyone you can imagine. The rats are deserting the ship, lining up to see who can tell the most the fastest."

"That's a good sign," I said. "Even after Bryant was murdered his closest friends still refused to talk. They were terrified of Ham."

"They should be," Fred said quietly. "So should you."

His statement brought me up short. I didn't know what to say so I just waited for him to explain.

"That's why Tom called you. We've been interviewing devotees recently about the Chuck St. Denis murder. Lots of people who are afraid of Drescher are starting to come forward now because they really think we might have him this time." Fred's jaw tightened, and I sensed how badly he really did want to nail Drescher.

"Anyway, we had this one devotee in last week, a pretty high-up guy in the organization. Been at New Vrindaban from the beginning. He had some good corroborating details on the St. Denis case, and validated a few things we already knew about the Bryant murder. I could tell he had good information so I asked him if Keith Ham had a hit out on anybody else."

Fred paused for effect then grinned. "He said, 'Yeah, that lawyer, David Gold.'"

I heard the words, then my mind froze. I could only hope I didn't look as scared as I felt at that moment. Fred seemed to scrutinize me as he continued.

"This witness said Drescher used to follow you out to your cabin."

He paused a moment to let me say something. I couldn't.

"You've got a cabin out at Rose's place, right? Dark brown wood, cement block foundation? Sits right above a little stream?"

I nodded.

"Yeah, well, that's the place Drescher described to this witness. Drescher said he followed you out there a few times."

"At night, I guess," I said. It was a stupid thing to say, but I had to say something. I thought of the many nights I had walked by flashlight through the half-mile of thick woods between the farmhouse and my cabin. Which times had Drescher been there, watching?

"Drescher told this guy, 'The only reason that son-of-a-bitch Jew boy is still alive is I couldn't find the right spot to blow him away.'"

Fred grinned at me again. Part of him was immensely enjoying my discomfort.

"At least Drescher's in custody now," I said.

"Yeah, but the Swami's not. And he's got plenty of other flunkies."

"I know." I stood up, anxious to leave. "Thanks for the tip."

Fred stood with me and gripped my hand with genuine concern. He was no longer smiling. "Watch your back, Dave."

As I stepped out of the courthouse and into the street my thoughts became more clear and I was hit with a flood of emotions. The main one was raw animal anger. I was furious. Not so much at the Krishna leaders who wanted me dead, but at all the compromised public officials whose fear, greed, and political ambition had, in effect, endowed the Krishnas with a license to kill. Then as I fumed and muttered I was suddenly stopped by an eerie, unfamiliar uneasiness. I shivered involuntarily and quickly looked behind me, then to both sides.

I hurried back to my office, eager to tell somebody about it. But the only person there was one of the secretaries, and I didn't want to scare her. I started to call Rose, but decided to wait until I saw him at home that evening. Then I remembered I wouldn't be going home until very late, probably after he'd gone to bed. That evening I was going to be on television for four hours in my capacity as president of the local bar association.

The presidency of the Marshall County Bar Association was a revolving position determined strictly by seniority. That year, it was my turn to be president. It was also customary for the local bar associations to do at least one community service project a year, and tonight was it. We had joined with the neighboring Belmont County and Ohio County Bar Associations to do a live call-in show, which was scheduled for that evening on a local station. As much as I loved having my face in front of a camera I'd have given anything to avoid going that night. But as president, there was no way I could back out.

I left the office in the late afternoon and drove to the station. The format was that a hundred lawyers would be manning the telephones and answering legal questions for free in the background, while the other two bar association presidents and I sat out front with the show's host, discussing legal issues.

At seven o'clock we went on the air. After a slow start the phones began ringing and behind us all the lawyers in the studio were soon occupied. In the foreground, the show's host did a good job of keeping us on legal topics that would be of interest to the common man. I tried to hold my attention on what I was doing, but I was still distracted by the events of the day and feeling very out of sync with the entire scene. Though I participated in the conversations, I probably spoke the least often and was the least eloquent.

I was surprised, therefore, when late in the show the floor director handed the host a slip of paper that thrust me into the spotlight. The host glanced at the message.

"It's a call-in question," he said, looking up, "and the caller asks that it be directed to Mr. Gold. Well, it's not really our format to have these gentlemen answer questions on camera, but we're nearing the end of the show so I suppose it's all right. Dave?"

"Sure," I said. "Why not."

The host read from the note. "This caller asks, 'Does the law recognize a person's right to defend his church against outside threats? You can legally kill to protect your home. What if you live in your temple?'"

I could not say anything for a few seconds and it was one of the others who spoke first. "We were expecting mostly questions on taxes and real estate," he joked.

"I, uh... I think the logic is twisted, here," I said slowly, trying to rise to the occasion and put coherent thoughts together. Whatever the true reality, in my mind I was now answering a question from a man who was planning to kill me, and who was watching me answer it on TV.

"The law does recognize self-defense when your home is physically entered or attacked," I went on. "And of course when your life is in danger. But what you seem to be talking about is a pre-emptive strike against some vague religious enemy. That's murder."

I started to say more but the host was becoming uneasy.

"Thanks, Dave," he said, quickly. "I'd like to turn now to a legal topic that many of us in middle age are becoming more conscious of — wills. Harry, when should a person think seriously about making out a will?"

I know the host was simply trying to segue to the next topic on his list, but the irony was so thick I almost started laughing. The others seemed oblivious to it and launched energetically into admonitions about how it was never too early in life for a will. I felt like I was on another planet.

Finally at eleven o'clock the director gave us the "All clear," and the lights dimmed. I left the studio and headed towards my car. I walked quickly, occasionally stealing a glance behind me or up ahead into the darkness. When I got to my car I jumped inside and locked the doors. Then, as I put the key into the ignition another thought hit me. I paused, then held my breath and turned the key. When the next sound I heard was the engine roaring to life, I exhaled deeply and told myself I'd seen too many gangster movies.

By now I was hoping Rose would be in bed when I got home. The small black and white TV in the kitchen only got one channel — the one I had been on all evening. I was sure that Rose had seen me, and undoubtedly had passed the evening poking fun at my posturing and ego for the benefit of my housemates. But as I climbed the steep cement steps that led from the street, I could see the light still on in the kitchen.

Rose was sitting alone at the table when I came in, working a crossword puzzle. When he saw me he stopped what he was doing and set the puzzle aside. Over the years I had seen him go through several puzzle phases, where he would work the crossword in the evening paper every night for a few weeks, then drop it and not do another one for a year. Once he started a puzzle, though, he would refuse to become distracted until he had completed it. The way he put the puzzle aside when I walked in told me that it wasn't part of a phase. He was just passing the time waiting for me.

"What's new," he said in a tired and friendly drawl. I did not see the familiar hint of mischief in his eyes that would indicate I was about to get the kidding I expected for posturing in front of the cameras. Instead, I sensed concern.

"We did that call-in show tonight. For the Bar Association."

"I know. I saw it. You have something on your mind."

"Tom White called a few days ago and asked me to stop by — said he had something I needed to know about. I went over there today."

"What's up?"

"One of the Krishnas they're questioning about the St. Denis case told him Ham put out a contract on me."

Rose raised his eyebrows but made no comment.

"Drescher bragged about following me out to my cabin. He said the only reason I wasn't already dead was he couldn't find the right spot to shoot me."

Rose remained motionless in his chair and seemed to be lost in thought. I continued to ramble on.

"So, I mean, Drescher's in custody now but who knows how many other nuts the Swami has floating around that would be—"

"Get a gun," Rose said, suddenly interrupting. His voice was matter-of-fact but his tone was firm. It was more than a suggestion.

"I've thought about it Mister Rose, but I don't know guns. I don't think—"

"Get a gun," he said again. Then he dropped the subject and went on to talk of other things, including how ridiculous I had looked on TV that night. We had a few laughs at my expense then went to bed.

It never occurred to me to ignore Rose's advice, even though I knew that with or without a gun I would still feel absolutely defenseless. If a Krishna hit man was lying in wait for me at my cabin or in a dark Wheeling alley by my car, a handgun in my pocket or glove compartment wasn't going to do me much good. I felt incapable of protecting myself against such a circumstance, and strongly believed the only protection I could hope for was intervention from a higher power. But Rose had told me to get a gun, so I started shopping.

The best consultants I could think of were the guys on the farm, but I wasn't sure how to approach them about it. Although I counted them among my closest friends, there was always a gulf between us. Real or imagined, I felt they regarded me as something of a sissy. I spent my days in comfortable offices and ornate courtrooms, while they perched on rooftops and hung from ladders. I spent almost every week-end with them at the farm, cutting firewood, clearing pasture, repairing buildings, or shoveling out the goat sheds. But no matter how well I kept up, I sensed that to them I would always be a week-end warrior.

The Krishna threat against me apparently boosted my stock with them, though. Rose had evidently made it clear that he regarded a threat against one of us as a threat against all. I didn't have to ask them for advice about guns, they came to me.

The following weekend I went out to the farm as usual to help with the endless chores. It was October and the weather was brisk and stimulating. We worked hard all morning, cutting and hauling firewood from the back end of the farm. Afterwards, Chuck, Larry, Mark, Jake and I were relaxing in the farmhouse, fixing lunch. Larry walked into the dining room with an iron skillet half-filled with something unrecognizable he had fried up for breakfast, or perhaps even last night's dinner.

I watched him for awhile, unable to resist smiling at his every move. Larry was one of the funniest people I'd ever met, and his sense of humor was magnified by the comic lifestyle he'd adopted at the farm. He had accumulated a rather eclectic wardrobe over the years by picking through Goodwill bins, and now kept all his clothes in a pile in the corner of his room. Each day he dressed in whatever shirt and pants his hand touched first—a selection method that invariably produced harlequin-like combinations of plaids, stripes and bizarre color combinations. He came from a rough rural town on the northern outskirts of Pittsburgh. He was tall and wiry, and before he met Rose his life was a perilous series of scrapes and jams and misadventures—often involving women.

As I watched, Larry placed his skillet on the table, then went to the refrigerator and pulled out a quart of goats milk, a stick of margarine, and a large jar of a generic-brand grape jelly. He held up the jelly and pretended to read from the label.

"'This product has grapes and leaves and bird shit all clumped together, but it's suitable for normal everyday use—as long as you feed it to someone else.' All *right!*"

He sat down and piled an enormous slab of margarine on a piece of bread, then spooned a heap of his jelly-substance in there with it. He took a huge bite and shook his head in satisfaction like it was the best thing he'd ever tasted. Then he started on the nameless food in his skillet. After a few bites he looked up at me.

"So our neighbors want to thin out the Jewish population around here, huh?"

"Yeah, they're driving down the property values." Chuck said. He was stomping around the kitchen and dining room putting together his lunch, looking sullen as usual. His perpetual scowl was an accurate reflection of his mood about half the time. The rest of the time he was indifferent to life. No one had ever seen him happy. His communications with people were very direct and literal, and he had little use for the formalities of social convention. Sometimes, however, he did show flashes of humor. During the time he was building my cabin he had occasion to phone me a few times at the office. Once my secretary asked if she could say who was calling.

"Yes," he told her.

After a long awkward pause my secretary said, "Well, who *is* calling."

"Chuck Carter."

"May I tell him what this is concerning, Mr. Carter?"

"Yes." Another long pause.

"Well, what *does* this concern?"

"It concerns my wife," Chuck said, his voice rising. "I want him to stay the hell away from her!" His call was put right through.

Now, as I watched Chuck gather the materials for his lunch in his deliberate manner, I realized how little I actually knew about him—how little any of us knew about him.

"Whoa, boy," Chuck whistled, looking in the refrigerator and spotting the smoked fish I had brought. "If it's open season on Dave Gold let's shoot him now and take his lunch."

Every week-end I brought out something to share, and every week-end we went through the same ritual. If it was something Larry liked he dug right in and ate as much as he could as fast as he could. Chuck, however, would always act surprised and wait for my invitation before eating any of it. He would take a minute portion, to show he wasn't greedy or obligated to me, then later go back for seconds, and thirds, and keep eating until the food was gone or he had made himself sick, whichever came first.

Chuck took the smoked fish out of the refrigerator and set it on the table. Larry picked it up by the tail, brought it up to his face and stared at it, eyeball to eyeball, for several seconds.

"He blinked first," Larry announced triumphantly, then tossed the fish back onto the white wrapping paper and turned to me. "So what kind of gun you looking for?"

"I don't know yet."

"Get one like this," Larry said, pulling his gun from his back pocket and putting in on the table.

Chuck stopped what he was doing and put his gun beside it. "I got one almost like it," he said. "They're good guns."

Hearing the turn in the conversation, Mark and Jake came in from the living room where they'd been eating and put their guns on the table, too. I stared at the four weapons like they were lit sticks of dynamite. Larry and Chuck extolled the virtues of their aluminum alloy Smith and Wesson .38 specials.

"You can walk around with it in your pocket all day and not even know it's there," Larry said.

Chuck's gun was identical, except that his trigger was rounded. "That way it doesn't get hung up on your pocket if you need to pull it out in a hurry," he explained.

Jake picked up his gun from the table. It was a smaller caliber gun but had a longer barrel.

"Those snub-nose things are only good for sticking in people's bellies," he said with an odd laugh. "I can hit a tin can at fifty yards with this."

"Yeah, but it's got no stopping power," Mark countered. "You may hit someone at fifty yards, but they're going to hit back. Now this," he said, lovingly picking up his black steel .44 magnum, "this will settle an argument."

I picked up Larry's gun. It was the first time I had ever touched a handgun. It felt foreign, unpredictable, dangerous. I remembered all the horror stories I'd heard of gun tragedies, and was almost overwhelmed with revulsion. I felt like I was holding a snake and fought off the urge to throw it down. But as I picked up and handled each gun in turn I began to feel less and less intimidated, and by the time I picked up Mark's cannon, I was almost intrigued by what I held in my hand.

Mark smiled at me. "We just might make a man out of you yet."

I decided on an aluminum .38 special, like Chuck's and Larry's, and began my search the following week. The first place I tried was Sullivan's Gun Shop on the outskirts of Moundsville. I had defended a juvenile who had broken into the store years before, and more recently I'd represented a member of the Sullivan family in a personal injury case. I thought I would feel more comfortable taking care of this unpleasantness with people I knew, but the reverse was true.

As soon as I walked in my antipathy to guns returned in the form of embarrassment. I felt uneasy and nervous, like a small-town teenager about to buy condoms from the family pharmacist. I was almost relieved when the clerk told me they had no aluminum .38's. I drove to Wheeling and tried several gun stores and pawn shops there, but none had the type of gun I was looking for. I began to wonder—even hope—that maybe I wasn't meant to own a gun.

The following week my other law partner, Jon Turak, returned from vacation. I was anxious to discuss all this with him. Jon was one of Augie's younger brothers. He had joined Lou and me in the practice several years before and had since become one of my closest friends, and definitely my most trusted confident. In some ways he was like Augie—and the other nine Turaks I eventually became friends with. He was gregarious, charismatic, loyal, and very family-oriented. But he was different from Augie in some fundamental ways. There was none of the domineering manipulation or bombastic diatribes that made Augie both an effective leader and a difficult taskmaster.

All of the Turaks were soft-hearted, but most had also developed an emotional armor that allowed them to protect their own feelings when necessary. Jon had not. He wore his affections and vulnerabilities very close to the surface, and seemed to get along just fine that way. Though he was not a student of Rose's, Jon had a profound understanding and respect for Rose and his teachings. He was close enough to the group to share its values and far enough away to give me an objective perspective when I needed it.

His first day back, I gave him a few hours to literally get his feet back under the desk, then about noon I went into his office and sat down. Jon was leaning back in his red leather chair, eyebrows furrowed, perusing a thick legal document.

"I can't believe it." He shook his head in bemused exasperation. "Bill Lemon has really outdone himself this time."

Bill Lemon was the prosecuting attorney for neighboring Wetzel County, and a throwback to the justice systems of a hundred years ago. He viewed us as bleeding heart crusaders and took special pleasure in trying to railroad our clients.

"Do you remember the Littleton case I have with Bill?"

I nodded. Some stolen farm equipment had turned up on the Littleton's property in rural Wetzel County. Lemon charged the son with stealing the equipment. I took the son's case, which we got dismissed. Lemon got mad about it and then charged the mother with Receiving Stolen Property. Jon took the mother's case and filed a Bill of Particulars, requesting discoverable information about the State's case against the mother.

"Listen to this." Jon leaned back again and read from the document. "Here's question 14 in my Bill of Particulars: 'State with particularity all evidence which the State intends to rely upon to prove that Sandra Littleton knew that the farm equipment which appeared on her property was stolen.'"

John put down his document and picked up the State's response. "Answer. 'Sandra Littleton received the farm equipment from her son, Ronald Littleton, and everyone in Wetzel County knows that all the Littletons are thieves.'"

Jon roared with deep, relaxed laughter, then tossed the papers aside.

"So what's new around here?" he said.

I leaned my chair back until it was balanced against the wall.

"Tom White called me right after you left."

"Let me guess. He wants you to represent him in his divorce."

"Not quite." I told Jon the whole story and realized as I spoke how much I'd been looking forward to talking with him about it. When I finished he was silent for a few moments before speaking. I knew what he was thinking. Jon had been involved quite visibly in some of the Krishna cases himself. Just because there was currently no evidence of a contract on his life, did not mean one didn't exist. There was no reason to believe he would be immune.

"You've talked to Mister Rose about it, right?"

"Of course."

"What did he say?"

"He told me to get a gun."

"Did you?"

"Not yet. What do you think about all this?"

Jon sat in thought for a moment. He was two years younger than me, and remarkably handsome, with boyish good looks and charm. At the moment, however, he looked old.

"We didn't ask for this," he said finally. "We just did what we thought was right, and this is where it dropped us off."

"So what are our choices?"

"None," he replied, smiling again. "Like Davey Crockett says, 'Be sure your right, then go ahead.'"

We sat in silence for several minutes, then Jon spoke again.

"You know," he said with a grin, "if you walk around with a gun in your pocket there's a good chance you'll just end up blowing your balls off."

"It's crossed my mind."

Jon leaned forward in his chair and spoke more seriously. "I know a guy, an iron worker I did some title work for. He's also got a federal firearms license. I could give him a call."

The next morning, Jon walked into my office, followed by a rather smarmy man with flabby arms and a thick mustache in need of trimming. He got right to business.

"Jon said you were looking for a handgun," he said as we shook hands.

"Yes, I am."

The man lifted his large black case onto my desk.

"He didn't know what you were looking for exactly, so I brought a selection." He opened the suitcase and removed his guns one at a time, placing them at intervals around my desk.

"Pick 'em up," he said. "Get a feel."

I started with an unintimidating .22. I examined it, aimed it out the window.

"A good gun for target shooting but not much good in a pinch," my consultant advised.

I nodded and picked up a western style Colt .45. It was incredibly heavy, and I wondered if cowboys really twirled these things on their fingers.

"A show gun," I was told.

I moved on to a .44 magnum. The gun man smiled.

"This is the type of gun I sold to your partner here. It's fast, dependable, and will do some damage no matter where you hit a guy."

I looked over at Jon with amazement. He never told me he'd bought a gun. I started to say something, but I could see from his expression he didn't want to talk about it, at least not now.

"It's a beautiful gun," I agreed, "but I need something I can put in my pocket and forget about."

"Then this is the piece for you," he said, picking up a .38 and handing it to me. Surprisingly I felt an immediate affinity for the weapon. It was light and fit perfectly in my grasp.

"It's called The Agent," the man said. "Colt makes it specifically for the CIA. Aluminum alloy, six shots—the Smith and Wesson aluminum .38's only have five—and it can take a lot of abuse."

I stood up, placed the gun in the right rear pocket of my suit slacks, and walked around my office.

"Can't even feel it," I said to Jon.

I asked about the price.

"I'm selling it for a friend's widow. I told her I'd get two hundred dollars."

I walked around the office some more, feeling the weight of it. I took it out and looked at it, then put it back in my pocket.

"It comes with bullets, right?" I said.

"For a friend of Jon's, *two* boxes."

"Is a check okay?"

"I prefer cash."

I carried the gun with me for the next few days and strangely, I was more afraid than when I didn't have it. It was as if the presence of the gun made the possibility of imminent death that much more real. Constantly feeling the weight of it in my pocket made it difficult to think of anything else. I told myself I would get used to it, and that someday I would think normally again.

The following Saturday I went out to the farm as usual to help with the work. I showed my new gun around and the residents all approved of my choice. I stuck it back in my hip pocket and felt better about it being there. We had been working the last few weeks clearing a small field for cultivation. That day we worked at digging out stumps. It was cool and sunny — a beautiful day for work.

About an hour later Rose arrived and began to work along with us. We'd been working in teams of two — one man with an ax, the other with a shovel. But with Rose there, everyone converged on the same stump to be near him.

We stood around the stump, taking turns with the ax and shovel work, talking, laughing at Rose's jokes, sweating in the cool autumn sun. Rose took a turn at the ax and swung it with the power and grace of a young athlete. When he stopped he handed it to me and smiled with true warmth.

I took the ax from him and swung it with a will, exalting in the joy of pure movement. As I did, Rose spoke casually of spiritual matters and the others who stood around the stump became motionless. I swung the ax and listened — no, *heard* — and his words penetrated more deeply than my own thoughts. Without warning I was moved to tears.

I swung the ax harder and kept my head lowered to hide my emotion from the others. And then, suddenly, I didn't care. I stood straight between swings and let my tears show. I swung the ax with a rhythm of movement so perfectly attuned to me it was almost effortless.

Each time I bent to chop the root I felt the gun in my pocket press against me. Each time I stood to swing the ax again the sun touched my back. I was simultaneously empty and full. There was nothing I would rather do, no place I'd rather be. If I were killed because I chose to come to this place and learn from this man, then surely this was the reason I was born. I swung the ax and wanted nothing more from life. In that moment an immense burden left me, and although I can't be sure, I believe that for a few hours that day I lost my fear of dying.

Chapter Nineteen

The Stagehand

A few weeks later I drove Mister Rose out to the farm. The guys who lived there had been putting up fence for three months. With winter coming on, Rose had put out a call to the outlying groups for help in hopes of finishing the project before the ground started to freeze. We were expecting a big turnout that weekend.

Usually, these were Rose's happiest times, working side by side with young men, talking and joking in the farmhouse after the work was done. But on the ride out that day he was pensive and uncommunicative, offering only an occasional comment about the traffic or weather. I stopped trying to make conversation and we drove most of the way in silence. It wasn't until we were almost at the farm that he spoke again.

"I've been walking through a dark place these last couple of days."

I waited for more, but he added nothing.

"What do you mean, Mister Rose?"

He paused a long time before answering. "I don't know if I can explain it to you," he said. His voice was flat and distant, and it made me uneasy.

When I pulled into the parking area, Rose got out of the car and without another word headed towards the road that led up the hill to where the work was going on. I followed, and we found the others already sinking posts and unrolling wire fence. Rose continued to be somewhat distant as we worked and soon everyone fell into the same mood. We worked steadily all morning with little being said beyond the necessities of the task. Along about noon the sky darkened and a cold rain began to fall. We gathered up our tools and headed for the house.

Inside there was a flurry of activity as people began to prepare their lunches. It was several minutes before I noticed that Rose had not come in with us. I went out to my car to get the food I'd brought and saw Rose some distance away carrying a few tools towards the east end of the farm.

Curious, I followed until I saw him arrive at the grave site he had picked out for himself several years before. I knew that periodically he tended and groomed this small plot of land. As I watched he began cutting the underbrush with a large scythe, stooping occasionally to pull on a root or toss something aside. He moved with thoughtful grace as he worked in the cold rain. After a few minutes I left, feeling like an intruder.

That night in the farmhouse, the wood stove creaking, Rose began talking about his Experience without anyone first asking a question. He talked about the Absolute with an almost indifferent familiarity, the way an immigrant might talk about the old country. As I listened to him, I had the sense that Rose wasn't really there, that he was not a part of our world. He was a stranger from the Absolute, marking off his remaining days in the prison of this dimension.

"Do you think you'll remember this place?" I asked him.

"Oh, I don't know, probably," he replied, leaving the distinct impression that it didn't matter either way.

The next morning we awoke early and prepared for work, but Rose lingered over coffee and conversation with us. It was after eight before we left the house. As we gathered tools and prepared to walk up the hill to the fence line, a red Jeep Scout stopped on the road in front of us. The driver was Keith Ham—"Swami Kirtanananda." Several other devotees were with him.

Rose walked over to the car and we moved closer, ready for trouble. Relations between the neighbors had never been worse. Krishna children called us names as they walked past, and one somewhat friendly devotee who had stopped by the farm told Rose confidentially that there were a dozen men ready and eager to kill him should the Swami give the word.

Rose leaned inside the driver's window. "So Keith, when are we going to get the rest of the fence?" he said.

The Swami hated to be called by his *karmi* name, but I don't think Rose did it to needle him—although Rose was perfectly capable of doing that. He just knew him as Keith when they met, that's all, and no amount of power or pretense would change it.

"It will be here by noon," Kirtanananda said. It was a different voice than I'd heard in court or on the evening news. While not exactly friendly, there was no arrogance or affected holiness about him.

"It was supposed to be here yesterday," Rose said.

"I called again this morning. It'll be here by noon."

They talked matter-of-factly for a few more minutes about the fencing, which was obviously a joint project between the neighboring farms—although Rose had never mentioned it to us. When they finished their business the Krishnas drove off. We followed Rose up to the fence line and worked until almost one o'clock.

After lunch Rose again seemed in no hurry to get back to work. He leaned back in his chair and looked us over one at a time.

"You know," he said, in a slow, reflective voice, "when a person gets inspired and makes a commitment to a spiritual path—and *acts* on that commitment—he *moves*. He changes. His *life* changes. But when he stops acting on his commitment, he stops moving. He stops growing. His *clock stops*."

He paused for a moment. "That's what it's like around here now—Brigadoon. None of you are moving. And if any of you want to pick up the torch again, you'll have to figure out why your clock stopped and do something about it."

We all stared at our boots or hands.

"But don't wait too long," he added with a slight smile. "I don't know how much time I have left."

No one said anything for what seemed like several minutes.

"Spiritual clocks stop for different reasons," Rose went on in an almost soothing tone. "Some of you have taken on wives and girlfriends, others want to explore the limits of your ego, others want to grab for the million bucks.

"But I'm not really disappointed," he said. "When people got into the group they were college kids, they had time and freedom. I always figured that eventually they'd have to buckle down—at least the ones who didn't figure out the secret of how to live *without* buckling down."

He stood up and got a can of soda from the refrigerator, then began to speak about each person individually, and where he thought they were in relation to the search. When he stopped talking I was the only one he hadn't mentioned. For a moment I considered leaving it that way, but I spoke up.

"What about me, Mister Rose?"

"I've watched you for years," he said, as if expecting the question. "Your heart's not in this work. You've suffered but you've never changed."

As we worked on the fence that afternoon I thought obsessively about what he'd said. It hurt, but I knew he was right. My heart wasn't in it anymore, and the more I considered it, the less sure I was it ever had been—at least not the way Rose meant it, anyway. But as for not changing? I was sure I had been making great strides all these years, even if my commitment level might have wavered at times. If I had been kidding myself about this I truly did not see it.

I tried to look at my life through Rose's eyes, but my ego kept rushing to my defense. All I could hear were my own rationalizations coming back at me. I knew Rose thought I was too wrapped up in my career, but I thought I'd done a respectable job of incorporating his principles into my business life. Exposing untruths was the essence of effective cross-examination, and intuition was every bit as valuable in the courtroom as in meditation.

I used determination and perseverance to win cases that seemed unwinnable. I did a fairly noble job of staying celibate in a distinctly un-celibate world, and of steering clear of the greed and compromise that I saw all around me in my profession. What did he expect from me? What was I doing wrong? What was I not doing that I should?

I refused to admit that I had abandoned the search. The flurries of egotistical ambition, the occasional interlude with a woman, the nights out with friends watching a ball game on big screen TV—these were merely amusements I tossed in to spice things up a bit. They were only enjoyable as long as I felt I had a "path" to return to. I did not want to think that they were what I had become, and that I no longer might hope that I would someday break through my ignorance and neuroses to discover my true Self.

Still, as hard as I argued with myself there was no getting around the fact that something was missing. What was it? The glue that bound together the hundred or so people who Rose considered serious enough to comprise the group was, of course, Rose himself. But what opened each of their minds to the possibilities that Rose presented? What inspired them to actually try and change their lives? It was the unexpected experiences that somehow "happened" to everyone who spent any time around him.

Healings, mind-readings, rapport, miracles of coincidence. These were the events that inspired and transformed people, far more than all the words in his remarkable philosophy. That was what brought me to him. That is what held my interest. This is what I now sensed was gone. I had lost the sense of wonderment—of unlimited expectation—that I had come to take for granted since meeting Rose. Without it, I was just going through the motions.

That evening as I drove Rose home to Benwood I tried to explain what I'd been thinking. I had a hard time putting into words what I'd felt so strongly earlier that day.

"I can't exactly point to anything in particular that's different," I said, "but there used to be a magic that you could feel in the group. I don't mean just specific events. It was like a crack that I used to be able to see through that kept this world from seeming so real. I don't know if I've changed, or the *zeitgeist* has changed, or what."

Rose smiled. "It's me," he said. "I've changed. I turned off the magic."

His statement shocked me. For as long as I had known him, Rose had never taken credit for any of the "surprises" that had happened. He also frequently spoke about how taking credit for phenomena would upset the delicate equilibrium of neutrality and indifference that supported acts of *between-ness*.

"I don't understand."

"When this stuff started happening it came as a big surprise to me. I always thought that healing was a trap to keep people tinkering with the props instead of breaking through and discovering what's behind the curtain. Then one day in the kitchen, Jean was complaining about a headache and the thought came to me that I could take that headache away if I wanted. So I just put my hand on top of her head and pulled it out. Her headache was gone."

"How did you know it wouldn't be a trap for you?"

"I knew it wouldn't trap me because I was indifferent to it. I knew what my direction was and I knew I wasn't going to let anything get in the way of it. So when minds got read, or people got zapped or healed, I didn't discourage it.

"But then it started turning into a circus. People were coming down to the farm just to see who'd get zapped. They weren't interested in philosophy, and they were wrecking the place for the people that were. So I pulled the plug. Magic and miracles attract people from too far down on the spiritual ladder."

I winced at his last remark and wondered if it was intended as a shot at me, knowing how big a part his magic had played in my spiritual interest. But he did not look at me or change his tone.

"A person can't wear too many faces," he went on. "I'm wearing the face of an advisor, not a miracle worker. Of course, I might change my mind if someone close to me was in trouble. But I'm looking for true seekers, people who want to find their ultimate definition. Not people who are merely impressed by magic."

Over the next week or so those of us staying in Benwood and at the farm began talking to Rose about what we could do to start moving again, to get our clocks started. He was evasive at first, as if waiting to see if we would suggest something ourselves. But a few days later he announced plans for a month-long "Winter Intensive" at the farm. It would begin January first.

Once the word got around nobody wanted to be left out. People who normally only came around for TAT meetings took time off from work or even quit their jobs to attend. I tried to shuffle my schedule, but the first two weeks were all I could free up.

On New Years Day, twenty-five of us gathered at the farm and Rose outlined the rules. There were lots of them. He had established a strict regimen and it was obvious he was dead serious about this Intensive. Up at six. Silence and meditation from six until noon. Work outdoors until five. Attend an evening meeting in the farmhouse from seven to midnight. Fasting was required for at least the first three days, and encouraged thereafter for alternating periods of three to five days. Strict celibacy was demanded, and to ensure compliance everyone was paired off in various rooms and cabins, and no one was permitted to go anywhere without his partner at any time. Rose made it clear that a breach of any rule would result in expulsion from the Intensive.

We all wondered why Rose, who generally not only refused to legislate routines but actively discouraged them, had come up with such a rigid program.

"There is no recipe for a lightning bolt," he had often said.

But this time it was different. It was as if Rose sensed that time was short, and that he had to pull out all the stops if there was to be any hope of helping someone break through. He was with us almost constantly, a combination teacher and comrade-in-arms. He fasted with us and led us on long silent walks to take our minds off our hunger. In the afternoons he worked along side us in the cold and snow, chopping trees and splitting wood. In the evenings he would hold rapport sittings and talk philosophy as we fought off the mind-numbing fatigue that threatened to overtake us.

About a week into it, Frank received a phone call from his wife informing him that his baby was sick. Rose told him to go home.

"Your first commitment has to be your family," he said, which was exactly what Frank wanted to hear. After Frank left, though, Rose spoke differently about how he had handled the delicate balance of raising a family while doing The Work.

"We used to meet Friday nights in Steubenville," he said. "It wasn't much of a group, mostly older women glad to get out of the house once a week, but I figured I'd work with what was in front of me until something better came along. Then I got to noticing that every Friday something would go wrong in the house. One of my kids would get sick, or my wife would go nuts about something. So finally I said to her, 'Listen, I don't care if you and the kids are *dying*, I'm still going to go the meeting.'"

There were a lot of puzzled faces. We all knew how protective Rose was of his wife and children.

"Honoring my commitment to that spiritual group was the only way I could keep my family from harm," he explained. There were still a lot of puzzled faces.

"If you're trying to take a vacation from nature in order to find your Essence," he went on, "the forces of adversity will attack you any way they can. And that usually means finding the weakest link. That can be your wife, your kids—anything you're attached to. If you let these adverse forces slow you down you're just going to encourage them, and that means more headaches for you and possibly even danger for those close to you.

"To have a chance of really doing something you have to set your psychic shield in place. That means a solid stance of pure commitment—no equivocation. This way you're protected, and though they may not know it or understand it, so is your family."

The exhausting regimen continued. One afternoon, about ten days into it, we dragged ourselves into the farmhouse wing after five hours of cutting, splitting and hauling firewood, too tired to even shake the snow and mud from our boots. We fell into seats wherever we found them. Those closest to the stove peeled off a few layers of clothing. Others waited for the warmth to reach their depleted bodies. The final rays of sunset lit up the windows and bathed the room in cool red light. No one spoke.

After several minutes Rose stood up and unbuttoned his long wool coat. His movements were stiff and he looked suddenly old.

"You look tired, Mister Rose," Nick said.

"It comes from trying to breathe life into twenty-five statues."

No one laughed. Nick stared at his work boots. "I'm sorry I asked."

"Don't be," Rose said, taking off his coat and sitting back down. "There's twenty-four statues who didn't."

Rose had repeatedly said that Nick was the most sensitive and intuitive among us, and perhaps the most likely to have some kind of Experience. The trouble was, he said, those same qualities made Nick the most likely candidate for a garden-variety nervous breakdown, too.

"I honestly don't know how you do it, Mister Rose," Nick went on. "You work harder at this than any of us, and you've already achieved, or become, or whatever. You're already *enlightened*."

"There's no point in getting a fat head about being in this work," Rose said. "I'm nothing special. Nobody's anything special. Everybody is working for God. Most people just don't know it. Maybe God doesn't even know it."

"But there is a difference between a person just living an animal life and somebody trying to find the Truth, isn't there?" Chuck asked.

"We're all living animal lives. Don't think you're better than nature. I don't believe in violating natural programming. But at the same time everybody also has the right to solve the mystery of life — to become who you are. That is your prerogative, and also your sacred trust. The complex web of nature is part of a blueprint that also gives every individual the chance for ultimate survival, ultimate definition. Not a guarantee, but a *chance*. And you don't have to violate nature to take a shot at it.

"There's nobody on earth who doesn't want to know the Truth. They're all moving towards it at the precise speed of their commitments, which is usually very slowly. People have no choice, really, but to try and find a way out. Everybody is miserable. A baby on his first day of life wakes up screaming. He doesn't like the atmosphere. Even the animals suffer. Everything's trying to eat them, and that's bound to be a headache. We're all just animals trying to survive in this jungle. I'm an animal, too. I've just seen a light, perhaps, that the other animals haven't seen."

He stood up and got a soda from the refrigerator.

"The irony is that animals and instinctive people — people who live like animals — pick me up better," he went on. "They know I'll be kind to them."

"Can you help people like that?" Larry asked.

"You can't help everybody, if that's what you're getting at. If you reach too far down the ladder, people end up dragging you down instead of you pulling them up. Even with the people who are receptive, whose heads have opened up for some reason or another, you can't necessarily help them in the way they demand to be helped. Sometimes even when you want to, you can't get too close. The formula for magic is to stay ten feet away from people. Love your friends, but keep your distance."

"Does that go for people in the group, too?" Chuck asked.

"Especially for people in the group. We're walking a tightrope. On one hand you have to have friendship, because without friendship, there's no hope of attaining anything of spiritual value. If people don't have the capacity for true friendship, they have no spiritual capacity, either.

"But if people are really serious about working together for the Truth, they have to hold up mirrors for each other. They have to stick their finger in their friend's face and say, 'Look, here's what you're doing wrong, this is what's hanging you up.' Because that person can't see it from where he's sitting — he's *in* it. The eye cannot see itself. This system is based on confrontation, not reinforcement. If I am to inspire anybody it will have to be because of the way I live my life."

The Intensive created an altered reality for me, one in which I sensed my clock could begin to run again, if I so chose. Fasting cleared out the physical, and perhaps even some of the metaphysical, poisons that had been plaguing me. The exercise and prolonged meditation gave me a sense of physical and even psychic power.

In his book, *Psychology of the Observer*, Rose outlines a system for climbing the various levels of the mind, or what he calls "Jacob's Ladder." When I'd read the book before it was just words. Now, with time and renewed energy I was actually able to see my thoughts, and to observe them as foreign entities separate from myself. Gradually I became conscious of this "observer" of my thoughts, and grew curious about who or what was observing them.

At odd times I would get insights into my behavior and persona so clear and true that they frightened me. When my two weeks was up I felt like I was just settling into the valuable part of the Intensive, and I left with the feeling that I should have tried harder to clear my schedule for the full month.

Once back in the office it was impossible to hang on to the fragile state of mind the Intensive had induced. The demands of the practice threatened to consume the small quantum of energy I had managed to bring back with me, and I found myself wishing I was chopping wood in the snow with Rose. I felt I needed him to administer some kind of jolt to me to keep me from sliding back into my old self, and I anxiously counted the days until he would return from the farm.

When he did, it was clear that the Intensive had exacted a heavy price from him. He looked drawn and pale, and he seemed to shuffle more than walk as he moved around the kitchen. I wondered if any of the "statues" at the farm had benefited from his loss of energy. I kept out of his way while he attended to his backlog of mail and paperwork, and waited for him to regain his strength and vitality.

A few days later I finally caught him alone in the kitchen. It was late evening. He seemed in good spirits and although we'd run into each other a few times in the past couple of days he greeted me like a long lost acquaintance. After a little small talk, I brought up the subject of the Intensive.

"How'd it go after I left?" I asked.

"Well, was you there when Nick had his experience?"

"No," I said, expectantly. "What happened?"

Rose put the kettle on the stove. "Nick picked up on my head one night and got a glimpse. It was genuine, but he didn't go too far. Put him into a tail spin, though. I ain't sure he pulled out of it before he left. He was still off the deep end."

Rose went on to describe Nick's experience, and how he acted afterwards. One night he had taken Rose's hunting cap and worn it for an evening, evidently putting himself in line as Rose's true successor.

"Hell, I ain't dead yet," Rose said with a chuckle. "Then a couple days later he and Phil ran in the snow with nothing on but their undershorts."

"They did *what*?"

"It got real cold up there, below zero. I was talking to the boys about *tumo* — the inner heat a man can generate that protects him from any cold. The Tibetans know this. There's some of them can run naked for hundreds of miles in the dead of winter.

"Anyway, I wasn't around at the time, but I guess Nick and Phil just cooked up this notion they'd give it a try. They stripped down and run from the house to the Chautauqua building and back. Phil come out of it okay, but Nick got frostbit toes and we had to take him to the hospital."

"Is he okay?"

"He's all right. No amputations. They kept him in the hospital three days, then he came back out to the farm for the last of the Intensive."

We talked for the rest of the evening about the Intensive and what had transpired there, then went to bed. Later that night I was awakened by the ringing of the telephone. I looked at my clock. Two-thirty. It took me a moment to force myself out of my warm bed into the freezing house. As I got to the door of the bedroom I heard Rose pick up the phone.

"Hello." It was the same neutral greeting Rose always answered with. No trace of concern over why someone would be calling in the middle of the night. No anger at being summoned into a frigid hallway. No impatience to return to a warm bed. Just "hello." I waited by the door to see if it might be for me.

After a long pause Rose said, "Where you at?"

For the next minute or so I heard only the "hmms" and "uh-huhs" someone makes while listening. Whoever it was evidently wasn't looking for me, so I gratefully climbed back into bed. Since the door to my room was left open in winter to catch what little heat made it upstairs from the wood stove, I could hear Rose as he spoke.

"I know, Nick. That's the way I felt in Seattle. I thought I'd gone insane."

Long pause.

"Yes, that's what happens. You're getting a glimpse of the mind from above. You're seeing that it doesn't exist, not as an individual unit. Right. Right. It's a contact point with another dimension. That's all it is. It isn't you. The human mind is just a matrix, a port where the larger Mind dimensions can anchor."

In the silences between Rose's comments I listened to the house creak.

"I know, I know. Right about now you wish you could stop what's going on and return to illusory life. When you walk up to the edge you think your head's coming apart. You get frightened."

Long silence.

"Yes. Yes, I know. But that's necessary. That total lonesomeness is what takes you away from all your contact with relativity. That lonesomeness comes from the realization that your essence is separated for all time from your loved ones and your attachments to the world."

Another long silence.

"Of course you're scared. You're afraid that if you let go, you'll crash into the sides of the bank and everything will fall apart. But believe me, Nick, you'll find that everything keeps moving as it should, even better than expected. Better than it would if you were still trying to control it."

Sometimes five or ten minutes passed between Rose's comments. Periodically I checked the clock. Three o'clock. Three-thirty. The hallway was freezing.

"Sure, I understand. I know that. Just try and keep yourself chemically balanced. You can handle this if you don't become unbalanced chemically."

A little later.

"You're becoming real. It's painful to part with what you thought was you."

Rose's remarks grew more frequent. I guessed that Nick was settling down on the other end. Rose's tone grew lighter, and more familiar. Finally there was laughter.

"Hell, no, I didn't cause this. I had my hands full just keeping an eye on you guys. Maybe something I said at the Intensive got your wheels turning, but whatever's happening is taking its own course, and that's the way it has to be."

After a short pause Rose laughed.

"Right, that's my function. I have to keep everybody on their toes. Zen is a system of shocks. But a teacher can't lay out in advance how he's going to do that. You can't tell somebody in advance that you're going to shock them. Otherwise they'll prepare for it and ruin the effect."

I heard Rose giggling and chuckling. I knew the crisis had passed.

"Well, as long as Tim's there with you, he'll keep you from doing anything really dangerous. Tell him to call me back if you try to join the Army or get married. Sure. No problem. We'll see you. Bye."

When I went down to the kitchen the next morning, Rose was sitting at the table. He wasn't watching the news or cooking breakfast or filling a book order, or any of his other morning activities. He was just sitting at the table in the darkness. I felt like I was interrupting when I came through the door.

We exchanged good mornings and he sat in silence while I fixed myself some toast. I checked the clock to see how much time I had before leaving for court.

Rose cleared his throat. His chest was congested, and he coughed a few times. "I feel like hell this morning," he said. His voice was low and weak.

"You have to start unplugging that phone after midnight."

"Nick was really shook up last night. He thought his head was coming apart."

"It frightened me just listening to you talk."

Rose turned towards me. "He got a glimpse. It scared the hell out of him."

He stayed quiet for a few moments, watching me butter my toast, then continued.

"This is what happens when you start backing away from what's unreal. When you start out, it's a wide path. There's all sorts of garbage you can get rid of. As you go on, the path gets ever narrower and the things you have to let go of are very precious to you. Finally there's no escape. You go through the funnel and that's all there is to it."

The image of a funnel terrified me. Like Rose said last night on the phone, it meant the end of everything I loved, especially myself, and there was no going back.

"Nick is scared and confused right now. It's pretty traumatic when you wake up and realize you've been living your life as a shadow in a stranger's nightmare. For awhile you're suspended over an abyss—not here, but not anywhere else either.

"That's why you can't just *transmit* to people. Most of the time out there at the Intensive the guys just stood around waiting for me to zap 'em, and save 'em the bother of having to work. Sure, I'm always looking for people on the brink that I can push. But even if the conditions were right and I found the right opening in their heads, I'm not sure I'd be doing them any favors. The difference between a breakdown and a breakthrough is the momentum you carry with you into the Experience. And that's something nobody but the individual can provide. I can't provide it for 'em."

A familiar intensity crept into his voice, a blend of resignation and impatience.

"I've always told you people, don't wait around for me to do this for you. Otherwise you'll look up after ten years and wonder where the hell they went and what you did with them. For a lot of the guys in the group ten years have passed already without them doing anything on the path. Then they put down their games for a month to take a vacation out at the farm and expect me to wave a wand and give them ten years worth of spiritual goodies. None of you are fighting for this. Nobody's knocking on the door. And even if they do, they run away when I answer it."

He began coughing again, then stood up and got himself a glass of water. After drinking it he remained at the sink. When he spoke again it was in softer tones.

"You know, when I was a kid, I used to hear about this great Shakespearean actor over in England who was famous for playing Shylock. I think his name was Peter Benson. I guess he could really play the part. Only trouble was he got so wrapped up in the performance that when the curtain went down he couldn't get out of the character. So after every performance a couple of stage hands would have to walk him through the streets of London, repeating over and over, "You're not Shylock, you're Peter Benson. You're not Shylock, you're Peter Benson." Rose looked up and caught my eye.

"That's all my job is in this place," he said. "I'm just a stagehand walking alongside a few people, saying, 'Hey, you're not that egotistical blob of flesh you think you are. You're *God*.'"

Chapter Twenty

Isolation

The winter Intensive and its aftermath left me with a confusing mix of thoughts and a compelling desire to make a change in my life. I had come to a crossroads. I became acutely aware of my own mortality—and Rose's—and felt the need to do something to get me back on the spiritual track before it was too late. But the same sense of mortality made the idea of living a "normal" life—whatever that is—more attractive, and I found myself wondering what it would be like to just drop everything and start over. The sense of wonder—the magic—that first drew me to Rose had vanished, and in its absence two seemingly conflicting desires had taken its place. I felt I had to make a decision. I had to either make a sincere spiritual effort for once in my life, or give it up and seek happiness as an ordinary man.

But even as I thought things through during those weeks, there was never any doubt which drive was the strongest. I'd been searching too long to give it up. And yet at the same time I realized how weak and half-hearted my spiritual efforts had been. I had pursued very little on my own. All I'd really ever done was put myself in proximity to Rose and hope he'd do it for me.

One thing was for sure, however. The more I thought about it, the more certain I was that I had become too entangled in my career, too identified with my role as a lawyer. Instead of a seeker who had started a law practice as the next step on the spiritual path, I had *become* a lawyer, a lawyer who used his profession as an excuse to keep from taking any more spiritual steps. In those weeks after the Intensive this became the focus of my thoughts, and in the end, I decided to take a sabbatical from the law practice.

I brought up the subject with my partners, Lou and Jon, and we discussed an arrangement where each of us could take a year's sabbatical. The more we discussed it the more I felt that a year away from the office could be my salvation. I let the idea percolate for a few days then decided to talk to Rose about it.

The kitchen was empty when I got home that evening but I could hear Rose moving about in his bedroom as I passed through the hall. I went upstairs, quickly changed clothes, and returned to the kitchen. Rose was just sitting down to read the Wheeling newspaper.

We exchanged greetings then he began looking around for his glasses. I decided to get right to the point before he got too far into the paper.

"You know, Mister Rose, I've been thinking a lot about how to get my head back into The Work."

He looked me over briefly. "I applaud the effort," he said, then patted some papers on the table and got lucky — his glasses were under one of them. He put them on and began reading the obituaries. I waited for him to finish before going on.

"I think I'm going to take a year off from the practice. We've been talking about it at the office, and I think it's what I need to get back on track."

As I spoke he turned to the supermarket ads and began checking prices. After a minute or so he looked up again. "Everybody's soaking the working man," he said. "It's open season on the little guy." Then he put the newspaper down and took off his glasses.

"A year off, huh?" he said, looking off to another part of the room. "I don't know. A person has to do whatever he thinks is right. But I wouldn't advise running away from your responsibilities."

"It wouldn't be running away, Mister Rose. My partners will keep the practice going, and I'll be back in a year. I really think I've forgotten what I came here for. I'm just a money machine. I want to get back in touch with some higher purpose before it's too late."

Rose glanced over at me briefly then looked away again. "Well, I don't pretend to know people's destinies. Maybe a new career will do you some good."

"It's not a new career, Mister Rose. I just need some time off. I want to make a real effort on the path. I want to—"

"Sometimes it's not so much *what* you do, that's important. But whether or not you know *why* you're doing it."

"I *know* why. I've been thinking about it for weeks."

"That doesn't mean you know anything," he said.

"I just really think this is what I need right now."

Rose smiled. "Well, things have a way of working out. That much is true." I let it drop. It was like we were having separate conversations. I told myself that his reaction was merely the result of my failure to communicate my intentions properly, not that my intentions were flawed and he saw through them. I felt sure that once he saw my sincerity he would understand and support my effort.

The next day I worked out the details of a revolving sabbatical with Lou and Jon. Each of us would get a year off after seven years in the practice. I had six years in, and would spend the next year disengaging myself from the caseload before I left. We were all very enthusiastic. It wouldn't be much fun for the two lawyers left behind, but the opportunity for a year off made it worth the price.

Once we made the decision to go ahead with sabbaticals things seemed to fall into place. We hired a fourth lawyer to help Lou and Jon while I was gone. Several of my most troublesome cases were suddenly resolved out of court. And after two years of looking for a bigger office, a perfect place suddenly fell into our laps at a great price. I interpreted these things as signs that I had made the right decision. The only problem was I had no idea what to do with my year off. I wanted to do work for the group, but I didn't know what to do or where to begin.

I had discussed my problem with Rose several times, or at least tried to. In the past he had always chided people in the group for not doing enough, for not being willing to take on a group project. But now that I had committed myself to a year off to do group work he seemed unenthusiastic about working with me, or even suggesting things I could do on my own.

Over the years I'd heard him itemize countless ways to expand the group— some practical, others requiring a bit more faith. The ones that appealed to me most, of course, were those in which I could picture myself on the road with Rose, working shoulder to shoulder, putting on lectures or Chautauquas. I even presented him with a few formal proposals of this type, but each time he became uncharacteristically subdued, and if I pushed it, downright negative. I was slow to admit it, but it became obvious that Rose did not want to tie his future to mine. I stopped making proposals.

A month or so later as we drove back to Benwood from the July TAT meeting he made it official, telling me I should go ahead and plan for my year off without him. I told him I already had. I told him I wanted to do something for the group, and joked that if I wasn't going to be someone he could push over the brink into the Absolute, then maybe I could at least bring him some other candidates. What I didn't say, but felt, was that I had a deep need to prove myself to him. I wanted him to praise me, to respect me. I wanted him to like me.

Wrapping up my involvement in the practice turned out to be almost as much work as starting it. I pushed all my cases as far along as I could, and those that couldn't be wrapped up before the end of the year had to be explained to one of my partners. I was under a lot of pressure at work and trying to figure out what to do with my year off at the same time was too much for me to handle. I put off any serious planning until January when I was going out to the farm for a month of isolation in my cabin. Surely then, in the quiet of the woods, I would come up with something.

But procrastination and indecision did not sit well with Rose. When he asked about my plans I'd try to float a half-baked idea by him, but it never worked. He'd immediately criticize my sloppy thinking and launch into stories of other group members who had "charged out half-cocked" and ended up doing the group more harm than good.

"I'd rather have nothing done than give people the wrong impression," he reminded me one night.

His attitude depressed me and increased the pressure I was feeling, making it even more difficult to think clearly about my plans. As usual, when I was having difficulties with Rose, my solution was to leave the house earlier and come home later, hoping to avoid him as much as possible. Someone in the group once joked that this was the standard path for a Rose student. First you make a commitment to work with him, then you start hiding from him.

During this time I did come home early a few evenings, and one of them turned into a real barn-burner of confrontation. It started routinely, with Rose complaining about someone clogging up the sink with food scraps again. But it took off from there, as he then launched into a strident litany of offenses that blew right through the eleven o'clock news.

He didn't mention anyone by name. He didn't need to. When he talked about the hundreds of books he was stuck with because the book salesmen had failed to keep their commitments, Craig's vacuous smile disappeared. When he spoke of the people who had grown weary of the search and were now projecting all their spiritual ambitions on a hunk of protoplasm of the opposite sex, Al's round face turned red. Rose's diatribe against women whose biological clocks launched them out the door once a month to find someone to father their babies made Carrie cry. And when he listed all the projects others had started and he had to finish, including the Chautauquas, I tried to assume my stone-faced courtroom demeanor, but my temples were pounding.

Maybe he was tired and overworked. Maybe we were just hopeless morons. Maybe he was fulfilling his role as teacher, lighting a fire under each of us to shake us out of our lethargy. Maybe all of the above. Rose was both a difficult personality and an enlightened spiritual teacher—and he didn't hold up a sign telling you which one happened to be speaking at that moment. His power lay in his unpredictability, and you discarded anything he said at your own spiritual, or at the very least, psychological risk.

His final comments that night were the most painful.

"I don't mind dying for you people," he said quietly. "I just don't want to put up with too much deception."

That night in bed I thought of death. For Rose, death was the bottom line of every action. His comment that evening about dying for us was made casually, and yet anyone who knew Richard Rose knew that he meant exactly that—that he was willing to die at any moment for someone else as long as it was in accordance with his sense of purpose, or "excuse for living," as he often called it.

As a young man Rose's obsession was to know with certainty where he would go after death, and his philosophy is geared to allowing others to answer that question for themselves. In Rose's eyes, the whole premise for spiritual work rests on this point: you are going to die, you don't know what happens next, and your actions in life will likely determine your status after death.

As I lay there that night words I'd heard from Rose over the years passed through my thoughts with full sound and inflection, as if he were speaking into my ear.

"If I thought everyone went to the same place, there'd be no point in me talking."

"Man isn't born with a soul, he has to create one."

"You're not going to go anywhere that you haven't been vaccinated for beforehand."

The next morning I got up early and dressed quickly. I hoped to get out of the house before Rose woke up. I tiptoed down the stairs and was relieved to see the hallway quiet and dark. Rose was probably fatigued from his expenditure of energy the night before, and I figured he had slept in. I walked softly past his bedroom and slowly opened the creaky door to the kitchen. There was Rose, barely visible in the dimness, leaning against the sink.

The gray light from the kitchen window did not reach his corner of the room. His "Good morning" came out of the shadows, in the hoarse voice that hung with him each morning until he was able to loosen the chronic bronchitis in his chest. As my eyes grew accustomed to the darkness I could see a softened, almost smiling expression on his round face.

"Good morning," I said, leaning against the stove. A quiet tranquility filled the room and I no longer felt in a hurry to go anywhere.

"I've been thinking about your vacation," he said.

"Sabbatical," I corrected.

"If you don't know what you're doing—if you don't have a vector—nature provides one for you. And it may not be in your best interest."

"I'm working on my plans," I said.

"My father used to say that the darker the black paint on the back of the mirror, the brighter the mirror's reflection." He paused to let the image sink in.

"That's the way it is with people in the group. A person conserves his energy for awhile, keeps himself clean and tries to rise a step above the manure pile. He builds up a quantum. But what happens? The king falls off of his throne. He meets a woman who's like the black paint on the mirror. He projects all his desires on this woman, who is doing nothing more than just reflecting back what the man wants to see."

"Mister Rose, I'm not heading out to find a woman. I just want to do some work for the group."

Rose smiled. "I was in the seminary for five years. Left when I was seventeen. That's when my real education began. Not long after, I tried to commit suicide. Hell, I *did* commit suicide, but I pulled out of it."

I sat down at the table.

"It was over a girl. She was a beautiful little thing with the sweetest smile and most beautiful voice I'd ever heard. I thought she was an angel. I wrote her poetry and treated her like fine china. I found out later she was the town whore. Everybody in Benwood had taken a crack at her but me. And when I discovered what a fool I'd been—projecting virtue and innocence and God knows what else onto her—it threw me into complete despair. I figured that if I could be so completely off base about something as basic as human nature, then what chance did I have of finding out anything about the really important things in life?

"To me, the thought of spending my whole life in ignorance was intolerable. I didn't want to live if I was going to be snowed by one thing after another, without any chance of ever knowing the real score. And since I was a Catholic and knew I was going to heaven, I figured the best thing to do was to get the hell out of here and move on to some place a little less abominable. I knew where my parents kept the rat poison, so I got it and drank it—the whole bottle."

He paused a moment to take a sip of tea.

"Strychnine's a rough way to go, believe me. The convulsions jerked my feet to the back of my head. And my teeth were locked tight—I'd have gnawed the doctor's fingers off if he'd tried to pull my jaws apart. That's where my mother took me, to this old doctor's office down the street. When the doctor saw how much I drank he said, 'Son, you've done a damn good job of it.'" Rose drawled the words out slowly, just as the doctor might have done.

"I heard him tell my mother I'd taken enough poison to kill ten men. At this point my sight was gone. Hearing was the only sense I had left, so I was just laying there waiting for the bugles to blow and the angels to come and carry me off to heaven. That's the way it's supposed to happen in the perfect religion of the most perfect person in the world—my mother.

"I kept waiting, but no one came. The convulsions are banging me up and down on the doctor's steel table and my teeth are grinding like sandpaper. There's no angels, no chariots. I'm just dying hard. And then I had a vision."

He turned his head to look right at me.

"I'm not talking about some fuzzy, dream-like vision. No, I saw everything very clearly, as clearly as I can see you right now. And what I saw was me, Richard Rose at seventeen, dead, laid out in a casket under ground. I was looking straight at him, as if someone had cut through the earth and the side of the coffin, to give me a cross-section view of the whole scene.

"And while I'm lying there on the doctor's table, somehow at the same time I'm also watching myself in the grave. And time is still passing on both fronts, because the next thing that happens in the vision is that Richard Rose in the coffin starts to rot.

"Since I'm seeing myself from the side, what's closest is my right arm."

Rose reached over with his left hand, grabbed his right shoulder, and slowly moved his hand down the length of his arm. "And that arm just rotted and withered away, right before my eyes."

"What did you do?"

"I did what I had to. I fought my way back. The reason I took the poison was that I didn't want to go on living in ignorance. But the vision made it clear that I couldn't expect to learn anything in death. Like Christ said, 'The dead know nothing.' So I figured I'd better get to work and find some answers while I was still alive."

He finished his tea in a long drink then put the cup in the sink and stared straight at me again.

"If a person can't take the tension and wants to throw in the towel on the search, I certainly won't stand in his way. But be careful. If you're going to surrender to illusion, at least make it an attractive illusion."

"Mister Rose," I said, somewhat exasperated, "I have no intention of surrendering to an illusion of any kind."

He softened a little. "No one ever *intends* to," he said.

Rose was clearly concerned about what I had in mind for my sabbatical, and because I had no plans he apparently assumed I was headed out to find a woman—any woman. It was true that I sometimes daydreamed about what a "normal" life would be like, but I fully intended—at least consciously—to use my year off to do group work and nothing else.

But as the end of the year approached I still did not know what I was going to do with my time. Rose brought the subject up frequently and all I could do was tell him that I was going to figure it out during my month of isolation in January. As the pressure built I looked forward to that isolation as if it were the magical cure for all my problems.

On Christmas day Rose hosted a big dinner out at the farm, as was his custom. On these occasions he laid aside all vestiges of his teacher persona and became the consummate host. We were honored guests at his table and all else was forgotten. That year, when the evening came to an end I drove him back into town. In the car he became the teacher again and immediately resumed taking me to task for my lack of planning for the upcoming year. In the wake of such an enjoyable day I was caught completely off guard.

I had recently been toying with the idea of writing his biography, even though I'd never written anything more than a letter in my life. In desperation I tossed this idea out to him. He immediately dismissed it, telling me flatly that I wasn't capable of it, and that any attempts to do so would be a complete waste of time. I sulked for the rest of the ride and prayed that during my upcoming isolation I would somehow come up with an idea that pleased both him and me.

On December thirty-first they had a little going away party for me at the office, then I stopped off in Benwood to pick up my things before heading out to the farm to begin my isolation. Rose was getting ready for the New Years Eve party he always threw at the farm, which over the years had grown into a sort of informal TAT meeting. The kitchen table was covered with food he was going to take out there.

"Coming to the party tonight?" he said.

"No, I'm starting isolation right away."

"Oh, yeah. Have you come up with any plans for your vacation yet?

My jaw tightened. "No, but I've got a few ideas I hope to refine while I'm out there."

He pulled out a chair and sat down at the table. "You know, I was thinking about your vacation the other day and I might have an idea for you."

I grabbed a chair. He began explaining his proposal and I nodded my head in disbelief. It was the plan of my dreams: Mister Rose and me, side by side, traveling the country, putting on lectures and hypnosis demonstrations.

"Why don't you give it some thought while you're loafing out there and see if you can come up with something." I promised I would, and left Benwood a confused, but very happy man.

I spent New Year's Eve joyfully hauling supplies out to my cabin. Each time I returned to my car for more gear I could hear Rose and thirty of his closest friends and students laughing as they drank wine, played euchre, and talked philosophy in the farmhouse. Even though it was cold and the mud sucked at my boots with every step, I wouldn't have traded places with anyone in the house. I had a whole month ahead to work up a plan based on Rose's ideas, and the rest of the year to carry it out with him.

It was difficult settling into the solitude at first. My body and mind were still whirling at the pace of the outside world. But after a few days I found some measure of peace in my cabin. Gradually, I lost interest in the Steelers and the stock market, and settled into a comfortable routine of meditation, exercise, and writing my "proposal" to Rose.

I worked with one of Rose's common complaints in mind: that everyone in the group viewed ladder work as a hobby, volunteer work performed in your spare time.

"If you want to succeed on the ladder, you have to work like it was your livelihood and you had ten starving kids to feed at home," he advised us.

I was determined that my proposal would not fall into the hobby category. I put together budgets, timetables, publicity packages, even charted out an itinerary on a map. When I was satisfied that I'd come up with a venture that would dwarf even the

Chautauquas, I placed my book-size proposal into a large brown envelope and deposited it in the farmhouse mailbox, addressed to Rose. That done, I began to settle into the quiet isolation I'd come for.

Several others were also squirreled away in their cabins, and though we were each alone, I felt joined to them somehow in our mutual solitary efforts. Occasionally we'd pass in the woods, sometimes pretending not to see each other, other times breaking out in laughter.

A bulletin board and calendar had been placed by the bunkhouse. Each day we signed in to let the others know we were okay. The board also served as a message center, and every morning I checked for some word from Rose about my proposal. After a week of not hearing from him I concluded he must be waiting for my return so that we could fine tune the plan in person. Then one snowy morning I saw a folded piece of paper tacked to the message board with my name written on it in an unmistakable hand.

Somehow I knew it was trouble. An overpowering uneasiness hit me and I actually felt sick to my stomach. I put the note in my pocket without reading it and went back to my cabin. There, alone at my desk, I unfolded the paper as if it contained my obituary. It was written in large, almost angry, block letters. Blood pounded in my ears as I read:

GOT YOUR NOTE. DON'T EXPECT ME TO ADJUST MY DIRECTION SIMPLY BECAUSE YOU HAD NO IDEA WHAT YOU WERE GOING TO DO ONCE YOU TOOK THE YEAR OFF. YOU TREAT <u>THE WORK</u> LIKE YOU DO YOUR CASES. BUT THE TRUTH CANNOT BE CAPTURED WITH A FLICK OF THE WRIST. IF YOU WISH TO PLAY GAMES WITH YOUR LIFE, NO ONE HERE WILL TRY TO STOP YOU. BUT DO NOT TIE UP THE VECTORS OF THOSE WHO ARE <u>SERIOUS</u>. WE ARE TALKING ABOUT MAN'S QUEST TO <u>BECOME A SOUL</u>.

R.

Everything I thought I'd accumulated in preparation for the sabbatical—the sense of power, the peace of mind, the detached optimism—all disappeared in a flash. I was devastated. How could he do this to me? Didn't he realize the effect this letter would have on someone shut away in a cabin? Hadn't I had taken the year off to do *his* work? Wasn't it his idea that we go out on the road together?

An angry debate raged in my head for days afterwards, but it was frustrating and futile. There was no one to argue with. And even if there was, and even if I won—if I was somehow proven right, and

Rose proven wrong—what good would it do? The situation would not change. No matter how I looked at it an empty year still lay ahead, with nothing to do and no one to do it with. The days and nights grew endlessly unpleasant. There was no running away, physically or mentally. I re-read Rose's letter dozens of times, trying unsuccessfully to see where I had gone so wrong.

I needed help. Years before I'd bought a copy of the *I Ching*, just a few days after Rose's copy had comforted me with words about "a strong and good friend." Now, I turned to it again. I tossed the coins, then looked up the corresponding hexagram.

The image was "Fire on the Mountain," and the judgment, "The Wanderer." The commentary spoke of a fire that has burned up all the grass on a mountain, and must either jump to another mountain or burn itself out. In material life, it was explained, an individual who achieves all he can in a particular field stagnates if he refuses to move on.

I closed the book and looked out the window at the icy woods. If the *I Ching* was advising the bird to leave the nest, I figured it might as well fly south for the winter. I decided to go to Florida because I had friends there and I liked the beach.

But there was still the problem of what to do. I had to think of some way to make my trip relevant to the group. What could I do? Start a group? Give lectures? I remembered that I'd occasionally receive circulars advertising stress management programs in my office mail. It occurred to me I might be in a position to do something like that myself. I had been teaching yoga off and on at the Wheeling YMCA for a couple years, and I could certainly adapt some of Rose's philosophy to that theme. I became excited again and threw myself into the task of putting together a stress management program I could offer in Florida. By the end of the month I had what I thought was a viable plan.

I returned to Benwood with apprehension. I worried that Rose might jump on me about my proposal again, or worse, criticize my new idea. But when I opened the kitchen door and saw him at the table all I felt was the familiar warmth of his presence. He was typing on his ancient iron Underwood and wearing a rather silly-looking hat with ear flaps.

At the sound of the door he looked up and smiled at my disheveled appearance. "Better shave that beard before you go to court or they'll hang you for a rabbi."

"Luckily I'm not going back to court." It was the first time I heard my voice in a month. It sounded like someone else's.

"Oh yeah, that's right, you're taking some time off."

I wondered if he really could have forgotten my plans, considering the note he'd sent me a couple weeks before. No matter, though. We talked like old friends. He brought me up to date on all I'd missed, and I told him about my experiences in the woods. The evening passed without mention of his letter or my new plans, which was fine with me.

The next morning we got down to business. I thanked him for his letter, and acknowledged that I needed tough medicine to finally get serious about the year ahead.

"In spiritual matters, sometimes you have to attack people to help them," he said. Then he asked me about my plans. He nodded when I mentioned Florida, and of trying to get on with a college in some sort of teaching capacity. He was not as receptive to my subject matter.

"I don't think 'stress' is going to attract the kind of people you're looking for. You're better off talking about 'success.'"

I wasn't about to start all over again, and when he saw that I was set on my approach, he let the matter drop.

I spent the next two weeks preparing for the trip, digging up the latest research on stress at the library, putting together a brochure, lining up a place to stay in Florida. When it looked as if I was as prepared as I was going to get, I packed up my car, made a few last minute phone calls, and went to bed with plans to leave at sunrise. The next morning Rose was waiting for me when I came down to the kitchen.

"Headin' out, are you?" he asked in a friendly West Virginia drawl.

"Yeah, I wanted to get an early start."

"Which way you taking?"

I started to verbally describe my route. Rose took a map from the shelf and spread it on the table. He studied with interest the route I had planned, then compared it to the one he'd taken twenty-five years ago in a borrowed Cadillac. I listened to his story of the trip and we laughed. That led to a few more stories, some old, some new, until finally he said, "Hell, I better let you go."

We walked over towards the door together.

"You know, it's good for you to leave," he said. "You get so close to people sometimes you forget who they are."

I fumbled nervously with the things I was carrying. "Thanks for all your help," I said.

He extended his hand to me for only the second time since I'd known him. The other was when I'd first entered his kitchen a decade before.

"I wish I could do more," he said.

Chapter Twenty-One

Seduction

About two o'clock the following morning I finally arrived at my destination, Florida's "Gold Coast." Eighteen hours alone on the road with my thoughts had already taken it's toll on the image of holy crusader I so desperately wanted to believe in. Now, the expensive oceanfront high-rises that lined the waterfront had an undeniable appeal that made me question even more what my real motives were in coming. Instead of the ascetic "Wanderer" in the *I Ching* that I romantically fashioned myself to be, perhaps I was just another starry-eyed snowbird fleeing to Florida, hoping to find a new, and happier, life.

Ernie, an old friend of the family, had arranged for me to stay with his parents in Boca Raton until I could find a place of my own. Because of the hour I stayed in a small motel that night, then called his parents the next morning. They turned out to be a very pleasant and friendly couple who remembered more about my family, especially my father, than I did. They seemed pleased to have me as a house guest and equally pleased a few days later when I rented an apartment in Pompano Beach.

My immediate plans were to find an entre into the stress management field in the area, then use that stage to find people who might be interested in more esoteric matters. I hoped to form a group of serious spiritual seekers, then, when the group was big enough, invite Rose down to speak and work with them. I even had dreams that he might want to spend his winters here—away from the cold that inflamed his bronchitis—and that we could work side by side on my turf, with the people I had assembled.

Ernie's father had clipped out some newspaper articles for me about stress programs in the area. My first call was to a hospital administrator who'd received a very favorable write-up about a program she was running at a local hospital. Despite my careful rehearsing, she clearly was not impressed.

"What credentials do you have to teach 'stress?' If you were so successful as a lawyer, why did you leave? Are you still in good standing with the bar?"

I chose another name out of the articles and called him, receiving similar questions and the same results.

"I'll be tied up for the next few weeks," he said curtly. "If you're still in the area next month, give me a call."

After a week of working the phones and cold-calling on colleges, businesses, and community centers, I still hadn't made any progress. South Florida was a haven for misfits and con-men, and nobody believed that a lawyer would abandon his practice—even for a year—unless he was on the run from the police or the ethics committee.

Finally, after two weeks I got a break. I stopped in at Florida Atlantic University and made my usual rounds. After being shuffled from one department to another I ended up in the office of the Assistant Dean of Continuing Education, who passed me off to their Center for Management and Professional Development. The Center's director misinterpreted the dean's hand-off as a recommendation, and the next day I was hired to teach a course in stress management.

After that things went more smoothly. With the credibility of the university behind me, I was able to get myself some speaking engagements, mostly at professional association luncheons—doctors, lawyers, dentists, architects, anybody who needed somebody to talk for free while they digested their meals. After each talk I was approached by one or two people who sensed a deeper message behind my public talk. Later, over lunch or at their office, I'd tell them about my plans to form a group. Some people from my university classes also expressed interest in forming a group, and within a month or so six of us were holding weekly meetings at the home of one of my students.

Jubilant, I reported in to Rose. He was cautious.

"Somewhere along the line you'll have to make a shift," he said. "That is, if you want to attract serious people. These burned-out professionals aren't interested in changing their lives. They just want to get up one last head of steam so they can make a final assault on fleecing the public."

I explained my opinions to the contrary. Stress management was opening doors for me, and I was convinced that people with ears to hear were getting the deeper message. Rose listened quietly for awhile, then when I ran out of steam he spoke again.

"If someone is serious about this work they have to be ready to give up whatever stands in the way of their search. If that means leaving the wife, burning down the business, sinking the boat, and giving the golf clubs to Goodwill, then they've got to do it and never look back. But people who've already put twenty years into a specific direction aren't just going to walk away simply because you tell them to. You need to catch people before they have everything invested in a certain way of life. Talk to young people. Talk to them about success. That's what they're interested in. They haven't got it yet, and they're not even sure what it means. Define success for them in spiritual terms. They're the ones who might be able to make the shift."

I persisted with my own views and when it became clear we weren't going to reach an agreement, he dropped it.

"Well it sounds like it's going the way you want it to," he said. "Maybe things will work out for you."

For awhile they did. Things worked out very well. Shortly after that phone call a man approached me at one of my luncheon talks and asked if I'd come speak at his health club, the Palm-Aire, which I knew to be a very exclusive spa. I eagerly accepted and it turned into a regular spot. Every Monday night I presented my thoughts on stress management to a gathering of millionaires, politicians, and professionals, many of whom seemed eager to help me get even wider exposure. Through them I picked up some consulting work, which generated a little income and gave me hope that the whole venture might actually succeed.

I did not go back to West Virginia for the July TAT meeting. It was the first TAT meeting I'd missed in ten years, but I felt I couldn't leave the commitments I'd generated for myself. I felt uneasy about not going, but I had to admit that secretly I did not want to go back anyway. I was feeling good about charting my own course in Florida and I worried what a weekend at the farm with Rose would do to my mood and resolve.

But a short time later West Virginia came to me in the form of Chuck Carter, the man who'd built my cabin. I'd bought a new car a few weeks after I arrived in Florida and called Chuck to offer him a chance to buy my pickup. Chuck had often borrowed it at the farm and said that if I ever wanted to sell it to let him know. We agreed on a price over the phone and he said he'd fly down as soon as he could get free.

Chuck was a "hundred percent-er," as Rose called him, which was the highest compliment he could pay. Chuck had moved to the farm in 1975 and seemed prepared to spend the rest of his life living in poverty and simplicity, maintaining the ashram and carrying on with the work. At the farm his single-minded intensity had always intimidated me, and I looked forward now to spending some time with him on my turf, in my new life.

I waited for him inside the terminal, my enthusiasm holding strong even through the hour and a half delay of his flight. I thought of the different restaurants where we could catch a late dinner and maybe run into somebody important that I knew.

But the dream world in which I was living and with which I had planned to impress Chuck vanished as soon as he walked through the gate. His presence personified everything I remembered from the farm, and everything I was not. His body showed the hardiness and fatigue of long hours of physical labor. His face reflected the frustration and determination that comes from boxing endlessly with the shadows of the mind. He was a man living under tension, the kind of tension I knew was necessary if one was to successfully court Enlightenment. I swallowed my guilt as we walked out to the car, and buried my tan, un-callused hands deep within my pockets.

Chuck's presence disoriented me. It was as if I'd been split in half and had two separate states of mind in the same head. Whether out of fatigue or discomfort he said little in the car, and for the most part we rode in silence to my condominium. It wasn't until later that evening, sitting on my balcony, twenty-six stories above the ocean, that the conversation began to flow.

"That's beautiful," he said, staring at the moonlit surf.

"I never get tired of it." I leaned back in the chair, my feet braced against the railing. "Before I knew anybody here, I used to spend whole evenings walking up and down the beach," I said. "Then I'd look up into the windows of some of the beachfront condos and see people sitting in front of TV. I couldn't believe they were watching anything but the water."

We listened a few minutes to the waves below.

"The farm seems a million miles away," Chuck said.

"So what am I missing up there?"

"Work. Lots of it. Mister Rose has a hundred things he wants to get done this summer. As soon as we finish one project, it's on to something else"

"So how's he been?"

"Oh, the same, as always. He's trying to do too much, and he gets irritated when he doesn't get any support. He says everybody on the farm is hiding from him so he can't put them to work. Says we're just putting in time waiting for him to zap us. He says nobody's changing. Same old stuff."

"Does he say anything about me?" It was a dangerous question. I knew Chuck would speak the truth regardless of my feelings.

"He says you're on a giant ego trip, and that this whole Florida thing is just an excuse for you to try and make a big splash. He says you want your name in lights and a girlfriend to impress."

"I don't have a girlfriend," I said indignantly, sitting up in my chair .

Chuck kept his eyes fixed on the black horizon.

"He says you will, sooner or later."

Chuck left the next day in the pickup truck, but it was awhile before I recovered from his visit. He had brought Rose closer to me, here on the personal turf I had begun to create, and I was left with the familiar sense of irritation, frustration and uncertainty that settled on me whenever I found myself in Rose's cross-hairs.

I was reminded of the old lawyers maxim to never ask a question in court unless you were prepared to deal with whatever answer you might get. For weeks after Chuck left I paid the price for violating that rule in our conversation on the balcony. I became conscious of how strong a role ego-gratification played in everything I did, even — maybe especially — when I was trying to deal in spiritual matters.

So I tried to hold my vanity in check. But when I did I lost confidence in myself. My speaking ability deteriorated and I was out of synch interacting with others. For awhile, nobody approached me after my talks, and a couple of the group meetings were absolute duds. I began to worry, something I hadn't done since things started falling into place for me in Florida. In the end, I decided I had to forget about Rose's criticisms and move on, otherwise I was dead in the water.

The following Monday, Donna, a stylish woman with a diamond ring the size of a doorknob, approached me after a talk at the health spa. I had mentioned that I used to teach hatha yoga, and she wondered if I'd be forming a class any time soon. I'd been considering starting a yoga class as a feeder group for the philosophic meetings, and I wondered if this might be a sign that the time was right. I told her I'd been thinking about it and that I would call her if it materialized.

I asked some of the people I knew if they'd be interested and most said yes. One, a graphics designer named Lee, even volunteered his house. I called Donna and told her the first meeting would be Sunday night.

"Great," she said. "I have a friend who's also interested. I'll bring her, too."

Sunday night I sat on Lee's front porch, joking with people as they arrived for class. Surrounded by lawyers and businessmen who called me "Yogi Dave," or their "Jew-ru," looking out at the BMWs and Mercedes that filled Lee's driveway, being cooled by the fresh breeze that blew off the ocean a few hundred yards away, I felt relaxed, happy, and in my element. The almost spontaneous formation of the yoga class had removed the last doubts I had about whether I'd done right in pushing ahead instead of remaining paralyzed by Rose's comments.

I was about to start without Donna when a sleek black Porsche pulled up. Donna stepped out of the driver's side and waved in our direction. A second later the passenger door opened and a young, dark-haired woman got out. I couldn't seem to take my eyes off her as she approached. Even though I'd never seen her before she looked somehow familiar.

Her name was Nicole, and that evening I had a hard time concentrating on the class. My thoughts and eyes kept turning back to her. The following week I asked her out and it wasn't long before we started seeing each other regularly. Two months later I moved in with her. She was a good companion and a close friend, and it didn't take long for both of us to become convinced we were in love.

For awhile my life seemed complete. I had done what I set out to do. I was accepted as a stress management expert and had started an esoteric group with people I'd met through that forum. I taught classes at a university, gave yoga lessons, did banquet talks. And now, with Nicole, I was experiencing what seemed like genuine love. I had everything I thought I wanted in life.

But the problems attendant to still being a part of Rose's world refused to go away. There was the feeling of hypocrisy that washed over me when I heard myself advise a celibate life, and the ring of insincerity I heard in my voice when I spoke of simplicity and inner work. I was forced to draw more and more upon the past when trying to make a point about how a philosophic life should be lived.

And then there was Rose himself. Our conversations on the phone remained cordial only so long as we talked of trivial things. As soon as I brought up anything having to do with philosophy or the group, he waded into me, often so loud that I literally had to hold the receiver at arm's length.

I pressed on even harder, determined to prove that I could still make it work. I waited for the big break, the quantum leap that would demonstrate some real progress and put me over the top, all the while fearful of the big bust Rose had predicted. Neither came. My life went on day after day, with small victories and setbacks, and no clear sign as to what I should do with my future.

I pushed on with the talks and groups with an intensity bordering on desperation. I felt I had to somehow generate a new career that would embrace both of my obsessions: happiness and spiritual work. Nicole seemed willing to go anywhere and do whatever was necessary to make it happen, and her trust and support only increased my despair at not being able to pull it off.

The months passed quickly and my year's sabbatical was nearing an end without much being accomplished that I could show to Rose as proof I'd not wasted my time. I resolved to give it one last push.

Early in the summer I had done some consulting work for Bob, the eccentric owner of a Palm Beach graphic design company. Bob had deep insights into marketing and an interest in Zen. For reasons I didn't understand but deeply appreciated, he put together a slick seminar package for me that he guaranteed would fill the seats — at a hundred bucks each.

"What you do with them once you get them through the door is your business," he grinned.

I called everyone I knew. The professionals I'd met during the last eight months may have been lousy candidates for a philosophic group but they knew how to get the word out. More than fifty people showed up for the seminar. The audience was a good blend of men and women, students and professionals, with quite a few familiar faces smiling back at me in the crowd.

For some reason I felt relaxed, confident and enthusiastic, and the morning session was a big hit. As we broke for lunch, a dozen people came to the front of the room with comments, questions, and promises to return with friends for the next seminar. I reveled in it, and began to feel that I'd finally hit on the formula. When they'd all left, I sat down, propped up my feet and opened a can of soda.

There was a tentative knock at the door. "Anyone home?" It was Donna, who had played a big role in promoting the seminar.

I stood up. "Come on in."

"I just have a minute," she said. "I have to run to the office during break."

"So, what do you think?" I said. "How's it look from where you're sitting?" I was confident her praise would be appropriately effusive.

"Great. I mean, I think I understand much better what you're trying to do down here. You have a lot of really good things to say about what's important in life and what's not."

My smile drooped slightly. She seemed hesitant about something.

"But...?"

"It's just that I overheard a group of people talking out in the hall awhile ago. About half of them were people who already know you, and the others were here for the first time."

"Yeah...?"

"Well one of the new people was really excited by what you were saying, and talking about how important it is to live the kind of life you describe."

"Sounds good so far."

"Then one of the guys who knew you said, 'Only trouble is he doesn't live that way himself.' Then everybody who knew you started laughing. I don't think they meant anything by it. It's just that..."

"Well," I said absently. The energy drained from my body so quickly I had to sit down again.

Donna looked concerned. "I'm sorry, I just thought..."

"No, it's okay," I said.

I went through the motions of the afternoon session, but it was over. I could feel in my bones and my heart that I could no longer maintain the sham life I had tried to create for myself. It no longer mattered whether I regarded Rose as my teacher, or if he still regarded me as one of his students. The truth remained the same: you become what you do.

Left to my own devices I had lived out the dreams of my youth and the result was that my life had turned into a lie. I had tried to justify a life of material ambition by wrapping it in a spiritual cloak, and it would never work. Besides, my time was up. My partners expected me back and I had created nothing in Florida that would justify my staying.

Leaving Nicole was a great agony that I had a difficult time disguising. I said I would call and write and return to visit. I said I would study for the Florida Bar and maybe set up an office there someday. I said many things. She nodded her head and said that she loved me, but she did not say she would wait.

Chapter Twenty-Two

Nostalgia

I drove the first five hundred miles in pain and sadness over the piece of myself I had left in Nicole's bungalow, and the last five hundred dreading what awaited me in West Virginia. As long as the car was moving I was able to remain fairly stable. But as soon as I stopped for gasoline or to stretch my legs I was overcome with such an overwhelming depression that I was compelled to get back on the highway just to hang on to what was left of my sanity.

The Ohio Valley was even darker and dingier than I had remembered it. I pulled into the high school parking lot across from Rose's house and turned off the ignition. A cold February wind swept through and whistled in the windows and doors. The car quickly gave up its heat, but the thought of walking into that house with this unbearable sadness and facing the man who had predicted it kept me imbedded in my seat. Maybe I could go out to my cabin for a week, I thought desperately, or bunk at the office for a couple of days until I readjusted to the surroundings.

But finally, cold and just plain fed-up, I stepped out of the car and locked the door behind me. As I slowly made my way up the steps I noticed that the white porch paint I'd helped put on was peeling, and that a new latch had been put on the gate. Otherwise, everything seemed painfully the same. I stood on the back porch in front of the door, keys in hand, debating whether I now needed to knock or if I could still walk right in. I thought of all of Benwood's unwritten rules, and wondered if I could actually adjust again to what had for so long been my life. Finally, I unlocked the door and entered Rose's kitchen yet one more time.

He stared at the unexpected intruder through dime-store reading glasses, then placed the book he'd been reading onto the cluttered table. I just stood there. He said nothing as he got up and walked over to me. Then he shook my hand and said simply, "Welcome back."

The pain was still there. The pain and sorrow over my lost life, and love. Reality did not change when he grasped my hand. He never took his eyes off me as I removed my hat and coat, tossed them on a chair and then took a seat beside them.

"You're sick," he said.

I nodded. "Yes."

"I'll help you unpack."

I put my coat on again and together we unpacked my car, making trip after trip up the steep cement steps. When the last box had been deposited in my room he turned to me and said, "You've had a long day. Better get some rest."

I laid on my bed and listened to his slow, purposeful footsteps descend the stairs and make their way into the kitchen. There was the familiar creaking, then closing of the hallway door, followed by the muffled sound of the eleven o'clock news.

I stared at the cobwebs and peeling paint and listened to the endless roar of trucks rumbling past into the night. And I knew without question, that my fling with elusive, illusory happiness had come to its inevitable end.

I awoke late in the morning to the sound of coupling freight trains instead of tropical birds. I pushed myself through my morning yoga routine, dressed, then headed down the steps. My initial disappointment at the empty kitchen was soon replaced by a sense of relief. Considering the importance of what remained to be hashed out with Rose, I probably wasn't ready for that confrontation.

I sat in the darkened kitchen, listening to the clattering of the overworked space heater and staring at Rose's empty chair. Through my nomadic Chautauqua days, my obsession with career success, and now my frantic search for elusive happiness, Rose was always the same, living the same life, following the same direction.

"The true measure of a man is his consistency and reliability," he often remarked. Suddenly I felt very small in the shadow of his presence.

A few minutes later Rose emerged from the hallway into the kitchen. He looked me over as if checking my condition, then smiled. He made small talk with me while he fixed himself some tea, then sat down in a rocking chair near the stove.

"You know, falling in love can be a beautiful experience," he said. "But for someone who has made a commitment to the Truth, it can be a toboggan ride into Hell."

I sighed and said a soft "Amen."

"People who stay around this work long enough get a sense of how incomplete they really are. But after a while they get tired of searching, so they project all their ambitions onto someone of the opposite sex. And for awhile there's a certain beauty and serenity in the surrendering of the ego. But it doesn't last.

"The earth can be a very lonely place," he said, firmly but without reproach. "And romance can be a great comfort. While you're in love you really think you've found something important, that this is it, and from now on life will be different." He seemed to be speaking from a memory of another life, another person.

"But you know what happens? As soon as it's over and you come to your senses and take a look around, there you are again. Back in the middle of the desert."

He lowered his gaze, and stared directly at me. "But there's no peace. There can't be, because the work's not completed."

I searched for my voice, but said nothing.

"Nobody can be blamed for trying to find a little company in this nightmare, someone they can count on, share a few laughs with, and maybe a little intimacy. Without friendship there's no communication, and without communication, there's no hope of spirituality. That's what I meant in *The Albigen Papers* when I said there's no religion greater than human friendship. Even the Absolute is attracted to pure Love."

I stared at him, studying him intently as his short legs rose and fell with each rock of the chair. I decided to say nothing. In the past I'd sometimes not ask a question out of fear of what he'd say. Other times I'd ask one question too many and upset the invisible equilibrium that had opened the psychic passageway between us. Now, I was afraid to open any link between us, afraid to inquire how much he knew about my life, my future, my battles and pains.

"Let's get some air," he said.

Rose was not a restless person. If he took a walk it was for a purpose—because he hadn't been able to get out to the farm to "swing an ax," perhaps, and felt the need for exercise, or when a visitor had something personal to discuss. Why he now wanted to go outside I didn't know. We both put on coats and stepped out into the cold. It had snowed overnight and the town looked clean and white. Stray flurries still dotted the air and the street was unusually quiet.

"Right here is where my father got killed," Rose said, pointing out into the street in front of his house. "He was always stepping out in front of cars and the last time he did it he finally made the trip." I looked over at Rose as we walked, surprised, as I always was when we were side by side, at how short a man he was.

"Sometimes I think he did it on purpose. He wasn't the type to put up with too many headaches. His solution was to take a drink." Rose laughed. "Unfortunately, that doesn't work for me."

I had watched Rose take on more and more headaches over the years, and had seen the toll they had taken on him. Maintaining and improving a 130 acre farm/ashram with no money, outdated equipment, and moody volunteer labor. Perpetually ruminating on better ways to get his message across to people who wanted to hear anything but the truth. Turning his house and farm, and even his life over to strangers. Never turning his back on anyone no matter how little they seemed to appreciate what he was offering. As we trudged silently down the street in the falling snow, I thought of all he was carrying and wondered again, why?

"My father was not an educated man, but he had a lot of wisdom. I don't mean stepping in front of cars was wise," he chuckled, "but he had a certain intuition about the world. Trouble is he never knew who he was or where he was going when the car finished flattening him.

"That's the advantage of going through the Absolute Experience," he added. "I know what's up ahead.

"But even though there's only one Reality, not everybody can face it. If my mother'd had the Experience, she would have thought she went to hell. Because you're only seeing one side of it, the outside, and that's a pretty terrifying reflection."

He was no longer speaking to me, or at least not only to me.

"No matter how enormous that which you become a part of is, it's still a very lonely place. The Absolute is a very lonely place. You're the only one there. Of course," he added, "*everybody* is the only one there."

Sometimes in the kitchen with Rose, or in rapport, or reading "The Three Books of the Absolute" — even sometimes in the silence of my own thoughtless mind — I occasionally got a fleeting appreciation of where he had been, and where his Real Self still existed. I sensed it and feared it and hungered to return home to it myself.

Now, in the snow and the residual loneliness, Rose had again brought me up to the door of the Absolute, and it's unending starkness drove me back into a longing for everything warm and secure and familiar I had ever known. My dead father. My lonely mother who thinks she has lost me. Trips with the family in a crowded station wagon. The smell of musty cabins at summer camp. My first dog. My first love. It was overwhelming, so pleasant and so forever lost I thought I'd go mad if the mood didn't let go and allow me to return to my worried, isolated ego.

"It's like hillbillies and hunting dogs," Rose said, suddenly breaking the silence.

"What was that, Mister Rose?"

"If a hillbilly has a coon dog he's particularly proud of, he'll castrate the animal and hide his balls under the porch. That way the dog will always come back home."

Sure that he had my attention, Rose continued. "That's the way it is with this stuff. Once you've got a taste, you're like a castrated hunting dog the rest of your life, searching for what you had when you felt more whole. You keep getting drawn back but you don't know why."

I smiled and shook my head at the analogy. "Do you mean a taste of love, or of spiritual aspiration?"

Rose raised his eyebrows mischievously. "Yes," he said, then walked awhile in silence. "Moods are powerful things," he said quietly. "Fear, seduction, and nostalgia. These are the three moods of man. And the most powerful of these is nostalgia.

"You know, somebody once said the most painful thing on earth is a pleasant memory. This nostalgia that sometimes comes over us isn't an accident. It's a message. It has something to tell us. We're programmed to indulge in life, but this haunting nostalgia is a subliminal message from another plane. It's the homing instinct of the mundane mind. It's what draws us back to the Father."

"But why such sadness?" I said. "Why the pain?"

"Because nostalgia is a window to the soul, and the soul is lost to man as he lives. Nostalgia is the soul's memory of prior experience. Touching it, you touch the Eternal."

His words seemed to find my thoughts and speak directly to them.

"Nostalgia is the door," he said. "The only door. It's the one mood that makes man hungry for union with the Soul. Without it we'd be lost. But with the nostalgic mood comes the feeling that, yes, there *is* something. Something to *become*. This is the evenness — mankind's voice of rectitude. This is the even voice of man."

Something in his words touched and soothed me, even though I wasn't sure I understood what they meant. I suddenly felt very light and comfortable. We walked a long way that morning in the snow, Mister Rose talking all the while of matters of the heart. We walked until we reached some unseen destination in his mind, at which point he turned around and we headed home. The whole town was impossibly silent and white that day — so silent I could hear the snow fall — and in my memory I cannot recall seeing anyone else on our entire walk, though surely there must have been someone.

Chapter Twenty-Three

Fear

For awhile after my return from Florida life with Mister Rose was much the same as it had always been—an unpredictable existence marked by extreme highs and lows. There were times I would leave the kitchen in a near-exulted state and literally fall to my knees in my room, thanking God for the incredible opportunity of living and working with Rose. And there were periods I endured almost unbearable frustration and anger as he picked and prodded and criticized and tore into me for character flaws I felt powerless to change.

But then, almost overnight it seemed, there was neither. Rose did not appear interested in my legal cases, or in my efforts to convince him of the depth and sincerity of my inner life. I found it difficult to engage him in serious philosophic conversation—or conversation of any kind, for that matter. If I told him about a book I was reading, or a dream I had, or some insight that crossed my mind during meditation, he would offer only a half-hearted comment, then either change the subject or turn away from me altogether and busy himself with something else.

I tried to figure out if it was something I had done, or left undone. I endlessly observed and analyzed the situation, trying to correlate Rose's moods to my actions. But there seemed to be no direct connection. In the end I concluded that the most likely explanation was the one most difficult to face—that Rose had simply lost interest in me, and in my spiritual aspirations.

It was a conclusion I desperately did not want to confront. I buried myself in my legal work and came home later and later, hoping to avoid Rose and any conversation or gesture that might confirm my suspicion that Rose had written me off. I ruminated and agonized and made elaborate plans to do something—anything—that would re-kindle Rose's interest in me. Then, in the midst of this extreme spiritual dis-ease, the physical suddenly jumped to center stage. I was diagnosed with a fast-growing tumor in my head.

My first indication was not a symptom but an observation. One day in the office bathroom I looked in the mirror and was startled by what I saw.

"Jesus," I said out loud to myself. "I'm cross-eyed!"

I looked again, wondering if the light or angle had played some sort of funhouse-mirror trick on my perception. But as I scrutinized the reflection in front of me there seemed to be no doubt. My left eye was obviously different. At first glance it appeared to be higher than my right eye, but as I studied it with growing concern I realized it was actually bulging out of my skull.

I turned away from the mirror, assuring myself that I'd slept on it wrong or been bitten by a spider or something, and tried to turn my thoughts back to work. But fear repeatedly brought me back to the mirror and the comical, almost grotesque, face that awaited me there.

Finally I walked into the adjoining office where Jeanne, a long-time assistant, was working on the books. I sat on the edge of her desk and tried to be casual.

"Look at my face," I said. "What do you see?"

She looked up from her ledgers. "Holy cow! You're bug-eyed!"

So much for the slept-on-it-wrong theory. After that, things started happening fast. As it happened Jeanne was seeing an eye doctor herself for early signs of glaucoma. She gave me his name and an hour later I was ushered into his examination room. He poked and prodded and tested, then announced there was nothing wrong with my eyes.

"But something is causing this bulging, that's for sure. Who's your family doctor?"

"My brother, actually."

"Good. Call him today."

I went back to the office thinking I would catch up on some work first, then call my brother, Gordon, later. But even sitting behind my desk with case files stacked three deep, work seemed a million miles away. I picked up the phone and called.

"Dave," he said. "What's up?"

"It's crazy. I hate to bother you, but the local eye doctor made me promise to call."

"What about?" His voice took on an immediate professionalism. I relayed the events of the morning and as I finished I glanced up at the clock. It wasn't even noon yet.

"So what do you think it is, Doc?" I said.

"We'll need to run some tests. I can get you into the hospital here today and—"

"Today? Whoa, I've got a big trial coming up. How about next week?"

"Well, I...I don't think so, Dave. You should probably come on in today. With any luck you'll be out by morning."

There was something in his tone of voice, or the way he used my name in the middle of a conversation, that convinced me to take his advice. So an hour and a half later I parked the car where he had instructed and walked through the main door of Passavant Hospital with my hastily packed gym bag. Surprisingly, Gordon's wife, Suzi, was waiting for me there. She almost ran over to greet me and gave me an unusually long, tight hug.

"Hey, good to see you, too," I said with a laugh.

The woman at the patient intake desk smiled when she saw me. "You look just like your brother," she said.

An orderly came with a wheelchair and insisted I sit in it.

"It's my eye, not my legs," I said.

Suzi squeezed my hand. "Go ahead. They make everybody do it. I'll wait for you out here."

I was quickly passed from person to person, then wheeled down for x-rays and three or four other diagnostics before being taken to my room. In a few moments my brother walked in accompanied by a portly young doctor with a serious, almost stern expression. Gordon introduced us and the young doctor put me through another examination. Both he and my brother were all business. When he was through the young doctor explained that my vision was fine, which led him to believe that the difficulty was not in the eye, but in something connected to the eye. Then he announced that I would be turned over to a neurologist. We shook hands briefly and he walked out.

Gordon remained standing by my bed. "You'll have a CAT scan this afternoon at four o'clock. After that it will be too late for any more tests. You'll definitely be here for the night."

"Yeah, I figured."

Gordon continued to stand silently by my bed, probably waiting for questions that, inexplicably, I had no idea to ask.

Later, after the CAT scan, the neurologist and my brother stood together in front of a wall of light, looking at my x-rays. I waited for awhile, then walked over to join them. The neurologist glanced at me and pointed to an area of the x-ray.

"You see this?" His finger circled a light spot the size of a golf ball near one of my eye sockets. "That's what's pushing against your eye."

"So what happens now?" I asked.

"Well, this is just a community hospital. We don't have the facilities to take care of you. Luckily, Allegheny General has an expert in this field, and we've lined you up an appointment with him tomorrow morning."

The expert was a man named Kennerdale, a world famous eye surgeon who was continually addressing some august medical body or another. Apparently the only reason he was able to see me on such short notice was that he had been scheduled to appear on a panel at the AMA convention in Seattle that week, but his plane had been fogged in at the Pittsburgh airport the night before.

He was in his early forties, tall, broad but not really overweight, with a full head of dark hair. Though personable enough, he had the detached, confident air of the professional that Mister Rose was always railing against. We briefly reviewed my symptoms, then he said he was going to perform an ultra-sound test. He explained that he would be running a sensor over my eye, which would be a little uncomfortable until I got used to it, and that he would be viewing an image transmitted to the screen in front of him.

I flinched the first time the sensor touched my eye, but Kennerdale held my head with a firm but gentle strength that had a curiously calming effect. I began counting my breaths as a simple meditation technique to help me relax, and gradually I was able to tolerate the procedure.

After about twenty minutes Kennerdale said, "There's the tumor."

My mind jerked suddenly to attention. My body must have jerked too, because I felt Kennerdale's grip forcefully squeeze the back of my head.

Jesus Christ! *Tumor!* Of course, what else would it be? Gordon and Suzi and everyone must have thought I was an idiot for not catching on, or at least asking questions before now.

"The tumor is a little bigger than I thought," Kennerdale said. There was that word again. I realized he was repeating it on purpose to be sure I got the message.

I have no idea how much longer he fooled with me. When he was done he told me the drops he put in my eyes to dilate my pupils for the ultra-sound would wear off in a half hour or so, and that I should wait out in the lobby until then.

Suzi put down her book and stood up when she saw me.
"How did it go?"
"He said something about a tumor," I said weakly.

She reached for my hand and sighed deeply, all pretense slipping away.

"I know. Gordon knew what it was right away," she said. "It was hard for us not to say something to you, but you never asked any questions. You really didn't suspect, even after you saw the CAT scan?"

I thought for a moment and tried to decide if maybe a part of me had known all along but perhaps just didn't want to face it.

"I don't think so," I mumbled. "I don't know."

I sat down heavily. "What kind of tumor is it?"

"They don't know yet," she said quietly.

It occurred to me then with sudden and devastating impact that I was a mortal being who was going to die—and possibly very soon. Rose had been trying to impress that fact on me—on all his students—since day one, but I never got the message until that moment. Nothing like a gun barrel between the eyes to focus the attention.

The nurse came back and told me the doctor would see me now. I followed her to a small room, and she closed the door behind me, leaving me alone with Dr. Kennerdale. Perhaps in deference to my dilated pupils the room was completely dark, except for a small antique table lamp with a rounded, stained glass shade. Kennerdale loomed large in the shadows behind the desk, almost too large for the simple chair in which he sat.

I found myself gazing directly into his eyes. I had often stared into the eyes of witnesses, opposing counsels, even judges, hoping to see some hint of deeper meaning behind the words they were speaking. Now I desperately searched Kennerdale's eyes for the truth behind the professional words I knew were coming.

"You've got a mass in your left occipital orbit," he said. "That's what's pushing against your eye. It's not common, but its not all that unusual either. I see maybe eighty to a hundred of these a year."

"Is it malignant?" I blurted out, almost before he stopped speaking.

"We don't know. Won't know for sure until we take it out."

I looked away from him for a moment. The office was new and clean. There weren't even any pictures or framed degrees on the wall.

"What do you think, though?" I said.

He paused, as if deciding how much to tell me. "The fact that it seemed to appear out of nowhere indicates that it's fast growing, which is consistent with a malignant tumor. Like I said, though, we won't know for sure until after the surgery."

Today was Wednesday, he said, and his usual surgical team worked Tuesdays and Thursdays, so he could either do emergency surgery tomorrow morning, or wait until the following Tuesday. He would make the final decision on which day after my medical tests were completed.

"I've scheduled a CAT scan for noon. I know you had one at Passavant, but that one was without dye."

"You seem pretty certain already. Why do I need more tests?"

"Because we've got to be absolutely sure before going ahead. Absolutely sure. This is a serious procedure, David, but we have made great strides recently."

"What do you mean?"

"The surgery used to quite disfiguring," he said. "They had to remove the entire side of the face, leaving the patient looking like a stroke victim. I've developed an entirely different approach, though. It will leave only a small scar that will follow the lines of your glasses. Barely noticeable."

"I guess there's no natural opening—eye socket, or whatever—to go through?"

"No. We remove the section of the skull adjoining the orbit. What happens next depends on what we find. If its malignant, we cut out what we can, then leave the skull section out and just sew up the skin—because we'll probably be going back in. You'll have six weeks of radiation, and depending upon how things look, we'll decide how to proceed from there.

"What's the prognosis."

His face was grim. "The ten-year survival rate for this form of cancer is less than ten percent."

"And if I don't get the surgery."

"That's not an option, I'm afraid." He sat forward in his chair and looked directly at me. "This is a particularly virulent type of tumor. Left untreated, it's fast-growing and painful. If it's malignant, you'll be dead in three months without surgery.

"And if it's benign?"

"If we see that it's benign, we just remove the tumor, replace the skull section and you go on your way like nothing ever happened."

"I like that scenario a whole lot better," I said, managing a weak smile.

Kennerdale smiled back. "Yeah," he said. "Me too."

I left his office in a daze. Reality had changed. I was now a dying man, and no matter what kind of tumor I had, or how long I lived, that would not change. The person who was going to live forever was now forever dead and I knew it. His sense of permanence, of lasting importance had vanished into the past. Even the concept of "past" seemed dead.

The change had taken place so fast that my defenses had no time to react or adjust, to prepare me with hopes, explanations, or spiritual platitudes. I was merely and only a dying man, and for the moment at least, the truth of that seemed to be enough. People die at all stages of life, some in their mid-thirties. There was absolutely no reason that one of them should not be me.

Suzi stood again when I entered the lobby and waited for me to speak.

"If it's malignant, the survival rate isn't good," I said. "Ten percent."

"You'll be in that ten percent," she said firmly, then linked her arm through mine and began walking.

We walked with no particular destination in mind, but soon saw a sign for the hospital chapel. Inside, we found an oasis of simple beauty no bigger than a living room, insulated from the noise and bustle of the adjoining hallway. There were three rows of chairs facing three long, rectangular stained glass windows. We sat in the front row and I immediately felt a powerful connection with all the prayers and fear and grief that had been offered into that tiny chapel.

Next to me I heard Suzi crying softly. I began to pray but was soon distracted and overcome by a vision of what my immediate future held: operations, recovery, treatments, debilitation, weakness, pain. I thought of my mother and what she would have to go through, watching helplessly as her son slowly died. I didn't realize I was crying until the tears fell onto my folded hands.

"I don't mind the dying so much," I said out loud to Suzi. "I just don't want to go through all the bullshit."

"I know," she said quietly. "I know."

When it was time for the CAT scan, we left the chapel and returned to the lobby. After a few minutes my name was called and I was led to a small examination room where I was injected with radioactive dye. Then I was led into a narrow room with an examination table attached to a large apparatus that I now recognized as a CAT scan machine.

A technician helped me get situated on the table, and as he walked away a female voice came through a speaker near my ear, introducing herself as the conductor of the test. She explained a few things about the test and asked me if I was claustrophobic. As soon as I said "No" I heard the hum of machinery, and the beige metal cowl began approaching from the bottom of the table. I found the noise and movement oddly disquieting, and immediately began breathing deeply and counting my breaths. Soon the metal cowl was fully extended and covering me, so close that I felt a rising sense of panic.

Yesterday I had practically slept through the CAT scan at Passavant, but today was definitely different. I don't know if was the shock of the morning's events or the technician's suggestion of claustrophobia or the comparison to a coffin that I couldn't get out of my head, but I suddenly became uncomfortable in the extreme. Once aware of the sensation, I expected the secondary panic also—the panic about being panicked—but blessedly this did not come.

Fighting the fear I closed my eyes and, as Rose had so often counseled, went within. After a few moments I was able to observe my state, and was calmed by this identification with the *Observer*: that impartial, objective and separate sense of self that sees everything—including thoughts and panic—as external, observable events. Rose often said that this Observer was a facet of, and a gateway to, the True Self.

The True Self. How often I had proclaimed that I was in search of it, and yet how little I had actually done. My God, this could be it! My life may be over and I've blown it. I'd been given the incredible gift of meeting Rose, and though I worked with him for fifteen years I never truly made the simple commitment he insisted was the key to the kingdom:

"Make up your mind you're going to find the Truth regardless of what it takes. Then you'll get somewhere. You make a commitment that you're going to see this thing through, that's all, even if it drives you insane or costs you your life."

With a sudden, wrenching sadness I realized that something was indeed about to cost me my life, but it most certainly was not my hunger for the Truth. I had never done what Rose said *must* be done in order to have any hope. I could almost hear his voice in my ear:

"It's simple. Make a vow to yourself and whatever God might be listening that you want nothing out of this life except the Truth."

It seems I have wanted everything *but* the Truth. God, how could I have been so blind, so greedy, so selfish. Rose tried everything he knew to get through to me, but he never actually interfered with my ignorance, with the direction I took in life. He didn't believe in it.

"*People have to find out for themselves what has value in their lives and what doesn't. What's worth living for. What's worth doing.*"

He even incorporated that attitude into his philosophy, insisting that formal spiritual practices were secondary to just "keeping your head on it" and working with what was in front of you.

"*Your everyday life will give you all the koans you need to get Enlightened. You've got to face adversity in this realm, and conquer it.*"

I almost smiled. Life had just given me the mother-of-all-koans and I felt helpless to use it for anything other than self-pity and remorse. Remorse. I scanned my life and memories, looking for unfinished business and unrealized dreams.

"*Success is the ability to look back without regrets.*"

What had I missed? I was going to die childless and alone, the greatest fear my mother held for me, and yet I felt no pangs of regret at that thought. There was really only one thing: The Path, and my failure to walk it. In the beginning it was easy and fun, but as the years went by I took longer and longer side trips, until finally I wasn't walking the path at all, only crisscrossing it now and then.

"*When you start out, it's a wide path. There's all sorts of garbage you can get rid of. As you go on, the path gets narrower and narrower and the things you have to let go of are very precious to you. Finally, there's no escape. You go through the funnel and that's all there is to it.*"

There it was. My fear of the funnel. On the other side was Truth, God, the Absolute, Infinite Awareness — the Reality I claimed to be seeking. But I knew it would not be Dave Gold that survived the funnel, and Dave Gold was all that I knew. Of *course* I was a half-hearted seeker of Truth — the Truth scared the shit out of me! How the hell could I go balls-to-the-wall after something that terrified me?

"*No matter how enormous that which you become a part of is, it's still a very lonely place. The Absolute is a very lonely place. You're the only one there. Of course, everybody is the only one there.*"

With a sudden almost physical pain I realized that it was never the Truth that I sought. All I really wanted was the approval and respect of people — especially Rose — who *really did* love the Truth! It had all been an elaborate subterfuge. I had spent years trying to convince a man who could see through me like water that black was white, that Dave Gold was a serious seeker of Truth. My whole life was a sham, and now, perhaps, it was over. I was gripped by an intense emotional pain unlike anything I had ever experienced.

Then, suddenly, the world became completely silent. In the void I heard a drop of sweat as it fell from my face and hit the table, and for a moment, my mind stopped. Like a switch had been thrown and everything had instantly shut down. All the noise that was Dave Gold just went away. I was totally empty and alone. I don't know how long it lasted and I have no memory of anything, but I think some part of me made a solemn promise in that moment.

"Okay, David. We're done."

The cowl slowly retracted. I continued to lay still for a minute, staring at the ceiling.

"We're done, David. You can go now."

I sat up slowly and got off the table.

I spent the weekend with Gordon and Suzi. On the day of my scheduled operation I awoke in the dark of early morning and looked out the window. The night was cloudless. Frosted grass glistened in the light of the full moon. As I did my usual yoga routine, I was struck by the sense of calm and timelessness I felt. For the first time in my life I was in no hurry.

When I went downstairs, Suzi was already waiting for me in the kitchen, car keys in hand.

"We better get going," she said.

At the hospital I was put into a room with a frail man in his eighties who had to struggle for every rattling breath. When they finally came for me I was placed on a gurney and rolled down ever-narrowing hallways, through a series of glass doors marked "RESTRICTED ACCESS," and finally into a small, dimly lit room with people in green gowns and serious faces talking in hushed tones.

Suddenly I had to go to the bathroom worse than I could ever remember. Reluctantly, they allowed me to get off the gurney, but it was clear from their attitude that I had moved onto the production line, and that there would be no more delays. I stood over the toilet for what seemed like several minutes as all the water in my body deserted me. Then I took one last look at myself in the mirror and hurried back.

As soon as I lay back down on the gurney a nurse leaned over me and said she was going to start an IV. A few minutes later a soft-spoken doctor introduced himself as the anesthesiologist, and explained what he would be doing. First, he'd give me a sedative, then the knock-out drops. He said I might wake up with a sore throat.

"A sore throat I can live with." We both smiled through tight lips, and then he was gone. A new face appeared and said he was taking me to final pre-op. I was rolled into a harshly lit room and helped off the gurney onto the operating table. A half dozen people in surgical masks told me their names as they fiddled with me and various pieces of equipment. I repeated each of their names out loud as they told them to me: Frank, Harold, Linda... I counted my breaths. I commanded myself to Observe. One of the doctors nodded to the anesthesiologist to begin. I could hear my heart. From out of nowhere the Jesus prayer flew across my mind: *Lord Jesus Christ have mercy on me a poor sinner. Lord Jesus Christ have mercy on me a poor sinner. Lord Jesus Christ have mercy...* And then there was nothing.

I emerged from oblivion more gradually than I had entered it. I was conscious of bright light on the other side of my closed eyelids, but I knew I was not ready to confront it yet. First, I needed to remember who I was. Nothing. I was at a loss. All I knew was that whoever I was had a pounding headache unlike anything he'd ever felt. Anyone with this much pain must be in a hospital.

"Nurse?" I called out.

A feminine voice came back, sweet and gentle.

"David. How are you feeling?"

With the mention of my name, my memory and life came flooding back.

"My head hurts."

"Here. I can give you some morphine."

I heard movement off to my right, and within a few seconds I was overwhelmed with a rush of well-being.

After a few minutes she asked, "How do you feel now?" God, what a beautiful voice. It pierced the fog in my head like a clear, crystal bell. I wondered what she looked like.

"My head still hurts pretty bad."

"If you think you need another shot, I can give you one."

I nodded, and moments later, the pain was gone. With its absence, a new imperative took over—the need for an answer to the big question. Malignant or benign. The answer, I knew, was an arm's length away. All I needed to do was touch my head. If they had replaced the skull fragment, the tumor was benign. If they had sewn back only skin, it was malignant.

I sent the message to my left hand, but it barely budged. I was so tired, and so weak, and then there was the morphine... "*Cut the shit,*" some disgusted internal voice said. "*You're stalling.*" I felt my left hand slowly rise until there was contact with my head. But the bandages were so thick I couldn't tell one way or the other. In a strange way I was relieved. Maybe I wasn't ready to know.

I could sense that the nurse with the musical voice was still nearby. Surely she knew. I had only to ask and the single most important question of my life would be answered immediately.

But something stopped me. I could not bring myself to ask the question. Perhaps I feared the answer. Perhaps I feared I already knew the answer. All I knew for sure was that for some unknown reason the question was, for the moment at least, not appropriate.

So I said something else instead and the nurse came to sit beside me. We talked for a long time about other things. At one point I opened my eyes and looked at her for a moment. She was even more beautiful than her voice.

Some time later an orderly came to take me from the recovery area back to my room. The beautiful nurse walked beside me and continued talking as the orderly wheeled my gurney down the hall and into the elevator. Her presence was a great comfort. When we reached our floor I was rolled down the hallway and into my room. Suddenly the world burst into noise as a crowd of people all started talking at once. I opened my eyes and propped myself up on my elbows. They were all there, crowding around me—Suzi, Gordon, my mother, sister, niece…

"Did they tell you? Did they tell you?" Suzi almost shouted. "It's BENIGN!"

My arms gave way like trap doors. I fell back onto the gurney and began crying in great noisy sobs of joy and relief. My sister stroked my hair. My mother kissed my fingers. The beautiful nurse put her hands to her mouth and began apologizing over an over. "I'm so sorry," she kept saying. "I'm so sorry. I thought you already knew."

I wanted to tell her that it didn't matter, but I couldn't stop crying. I wanted to tell her that nothing that had happened to me in my entire life up to that very moment mattered in the least.

Chapter Twenty-Four

Outcast

There were some beautiful moments with Rose in the kitchen following my return from the hospital, but they proved to be a brief respite. Within a few weeks Rose was as irritated and dissatisfied with me as ever. Maybe even more so because the "knock on your head," as he called my cancer scare, had not gotten through to me, had not awakened or transformed me.

Every day I reminded myself that Rose's conception of me was not the issue. His favorable opinion did not change my "eternal fact status," nor did his good graces guarantee the Grace of God. But like the trained seal that Rose had compared me to during simpler times, I could not help but perform for his approval.

I picked more fights with the cops and judges. I worked longer and harder at the farm. I made fewer trips to visit my family in Pittsburgh, and avoided those group members whose sincerity Rose questioned. I redoubled my inner efforts, seeking insight into whatever it was that stood between Rose and me. Nothing helped. I remained all but invisible to him. More disturbing, Rose did not seem particularly angry with me. He seemed to have adopted an attitude of resigned sociability, as if stuck on a bus with a unpleasant boor whom he could not escape, leaving him no choice but to make the best of it for as long as the ride lasted.

The only remaining solace for me was the weekends, when I would immerse myself in physical labor at the farm. I had finally earned the respect of the guys who lived on Rose's farm, and no longer felt like a soft city Jew around them. Here, at least, was one place I felt productive and needed. And as long as my body was engaged my mind seemed to disengage and free me from my worries. Each weekend I worked myself to near-exhaustion chasing a temporary sense of well-being that the rest of my life denied me.

But in time even this was taken from me. The camaraderie I had come to feel working side-by-side with Chuck, Don, Eric and the others, suddenly disappeared, and they no longer treated me like a comrade-in-arms. I studied their moods and faces for clues and reasons.

First I sensed the anger and negativity that manifested when Rose was complaining about you behind your back. Occasionally I'd catch them glancing over at me as we worked, no doubt replaying Rose's words and gauging the truth about whatever indictment he had leveled against me. Gradually, however, their mood shifted from distrust to one of distance, and even pity. No matter how hard I tried to either dismiss or ignore these perceptions, it was painfully obvious that something was going on.

By now it was mid-July. Rose came out to the farm one weekend and began giving specific orders about what he wanted done. We were told to abandoned our summer-long project of clearing more pasture for the goats, and to begin cleanup and repair of the farmhouse and outbuildings — which he personally supervised over the next few weekends. It was clear to me that Rose had shifted into the driven micro-manager he became when gearing up for a specific task or event, and yet there was no event planned that I knew of. The nearest scheduled group function was the Labor Day TAT meeting, almost two months away. To make matters worse, Rose and Chuck were perpetually huddling in the farmhouse kitchen, and whenever I walked into the room they immediately quit talking. I began to get an uneasy feeling.

As Rose had pointed out to me on many occasions, the one thing Dave Gold the egomaniac could not stand was to be left out of something. Mindful of this criticism, I tried to go about my business as if nothing was happening, but occasionally my ego and curiosity would override my intentions, and I'd drop a seemingly innocuous hint to one of the guys.

"What do you figure has gotten into Rose?" I said to Chuck one day. "He had such a burr up his ass about getting that pasture cleared before fall. Now he's got us doing yard work instead."

Chuck didn't look up from his task. "Oh, well...you know Rose..." he said with a shrug.

By the third week of this I felt like a ghost walking among the living. Worse, I hadn't the courage to bring matters to a head and find out once and for all what, if anything, was going on. By now our farm workdays had been lengthened and the pace quickened. Several guys from Pittsburgh even showed up to help. I knew that whatever Rose was planning must be rapidly approaching, but I still had no clue as to what it was. Finally, as Rose would say, someone "put me wise."

It was dusk on Sunday evening. I was helping Bill, one of the guys from Pittsburgh, pack up his tools after he'd spent a frustrating weekend trying to repair the old farm tractor. Bill and I joined the group in Pittsburgh about the same time, and I had enjoyed spending some time that day with someone who wasn't part of the farm clique from which I felt so estranged.

"So," he said, putting the last of his tools away and snapping shut the toolbox lid, "you live with Mister Rose. Do you think the meeting next weekend will really change anything?"

My stomach twisted. "What meeting?" I heard myself ask.

Bill stared at me for a few seconds, his face flushing with embarrassment. "Dave, I'm sorry I...I guess Rose...I mean he probably..."

I mumbled something like "Don't sweat it," and we awkwardly said our good-byes. A few minutes later I got in my car and drove directly to Benwood, a thousand thoughts running through my head, none of which lasted long enough to become words.

Rose was not home when I arrived. I waited for him in the kitchen, with no clue as to what I would say. He showed up a half-hour later. We exchanged brief greetings, then he made himself a cup of tea and sat down across from me at the table. He looked at me a moment, then picked up the newspaper and began reading the obituaries.

"I heard there's going to be a meeting next weekend," I said suddenly.

Rose looked up from the paper. "That's right. I've called together all the people who are still in the group. We've been going nowhere for ten years and I hate to see anything die slowly. Either we do something now or we call it quits."

He put down the paper and looked directly into my eyes as he continued.

"I don't have any more time to waste with people who aren't serious. Everyone wants to believe they're spiritual, but most people are just playing at it. If I'm going to devote the rest of my life to this group, it might as well be with *real* people. People with a spiritual vector. So some people aren't invited. Paul and Steve and Jay and Dave Gold and..."

I'm sure there were other names, other words, but I didn't hear them. My consciousness was caught in a tidal wave of anger and humiliation. The room receded and Rose's voice faded into a background hum.

I must have asked him a question, because when I returned to the room he was answering me.

"You're not a spiritual person, that's why. You're a friend to the group so you'll always be welcome in my house and on my farm.

But I intend to spend the rest of my life working with people who have a shot at a spiritual future."

I sat motionless, unable to speak or even think. Rose had apparently said all he was going to, so we spent the next few minutes in silence. Finally, I got up and made my way to the door. With my hand on the knob I turned back to him, perhaps hoping he might smile, or toss me some palliative remark. But his face was obscured by the newspaper. He had resumed reading the obituaries.

The following week was a nightmare. My mind was a morass of fragmented thoughts and emotions. Anger, shame, confusion, fear. I couldn't concentrate at work, or even on the most mundane daily tasks. All I could do was watch helplessly as my mind endlessly replayed events and ruminated on my sorry state.

It had been such a short time before that the doctor told me I may have only months to live. Now, with a second chance at life, with a renewed commitment to the search, Rose tells me I have no spiritual future. *No spiritual future!* I would not have thought it possible, but the drained, hopeless, fearful feelings that now wracked my mind and body were worse than when facing my physical death. My interior life was an agonizing landscape of pain and humiliation, and yet I knew that what I needed most was to be alone with it. I hastily arranged with my partners to take a week off and go into isolation in my cabin.

That Friday night was the beginning of the weekend meeting of those people *still in the group*, people who Rose had deemed to have *a hope of a spiritual future.* I stayed at the office until very late, agonizing, obsessing, not wanting to face the dark empty house in Benwood, or go out to my cabin while people were still arriving for the meeting. Finally, around midnight, I left the office, stopped by Benwood to pack a few things, then drove out to the farm. The parking lot was crammed with cars, and lights were still on in the farmhouse.

I parked out of sight on the far side of an overgrown outbuilding by the road, my front bumper pushing down the tall weeds, the branches of a scrub tree noisily scraping my side door. I hurriedly grabbed my bags and made my way, furtively, like an intruder, through the goat-gate and down the old logging road to my cabin. There was no moon and I had forgotten to bring a flashlight. As I got deeper into the woods I began walking more slowly, giving my eyes time to adjust.

I had never become completely comfortable in the dark, even though I had spent hours forcing myself to walk through the woods at night, trying to conquer my fears. I still retained a deep terror of the dark, of the unseen, of the unknown, that no amount of practice or counter-conditioning seemed to touch. Now, as I almost blindly made my way through the woods I felt even more vulnerable to whatever may lurk there. I was, after all, a man *with no spiritual future*, a man no longer under the protection of Rose and the group.

I thought of Thomas Drescher, the Krishna hit man, and how he said he had stalked me in those woods, waiting for the right time and place to shoot me. I thought of entities and wild dogs and hungry ghosts. I began jogging, trusting my memory of the way to keep me from slamming into a tree. When I got to my cabin I locked the door behind me.

I put away the few food items I'd brought, then opened all the windows. I could faintly hear the babbling of the creek a hundred yards away, and in my mind I imagined I heard the conversation and laughter of the "chosen ones" at the farmhouse meeting, those who were still in the group, those *with a spiritual future*.

Rose's devastating words would not leave me alone. My entire spiritual search was tied to Rose and the group. By excluding me from that meeting, from the group, Rose had passed the equivalent of a spiritual death sentence on me. Every fiber of my being cried out against it. I desperately did not want to believe what he said was true. And yet the only other explanation was that Rose was wrong.

But how in God's name could he be? He was the most penetratingly perceptive man I'd ever met and, quite literally, a mind reader. I had opened up my life to him, and even that which I tried to hide, he unerringly knew. With the possible exception of his wife Cecy, there was no one in the group who had spent more hours in his presence than I had. He knew me, all right. Better than I knew myself.

I slumped back in my chair, overcome by the hopelessness of my situation. It didn't even matter whether Rose was right or wrong about me. Either way, the result was the same. If he was right, I was not a spiritual person and never would be. If he was wrong, wrong about something this important, then he could be wrong about anything, or everything. And if Rose could be this fatally flawed, if he could mistakenly snuff out my spiritual hopes with a single decision, then the effect was the same as if he had been right. My spiritual destiny, the whole of my spiritual search, had been bet on the wrong horse. Either way, I had lost everything.

In a sudden fit of anger I jumped from my chair, knocking it to the floor.

"Why me?" I yelled out the window in the direction of the farmhouse. "Why *not* me? What have they done that I haven't? What have they got that I haven't got?"

Those last words, which rang in my ears as if spoken by someone else, stopped me. For in the question I also heard the answer. It wasn't what the others had that I lacked. Rather, it was something I had in such great abundance that Rose no longer believed I could be disabused of it by him, or even by Grace. Vanity. Ego. Self-absorption. I remembered the first words Rose ever spoke to me as if I had written them down:

"Now this guy here… There's no doubt in his mind that he thinks he's very clever and someone of great importance. He likes to think that he's blessed with a superior intellect and is destined to do great things…"

Rose had been pummeling me about my enormous ego for years, both with sledgehammer directness, and with humor…

"I'm a firm believer in fattening up your head before you chop it off. But with Dave Gold it's getting so we're not going to have an ax at the farm big enough to handle the job."

But I never got it. I endured the confrontations and admitted my culpability, but I never got it. Rose pegged it exactly:

"I've watched you for years. Your heart's not in this work. You've suffered, but you've never changed."

He was right. God, was he right. All I ever did was endure and suffer. It was my way of avoiding actual change. "See how much pain I'm in?" my suffering was saying to Rose and the world. "Surely that's proof enough that the spiritual fires are purging my soul."

And then, hoping I had fooled everyone, I would go about the business of being the same old Dave Gold. Yes, it was my giant ego that couldn't fit in that farmhouse with the serious seekers. I righted my chair and sat down, convinced I had gotten to the painful root of it.

And then a secondary realization caught me completely unawares and rocked my foundations. I suddenly knew what Rose had been up against with me all these years. Not only did I have a huge, unwieldy ego, but *I was proud of it*. I took secret pleasure in admitting I had a big ego, because subtly I was saying to everyone, "Yes, I have a terribly unwieldy ego, but of course the ego naturally grows in proportion to the greatness of the man, and so I am cursed with a great ego because of my greatness. A terrible spiritual burden, true, but that is the price one must pay for being great. How lucky you lesser mortals are to have such limited gifts, and therefore such manageable egos."

My entire being recoiled in shock and shame. It was pathetic. I was thirty-six years old and had lived in the same house with a living embodiment of the Truth for more than ten years, yet never in my entire life had I experienced a single moment of genuine humility! I was filled with an immense self-loathing. How could Rose have stomached me for as long as he did?

"Sure I'd like to work with more serious people, people who are already on the edge, people I could push into something enormous. But I have to figure that everyone who crosses my path is sent for a reason, even if I don't know what that reason might be."

I had, I suppose, merely been one of those people who happened to cross his path, even though he couldn't see any reason for it. He probably *never* thought I had any spiritual potential. It just took him fifteen years to completely give up on me. I was disconsolate. I laid down on my bed and prayed for sleep.

The next morning I awoke disoriented. When I opened my eyes, I was surprised to find myself in my cabin. Even when my memory returned, my conventional sense of time and place didn't completely come with it. It was 9:30, shamelessly late to be sleeping in my cabin. Normally on Saturday mornings we'd meet in the farmhouse at 7:30 and were working by 8:00. Then I remembered that this weekend was different. With that thought I expected to begin sinking back into the abyss I had been wallowing in. But, surprisingly, it didn't come.

I got up and began dressing. Something had changed. Something felt different. I figured it was simply disorientation caused by sleeping in, but as I went through my yoga routine, I realized that it wasn't going away. A different state of mind had settled in.

When I was finished the yoga I sat at my desk, where I had ruminated on so many other traumas over the years, all somehow connected to Rose. I glanced about my cabin. Everywhere were reminders of my supposed "search for truth," some written, some etched in memory.

Facing me on the window ledge was the wooden Buddha I had used so often as a concentration aid during numerous isolations and weekend retreats. Above the window frame was a faded yellowed sign on which, during a particularly rough isolation, I had thickly printed a single word: **ABIDE**. Could it really be that it was over, that it had all been for nothing? I sat for a moment with that thought but for some reason it did not produce the same sense of bleak devastation I had lived with for the past week. What was going on here?

Normally I meditate with my eyes open, but I had an urge to shut them. When I did, I recognized a faint sensation that made my heart beat faster. Hope. But why? Where did it come from. I stayed silent for a long time and listened. Then I remembered something Rose had said long ago:

"In spiritual matters, sometimes you have to attack people to help them."

My heart leapt. Was this what was happening? Was he still trying to help me? Was that what this was all about? I hardly dared think it was true. And yet there was no doubt that this thought was the source of the newfound hope that had crept up on me during the night, perhaps in a dream. Maybe, just maybe, this was an orchestrated move on Rose's part to finally chop off my fattened head and propel me into something.

"I don't want to bring you peace of mind. I want to bring you trouble."

I suddenly remembered a time several years back when Rose had kicked Larry out of the group and off the farm, where he had been living for eight years. Rose also instructed all remaining group members to stay away from Larry. Larry was devastated. He had no money, no place to go, and thanks to Rose's proclamation, no friends to turn to. A few days later he came to see me at the office. He had hit bottom, he said, and desperately needed help. Without hesitation I gave him some money, and even got him a job and a place to stay. Larry and I had been friends. It seemed only natural.

When Rose heard about it he was furious with me.

"You ruined it!" he said. "You killed Larry's one chance at an Experience. It took me eight years to set him up for it and you destroyed it in a day." For weeks afterwards Rose told everyone what an idiot I'd been.

Oh how I wanted to believe that Rose now had the same plans for me, that this whole affair was an elaborate scheme to push me over the edge into something enormous.

"Everyone has to take off some day. That is, if they're ever going to have any sort of spiritual realization of their own. If they didn't leave, I'd have to kick 'em out."

For a few seconds I was almost jubilant. Then a new thought stopped me in my tracks. If what I had just realized was true, then by realizing it I had just killed my chance for an Experience as surely as

I had killed Larry's by bailing him out. My heart sank to a new low. I buried my face in my hands and stifled a scream. There seemed to be no end to the mistakes, the wrong turns. I was truly a hopeless case. All the energy drained from my body and I became suddenly weak and exhausted. I lay back down on my bed and stared at the ceiling, too tired to even think.

Sometime later I awoke. I had fallen asleep in the middle of the day—something unheard of for me. As I lay there I became gradually aware of a feeling of pressure, of heaviness surrounding my body. It steadily increased in strength, giving me the overwhelming, but not uncomfortable, sensation of being surrounded—perfectly evenly across the body surface—by a suit of heavy air or water. There was no feeling of claustrophobia or suffocation or any of the other negative sensations one normally associates with being surrounded or pressed in upon. Instead, there was a secure and comforting sense of irresistible yielding to the pressure, of being absorbed back into my self, smaller, ever smaller, as the pressure grew greater.

Soon I was nothing more than a pinpoint surrounded by pressure, a dense, all-encompassing, overpowering pressure. The shell surrounding what was left of me grew thicker and thicker against the pressure, while I grew smaller and smaller, until the pinpoint of "I" receded into nothingness, and there was only an all powerful, unyielding Everywhere.

I waited breathlessly. There was an interval of time when the pressure wavered, seeming almost to recede. Then he came. I saw nothing, but I knew without a doubt who it was. My True Teacher. In the Hindu tradition he is called the *Satguru* – literally, the "Truth teacher." Each of us has many gurus, or teachers, but only one *Satguru*. The *Satguru* can be an incarnate being, or exist in spirit only. Until that moment I had always assumed my *Satguru* was Rose. No longer. There was no doubt that He who was with me at that moment was He who had guided me throughout my life. I trembled in awe.

"Are you coming for me?" I asked in my thoughts.

Then suddenly, as if in answer, he receded back into the darkness.

"Wait! Take me with you. Take me home!"

But even as I thought it, I knew I couldn't go. I wasn't ready. I heard Rose's voice again, speaking through the fog of my body's memory:

"The experience of Truth is a tremendous shock. In order to make use of it, or even survive it, you need to be vaccinated for that dimension."

I began crying and couldn't stop. The brief touch of my True Teacher had left me with an aching and a longing that was almost too painful to bear. And within that loss I felt more deeply than ever the pain of losing my earthly teacher, Mister Rose. As if on cue the memory of his words again surfaced.

"You don't need me. Nobody needs me. All you need is your own inner determination."

The tears and sobs came even harder as a strange joy mixed with my despair. For fifteen years I had studied under Rose, desperately seeking his approval, assurance, acceptance — some sign I was going to make it, some sign that *I was doing it right*. But there was no *right*. There was no *doing*. There was no *I*.

There is no recipe for a lightning bolt!

The rest of my week's isolation was spent taking long walks, or just sitting on a stump in the woods. I had no sense of time, and it seemed I never got hungry, although I would occasionally eat. At one point I lost track of which day it was and spent a long time trying to figure it out. On Sunday morning I packed my bag and headed through the woods to my car. A light rain began to fall.

When I got to the farmhouse I was surprised to see Rose's van in the parking lot. Equally surprising, there were no other cars around. The farm residents were apparently all elsewhere. I had not planned on talking to Rose so soon, and the thought of it set off butterflies in my stomach. But I decided that catching him alone in the peaceful environment of the farm was too good an opportunity to pass up.

I took a deep breath and walked up the steps to the back porch. He must have heard the noise because the curtains on the kitchen door parted before I knocked and Rose's head appeared in the window. He opened the door without a greeting and I stepped inside. Immediately I was overcome by a strong odor. In a cast iron pan on the stove were four eggs swimming in crackling bacon grease.

"Still raining?" he asked, carefully flipping his eggs.

"I'm not sure. I mean I think so," I stammered.

I had eaten almost nothing in the past four days, and the sight and smell of the greasy eggs made me queasy. I took a few steps away from the stove, and finally settled into a seat at the far corner of the dining room.

Rose finished cooking his eggs then came to join me at the table. I watched him go about the business of eating his breakfast as I had on hundreds of occasions in Benwood. Like everything he did, Rose ate slowly, purposefully, and without any noticeable pleasure. I waited until he was finished before speaking.

"How was the meeting last weekend," I asked.

He wiped his mouth on a paper napkin. "Everybody's forgotten why they came here in the first place," he said. "Most of 'em have quit working on themselves, so naturally nothing is happening. Then they go ahead and figure as long as nothing is happening anyway, they might as well cut their losses and go for the million bucks." He got up from the table and opened the refrigerator door. "Well, now they've got their million bucks and they're mad at me because they don't have the spiritual goodies, too." He took a pitcher of orange juice from the refrigerator and held it out to me.

"You want any of this?"

"No. Thanks."

I watched as he poured himself a large glass.

"I understand why you don't want me in the group," I heard myself say. "But I want you to know I'm not quitting the search. I'm not giving up."

He looked at me without expression. "That's up to you," he said.

"In my cabin this week I felt like I was right at the door of something."

"You break down the goddamn doors if you have to, that's all!" Rose said quickly, almost reflexively. Then he softened slightly. "But of course there's all kinds of ways to break down the doors. Even the Absolute is attracted to pure love."

"I intend to become Enlightened, Mister Rose—with or without your help."

"I wish you the best."

"I think I'm finally ready to change."

"Don't get your hopes up," he grinned. "There's some things even Enlightenment won't change. If you're a son-of-a-bitch before you visit the Absolute, you'll still be a son-of-a-bitch after. I'm living proof of that." We both laughed, and for a few seconds I basked again in the incredible warmth and power of his company.

We talked for awhile about other things, then in the middle of a short silence I said, "I better go. Thanks for everything, Mister Rose."

He looked at me briefly with the barest trace of a smile, then glanced out the window. What he said was, "It's stopped raining." What I heard in my heart was: *Just pass it on*.

Epilogue

It was the summer of 1989 that Richard Rose told me he would no longer be my teacher, but that I would continue to be welcome in his house. I took him at his word, I guess, because I continued to stay with him until 1991, when I moved out to my cabin and took on a larger role in the maintenance of the farm. Two years later I left my law practice for good, and began searching for ways to spend my time on something more meaningful than "going for the million bucks."

One thing I've done is finally get this book written—something I've felt compelled to do for twenty-five years now, ever since that first summer Intensive in 1973 when Rose told me to "Just pass it on." It's been a labor of agony and love.

A lot of people who have read drafts or advance copies of the book have asked, "So then what happened? Where is everybody now?" And so I'm back at the keyboard for an Epilogue. As I write this, it is sometime in the early morning hours of December 30, 1997. I am in my cabin after a long absence, halfway through a two week isolation. A light snow has been falling since late yesterday afternoon, and the view from my window is of tall snow-encrusted pines and vast acres of still, silent white. Nearby, two does graze with their fawns on the tips of tiny maple branches.

Keith Ham—"Swami Kirtanananda"—was tried and convicted of racketeering charges stemming from a variety of offenses, including the murder of Steve Bryant, the kidnapping of Devin Wheeler, and the multi-million dollar begging operation he orchestrated from New Vrindaban. His conviction was overturned on appeal, however, and in April 1996 he was re-tried. Mister Rose and I were subpoenaed as witnesses.

Thomas Drescher was convicted in California of the murder of Steve Bryant and sentenced to death. He was also convicted in West Virginia of the murder of Chuck St. Denis, where he is now serving a life sentence without parole in the Moundsville penitentiary. At Keith Ham's re-trial, Drescher was a witness for the prosecution. His testimony was so precise and devastating that Ham's lawyers threw in the towel and Ham changed his plea to guilty. Keith Ham is now doing twenty years in a federal pen. Not long after, one of the two main Krishna lawyers was paralyzed by a severe stroke. The other has recently become a near-invalid after a heart attack and triple bypass surgery.

In 1987, after a ten-year absence, Augie Turak came back to Rose. A year later he settled in Raleigh, North Carolina and started the Self Knowledge Symposium (SKS), a spiritual group based on Rose's teachings. He now oversees four highly successful SKS groups in the area, including campus groups at Duke, North Carolina, and North Carolina State. In 1994 I also moved to Raleigh, and am now working with Augie again on group matters, much as we did in the Chautauqua days.

Not surprisingly, Augie has grown into a teacher. He's always had the drive, the brilliance, the charisma, and an incredible repertoire of spiritual references and anecdotes. Now, in the last year, he's been blessed with the final piece — the capacity to love.

If you asked the students of the North Carolina State chapter of the SKS, they would probably tell you I function as something of a teacher as well. It makes me uncomfortable to think of myself in those terms, though, because as Rose always said, "You don't know anything until you know Everything." But I would be dishonest if I did not admit that I love the work and the people, and the profound impact that the SKS has had on so many lives. Including my own.

Several years ago Mister Rose began to show signs of forgetfulness and memory loss typical of many older people. It became considerably worse, however, and Mister Rose was finally diagnosed as having Alzheimer's disease. The last time I visited him at his house he didn't recognize me until Cecy, his second wife, reminded him who I was. Most of the fire and stern methods of the Zen teacher had faded, but their absence seemed to accentuate the incredible warmth and affection Mister Rose has always had for people, especially his students. Being with him, I experienced an almost overwhelming feeling of love. When I left he walked me to my car and put his arm on my shoulder — a gesture I had never seen him use before.

"Come back soon," he said. "Don't forget they way."

"I'll make you a deal," I smiled, ever the lawyer, "I won't forget the way if you won't forget who I am."

He laughed. "I don't know if I can hold up my end of the bargain."

Mister Rose now lives in a nursing home that specializes in Alzheimer's patients. The disease has taken his memory and words and personality, and left only the all-compassionate Buddha behind. He smiles and laughs and looks after the other patients, bringing them food or just standing next to them with a hand on their shoulder. Watching, you can almost "see" him using his direct-mind abilities to send silent messages of pure love to the ravaged minds of the others in the home.

It is hard for those of us who know and love him to watch as he slips farther from this world, even though in many ways he has never really been a part of it anyway — in it, but not *of* it, as the saying goes. But in the end the body betrays us all, and it must inevitably find a way to die. One way is no better or worse than another, I suppose. Still, it is difficult to know how to understand this particular way for Mister Rose, a man who once said that the difference between him and most people was that, "They live to live; I live to think."

What does it mean when an Enlightened man slowly loses his mind? He never spoke of this, and perhaps there is nothing to be said. The death of the body and it's manner of leaving have nothing to do with one's true nature. Mister Rose would probably say that he is dying an ordinary death, as he must, like any other man in this madhouse. The only difference, he might say, is that he knows exactly where he is going afterwards, that this is the great gift of his Enlightenment experience. In a short, haunting poem he wrote many years ago he seemed even to foresee the particular manner of his passing. Reading it now, I am strangely comforted. It is called, "I Will Take Leave of You."

I will take leave of you
Not by distinct farewell
But vaguely
As one entering vagueness
For words, symbols of confusion
Would only increase confusion
But silence, seeming to be vagueness,
Shall be my cadence
Which someday
You will understand.

Made in the USA
Monee, IL
12 August 2022